The Changing Food Law Landscape

This book analyses the current debates within food system governance, covering different aspects of food systems (from production to consumption) as well as different fields of law (from human rights law to environmental law). Recognizing that the law, in interacting with multiple disciplines, plays a major role in setting binding targets for sustainable innovation and business transformation, it brings together contributors from a wide range of professions, including agriculture, law, and business to examine the dimensions of food systems and the challenges in transforming them.

The contributors to this book examine some of the most significant aspects of food law and regulation, including the effects of global warming, intellectual property rights, and human rights, as well as local and international viewpoints on food safety, information sharing, and systems transformation. They consider the history and present challenges of food production, the different approaches to addressing the issues faced, and the factors of human biology, psychology, cultural norms and religion that shape our food environments. The analysis of knowledge, values and institutions provides a holistic analysis of human food systems. Topics such as regenerative agriculture, novel and alternative foods, and health-enhancing foods are also covered.

With its interdisciplinary approach, this book will interest researchers in agricultural law, food policy, environmental law, transdisciplinary food studies, and food science.

Siva Barathi (Sharl) Marimuthu is Senior Lecturer at the University of New England, Armidale, Australia and the co-chair of the IUCN Academy of Environmental Law Teaching and Capacity Building Committee.

Anu Lähteenmäki-Uutela is Doctor of Laws and Research Professor at the Finnish Environment Institute.

The Changing Food Law Landscape

Food Security, Sustainability and the Environment

Edited by Siva Barathi (Sharl) Marimuthu and Anu Lähteenmäki-Uutela

Routledge
Taylor & Francis Group
LONDON AND NEW YORK

First published 2025
by Routledge
4 Park Square, Milton Park, Abingdon, Oxon OX14 4RN

and by Routledge
605 Third Avenue, New York, NY 10158

Routledge is an imprint of the Taylor & Francis Group, an informa business

British Library Cataloguing-in-Publication Data
A catalogue record for this book is available from the British Library

Library of Congress Cataloging-in-Publication Data
Names: Marimuthu, Siva Barathi, editor. | Lähteenmäki-Uutela, Anu, editor.
Title: The changing food law landscape : Food Security, Sustainability, and the Environment / Siva Barathi (Sharl) Marimuthu, Anu Lähteenmäki-Uutela.
Description: Abingdon, Oxon [UK] ; New York, NY : Routledge, 2024. | Includes bibliographical references and index.
Identifiers: LCCN 2024035950 | ISBN 9781032491301 (hardback) | ISBN 9781032491325 (paperback) | ISBN 9781003392279 (ebook)
Subjects: LCSH: Food law and legislation. | Food supply—Law and legislation. | Food—Safety measures—Government policy. | Food supply—Government policy. | Sustainable agriculture.
Classification: LCC K3626 .C423 2024 | DDC 344.03/3—dc23/eng/20240806
LC record available at https://lccn.loc.gov/2024035950

ISBN: 978-1-032-49130-1 (hbk)
ISBN: 978-1-032-49132-5 (pbk)
ISBN: 978-1-003-39227-9 (ebk)

DOI: 10.4324/9781003392279

Typeset in Galliard
by Apex CoVantage, LLC

We dedicate this book to all the tireless researchers and teaching academics in the field of environmental law. Some of you are those we currently work with, while the others we look forward to meeting as we continue our journey in an area we are heartened to say is growing in both importance and relevance. Increasingly also, it is an area that is fast becoming truly multidisciplinary, hence highlighting the essence and nature of this book.

Contents

List of Contributors *xiii*
List of Tables *xviii*
Preface *xix*
Acknowledgement *xxi*
Abbreviations and Keywords *xxii*

1 **Introduction: Future Food Landscape – Towards Sustainable Food Systems Through Innovations, Cultural Shifts, and Transformative Law** 1
SIVA BARATHI (SHARL) MARIMUTHU AND ANU LÄHTEENMÄKI-UUTELA

1.1 Introduction: Sustainable Food Systems as a Target and Duty for Humanity 1
1.2 The Contents of This Book 4
1.3 Conclusion 8

2 **From Colonialism to the Commodification of Food: The Criticality of a Globalised Food System** 11
ALESSANDRA TELCH AND SIVA BARATHI (SHARL) MARIMUTHU

2.1 Introduction 11
2.2 Colonialism, Capitalism, and Commodification of Food 13
2.3 Food as the Colonising Force in the Past and the Present 14
2.4 Capitalism and the Commodification of Food 16
2.5 Management of Natural Resources 19
2.6 Criticalities of the Current Food Systems and the Call for Sustainable Food Systems Governance 20
2.6.1 Health Sustainability 21
2.6.2 Social Sustainability 22
2.6.3 Environmental Sustainability 23
2.7 Conclusion 26

3 The Role of Regenerative Agricultural Practices in Balancing Food Security Concerns and Natural Resources Management 31

ALESSANDRA TELCH AND SIVA BARATHI (SHARL) MARIMUTHU

3.1 Introduction 31
3.2 Food at the Centre of Sustainable Development Goals (SDGs) 31
3.3 Importance of Food Systems and SDGs 32
3.4 Balancing Food Security Concerns with Fair Natural Resource Management 37
3.5 Agroforestry to Reconcile Conservation with Social and Economic Benefits 42
3.5.1 Chestnut Groves as An Excellent Example 43
3.6 Conclusion 47

4 The Human-Food-Environmental Nexus: Anthropological Perspectives on the Impact of Human Food Choices Through Time 51

MELANIE FILLIOS

4.1 Introduction 51
4.2 In Brief: The Impact of Human Food Choice on the Present 51
4.3 The Impact of Human Food Choice on Past Environments 53
4.3.1 Food Production as a Driver of Past Climate Change 53
4.4 Archaeological and Historical Case Studies 54
4.4.1 Australia and the Introduction of Sheep 57
4.4.2 Cattle Grazing in the Americas 60
4.4.3 Cereal Agriculture in the Near East and Mediterranean 62
4.5 Conclusion: Drawing on the Past to Change the Future 64
4.5.1 Cultural Change as a Way Forward 65

5 Post-COVID Future: Living and Managing Life After COVID From Food Security Perspective 71

VANDANA GULATI AND SIVA BARATHI (SHARL) MARIMUTHU

5.1 Introduction: Food as a Necessity 71
5.2 Traditional Food Cultures 72

5.3 Globalisation and Industrialisation: A Threat to Regional and Traditional Cuisines 73
5.4 Impacts of COVID-19: Food Supply Chain Disruptions 74
5.5 Future Policies for More Resilient Food Systems 77
5.6 Conclusion 79

6 **Alternative Protein Products and the Legal Rules on Novel Foods: A Global Comparison** 84
ANU LÄHTEENMÄKI-UUTELA, ANNIKA LONKILA, AND SIVA BARATHI (SHARL) MARIMUTHU

6.1 Introduction 84
6.2 Novel Food Legislation Across the World with Alternative Protein Cases 84
6.2.1 European Union 84
6.2.2 United States 88
6.2.3 Australia 90
6.2.4 Singapore 92
6.3 Conclusions and Discussion 93

7 **Health Claims and Their Regulation: Comparing Australia and Europe** 98
SIVA BARATHI (SHARL) MARIMUTHU AND ANU LÄHTEENMÄKI-UUTELA

7.1 Introduction 98
7.2 Medicalisation of Health Claims Escapes Regulation 100
7.3 The Dilemma in Classifying Functional Foods as Medicinal 100
7.4 Codex Alimentarius 1997 Guidelines on Nutrition and Health Claims 102
7.4.1 Requirements in Codex Alimentarius 102
7.5 Regulation of Health Claims in Functional Food 104
7.5.1 Australia's Regulation of Health Claims 104
7.5.2 European Union Regulations on Health Claims 106
7.6 Critical Appraisal of the Australian System and the European Union 108
7.7 Towards Better Regulatory Control in Australia 108
7.8 Way Forward for the European Union 110
7.9 Commentary 111
7.10 Conclusion 113

8 Enriching Environmental Law and Improving Food Security Through an Innovative Interpretation of Human and Natural Rights 119
ALESSANDRA TELCH, SIVA BARATHI (SHARL) MARIMUTHU, AND ANU LÄHTEENMÄKI-UUTELA

8.1 Introduction 119
8.2 What Does Granting Rights to Nature Mean? 119
8.3 Human Rights-Based Approach and Legal Rights to Nature 121
8.4 The Birth of Rights to Nature 122
8.5 Legal and Cultural Prerequisites 126
8.6 Transitioning from Food as Commodity to Food as Common Good: Legal Instruments and Policies 129
8.7 Conclusion 131

9 Intellectual Property Supporting a Green Framework for Sustainability 135
ELHAM GHAFFARIAN, MARK PERRY, AND SIVA BARATHI (SHARL) MARIMUTHU

9.1 Introduction 135
9.2 Food Security 136
9.2.1 The Role of the Sustainable Agriculture Sector on Food Security 137
9.2.2 Agricultural Sustainability Challenges 137
9.2.3 Role of R&D in the Agriculture Sector 138
9.3 The University – R&D in Innovation and Technology Accessibility 140
9.4 Intellectual Property Rights as a Mechanism for Knowledge Flow 141
9.4.1 Diverse Perspective on Intellectual Property Rights' Effect 141
9.4.2 Weak Intellectual Property Protection System 142
9.5 Green IP Boost R&D in Different Intellectual Property Systems 143
9.6 Conclusion 144

10 Corporate Social Responsibility and Embedded Sustainable Business Practices 148
PETER DAWSON AND SIVA BARATHI (SHARL) MARIMUTHU

10.1 Introduction 148

10.2 Corporate Social Responsibility in Perspective 149
10.3 Corporate Social Responsibility Globally 150
10.4 Does Corporate Social Responsibility Matter 154
10.5 Evidence Suggesting the Adoption of a Corporate Social Responsibility Approach is Gaining Momentum 156
10.6 Is There a Need for the Adoption of Mandatory Reporting of Aspects of Corporate Social Responsibility, including the Australian Position 157
10.7 Conclusion 159

11 Eradicating Malnutrition: Capacity to Access Nutritious Food 161
MIA MAHMUDUR RAHIM AND ABHAY VIR SINGH KANWAR

11.1 Introduction 161
11.2 Nutritious Food, Malnutrition, and Capability Approach 161
11.2.1 Nutritious Food 161
11.2.2 Malnutrition 162
11.2.3 Capability Approach 162
11.3 Capability Approach Towards Access to Nutritious Food 164
11.3.1 Poverty – An Absolute Capability Failure for Nutritious Food? 166
11.3.2 Education – A Basic Capability to Access Nutritious Foods? 167
11.3.3 Health as a Basic Capability – Need for Bifurcation? 168
11.4 Access to Nutritious Food – A Basic Capability 169
11.5 Conclusion 170

12 Future Food and Islam: A Perspective From Malaysia 174
ASRIL AMIRUL ZAKARIAH, MOHD LOTPI BIN MOHD YUSOB, AND MURSHAMSHUL KAMARIAH MUSA

12.1 Introduction 174
12.2 The Intersection Between Future Food and Islam 175
12.3 General Principles of Permissibility and Non-Permissibility Under Shariah 177
12.4 Specific Reasons of Permissibility and Non-Permissibility 180

12.5 Halal Certification in Malaysia: Process and Regulations 182
12.6 Understanding the Concept of Halal Certification in Malaysia 183
12.6.1 Halal Certification Challenges 184
12.7 The Impact of Halal Certification on the Economy and Trade 185
12.8 Regulatory Framework for Halal Certification in Malaysia 186
12.9 Thoughts on Future Food: Halal Considerations 187
12.10 Addressing Food Scarcity: A Muslim Challenge 188
12.11 Conclusion – Malaysia's Stance on Future Foods and Islam 189

Index 192

Contributors

The Authors

Siva Barathi (Sharl) Marimuthu

Anu Lähteenmäki-Uutela

Mark Perry

Melanie Fillios

Mia Mahmudur Rahim

Alessandra Telch

Annika Lonkila

Vandana Gulati

Asril Amirul Zakariah

Peter Dawson

Elham Ghaffarian

Abhay Vir Singh Kanwar

Murshamshul Kamariah Musa

Mohd Lotpi bin Mohd Yusob

Siva Barathi (Sharl) Marimuthu is a Senior Lecturer at the University of New England, Armidale, NSW. She holds a PhD in Law from Monash University, Australia, a master's degree from the University of Malaya, and an LLB (Hons) from the University of London. She serves as the Higher Research Degree Coordinator (HDRC) and LLM Program Coordinator. Internationally, she co-chairs the IUCN Academy of Environmental Law's Teaching and Capacity Building Committee. She also leads a global, international and interdisciplinary Food Law Science Research Group and serves as an editor of the *International Journal of Regional, Rural and Remote Law and Policy*.

Dr Marimuthu's research centres on strengthening the legal frameworks and governance structures that support the sustainable use of natural resources and food production. Her doctoral work focused on the regulation of medicinal product advertising, particularly the interactions between food and medicine, functional foods, labelling, and health claims. Over time, her research has expanded to consider the wider impacts of food production on biodiversity. Her research also explores innovative solutions, such as climate-resilient crops and the use of insects for food and feed. Her work is highly interdisciplinary, drawing on environmental science, law, and policy, and aims to influence both scholarly discussions and policy development.

Anu Lähteenmäki-Uutela is Doctor of Laws and works as a Research Professor at the Finnish Environment Institute. She is interested in the value of nature, ecosystem services, rights, and justice. Her previous research projects have related to food systems, just transition, insects, and algae. Currently she leads the international BIO-TRADE project on biodiversity and trade, a work package on effective and just ways to govern nutrient emissions (Horizon Europe project NORDBALT-ECOSAFE), a subproject on marine ecosystem services and rights (EU Horizon Europe project SELINA), and a subproject on the justice impacts of land use decisions (EU Just Transition project SATUMAA).

Mark Perry is Professor and Head of School of Law at the University of New England in Australia and is also Emeritus Professor (Computer Science and Law) at the University of Western Ontario in Canada. He is Barrister and Solicitor at the Law Society of Upper Canada. His expertise is in the intersection of law and technology, with research emphasis on intellectual property rights, innovation, licensing, technology, and regulation in the field of biotechnology. He has led novel research into material transfer agreements, the patenting of lifeforms, and the deployment of advanced information technology. In addition to law, he has also led research into integrating legal externalities into autonomic computing systems and programming patterns. At the University of New England, NSW, he has served as the Chair of Academic Board, on the governing Council, as well as providing support and oversight to many committees. He lives outside Armidale, NSW, Australia.

Melanie Fillios is anthropological archaeologist with an interest in the relationship between humans and animals throughout history. Educated in the United States, she has extensive field experience in Greece and Australia, and has taught a range of theoretical and practical, field-based subjects in the United States and Australia. Melanie holds concurrent roles as the Director of Place Based Education and Research and as Associate Professor of Archaeology at the University of New England, Australia. Melanie is an avid advocate for sustainability and is intensely interested in exploring the nexus between people, animals and the environment and the resulting impact on diet.

Mia Mahmudur Rahim is Associate Professor in the School of Law at the University of New England, Australia. He pursued his studies in law and policy at the National University of Singapore, the University of Warwick, the University of Dhaka, and Macquarie University. Prior to his academic career, he worked as a judge, a lawyer, and a freelance legal researcher. Some of his recent research monographs include *Legal Regulation of Corporate Social Responsibility*, *CSR in Private Enterprises*, *Social Audit Regulation* and *Code of Conduct on TNCs*. Two of his forthcoming research monographs are *Corporate Criminal Liability in Environmental Jurisprudence* and *Regulating FDI for Development*.

Alessandra Telch is a jurist, obtaining her LLM from the University of Trento with a thesis on the nexus between Food Systems and Climate Change, and how both impact on the enjoyment of Human Rights. While working as Head of Legal Department in the inspiring environment offered by Rotho Blaas, a multinational company based in South Tyrol, she continues cultivating her interest for Food Law both through research, publications and volunteering for local and global organizations. She is member of the IUCN World Commission on Environmental Law and she is currently engaged in the development of the recently founded Slow Food Italian network of chestnut cultivators. She is committed to raise public awareness about the importance of a transition towards sustainable food systems, as an essential requirement for the achievement of the sustainable development goals set by the international community.

Annika Lonkila (Ph.D., LL.M.) is Senior Research Scientist at the Finnish Environment Institute. Her multidisciplinary work focuses on social scientific and legal studies on just sustainability transitions in the context of food systems.

Vandana Gulati is a senior lecturer in Biomedical Sciences at University of New England. Dr Gulati has been teaching in tertiary education over more than fifteen years in Australia in multi-disciplinary disciplines due to her multi-disciplinary qualification and experience. Dr. Gulati is very passionate in areas of food security, nutritional medicine and use of plants as medicinal agents. Dr Gulati finished her PhD in Life Sciences from Swinburne University of Technology in 2013 and investigated Aboriginal Australian plants for the management of type 2 diabetes. Dr Gulati worked as a post-doctoral research fellow at Swinburne University of Technology in Microbiology.

Asril Amirul Zakariah holds an LLB from Universiti Teknologi MARA (UiTM), an LLM from Universiti Malaya, and a PhD in Innovation from the University of New England, Australia. As the Deputy Director of Innovation and Commercialization at the Research Management Center of Universiti Sultan Zainal Abidin (UniSZA), Dr. Asril leverages his extensive expertise in environmental law and legal reform to drive research initiatives and foster advancements in sustainable legal practices. His academic and professional journey underscores a profound commitment to enhancing legal frameworks and promoting innovative solutions in the realm of environmental protection.

Peter Dawson holds a degree in business management and is a fellow of the Institute of Public Accountants in Australia. Peter has worked in New South Wales (NSW) Government public sector management for almost 50 years. Peter's work experience covers administration, finance, communications, and managing large teams delivering diverse transactions for the citizens of NSW. Peter has worked with the former NSW Roads and Traffic Authority, NSW Roads and Maritime Services, and Service NSW. Peter's interest in Corporate Social Responsibility (CSR) stems from his extensive experience in staff and business management and the need for business to deliver tangible benefits to local communities in a socially responsible way. Peter also has a keen interest in aligned topics such as dispute resolution and staff behavioural matters with the objective of sourcing the untapped potential of individuals, once again for the benefit of all. In addition, Peter has roots in the agricultural community and his parents were lifetime graziers in the sheep and cattle industry. Peter continues to be involved in that industry and has introduced sustainable business practices into his current farming business.

Elham Ghaffarian is PhD scholar at the University of New England. Her research focuses on Intellectual Property, Technology, and Sustainability. She holds a Master of Private Law from Azad University, Tabriz Branch, Iran (Sep. 2010 to Oct. 2013), and a Bachelor of Law from the same institution (Sep. 2003 to Feb. 2007). Currently, she is pursuing a Ph.D. at New England University, specializing in intellectual property rights, Smart technology and agricultural sustainability. Throughout her career, she has engaged in various sustainability projects and corporate social responsibility (CSR) management initiatives. From 2008 to 2017, she practiced as a Barrister and then served as a university lecturer at Azad University, Tabriz Branch, from 2013 to 2018. During her tenure, she taught courses on environmental law and intellectual property law, overseeing the publication of three papers where she contributed as both main author and co-author.

Abhay Vir Singh Kanwar is a PhD scholar at the School of Development Studies, Tata Institute of Social Sciences, Mumbai. He holds an MPhil in Planning & Development from IIT Bombay and a master's in Sociology from Jawaharlal Nehru University, Delhi. His research interests include the Capability Approach, Climate Change, CSR, Environmental Degradation, ESG, Malnutrition, and Public Health. He has previously served as faculty at the National Institute of Technology, Jamshedpur. This book chapter extends his MPhil dissertation, "Capability to Access Nutrition: A Case Study of an NGO Intervention in Mumbai." Additional publications can be accessed at: https://www.researchgate.net/profile/Abhay-Kanwar.

Murshamshul Kamariah Musa holds an LL.B from the International Islamic University Malaysia (IIUM) and an LL.M from Universiti Kebangsaan Malaysia (UKM). Although a non-practising advocate and solicitor, Murshamshul Kamariah is actively engaged in research and publication in the fields of intellectual property law, environmental law, and gender issues. In addition to academic pursuits, she serves as a Moot Master for the UniSZA Moot Club, guiding and mentoring students in moot court competitions. Through these roles, she contributes to the development of legal knowledge and practical skills in future legal professionals.

Mohd Lotpi bin Mohd Yusob is currently Deputy Dean of Academic Affairs and Postgraduate, and a Senior Lecturer at the Faculty of Law and International Relations, University Sultan Zainal Abidin. He holds Phd in Islamic Jurisprudence and Law from University Malaya, Master of Law (LLM in Administration of Islamic Law), Bachelor of Laws (Honors), and Bachelor of Laws (Shariah)(Honors) all from the International Islamic University Malaysia (IIUM) respectively. He specializes in Islamic legal theory and Comparative Islamic Jurisprudence.

Tables

3.1 SDG Goals and Their Relationship to Food Security 33
7.1 Institutional Framework for Health Claims on Functional Foods 109

Preface

The global climate crisis now overlaps into many fields and is one of the most significant challenges that we face. Within this context, two interesting and interconnected elements are rapidly gaining attention. First, there is a growing awareness of how food systems and agrifood policies depend on and impact the ecosystem and the climate. Given this, protecting ecosystems and biodiversity as well as mitigating climate change are vital for food security. Second, there is a growing recognition of the influence of law, particularly the judiciary, but also governments at every level via the drafting and passing of new laws and regulations that are then delivered by agencies in the form of policies and guidelines. This, in turn, reshapes our approach to conservation and protection of nature and the environment.

Our interactions with food are constantly evolving. The demand is for not only highly nutritious and safe food but also with the latest eco-friendly and sustainable flavours. Food chain operators must comply with a set of laws and regulations created by the individual nations to ensure food safety and quality but there is also a demand for food to be sustainably produced. We found that there are parts of the current food system that require a greater response than the capacity to provide safe and nutritious food to a growing population. As environmental degradation and climate change continue to worsen, the misuse of agricultural land, water, and energy contributes to an increase in global famine.

Furthermore, as the global population grows, balancing food security, safety, innovation, and environmental protection becomes increasingly important. Many factors lead to the conclusion that the existing approaches to food governance are inadequate. This book takes the lead in discussing the most salient features of the current situation and the next steps to address them in a timely manner. The book is primarily aimed at a legal audience, including those studying food law, agricultural law, natural resource governance, and environmental law. The discussion about the required legal reform is framed by the difficulties encountered by three (3) different nations. To learn from the best practices of other countries, this book compares the legal systems of the European Union (EU) and Australia.

Even though the book is aimed at a legal audience, it is increasingly becoming apparent that this legal focus is a subset of a bigger interdisciplinary picture that shall be factored into our discussions. Therefore, we believe students of interdisciplinary food studies and food science who are enrolled in food law courses, as well as researchers, regulators, and the food industry, can benefit from this book. Moreover, students of economics, finance, business, land planning, and the like will find the many interconnections contained in this book noteworthy.

As a reader, please now join us on an important journey via the chapters ahead. The chapters provide a holistic evaluation of the many connected and complex elements of our food landscape, both nationally and internationally. These elements range from the need for a sustainable and secure food system, the connection between the sustainable production of food and its interrelationship with the UN's sustainable development goals, the importance of agriculture and communities related to it, the evolution of human nutrition, our modern diet and ever-changing food choices, the legal rules pertaining to alternative food choices, the harmonisation of intellectual property rights to ensure access to the latest food production technologies, corporate social responsibility for producers of goods and services, malnutrition viewed as a capability framework failure, the allocation of legal status to the environment and, lastly, cultural sensitivity in food choices. Each element of the discussion highlighted in the chapters forms a part of the whole. The whole being a rich tapestry of elements that make up the drivers of food production in a sustainable and secure way.

Acknowledgement

Thank you to the many people who have been a part of the journey in completing this book. The book would not have been possible without the support of all the contributing authors, my family and friends. In addition, I would like to extend my appreciation to the School of Law at the University of New England for the Special Study Program (SSP) Leave granted to me to complete the co-authored chapters as well as to edit the book. In particular, I would like to thank the former Dean of the Faculty of Science, Agriculture, Business and Law (SABL) Prof Birgit Loch, former Head of School Prof Michael Adams, and Interim Head of School Prof Mark Perry for their support for my SSP leave.

A special mention of thanks to Mia Rahim for his guidance throughout the writing of this book, and last but not least, Peter Dawson, who I was able to bounce ideas off and who read many of the chapters and assisted with proofreading.

My heartfelt thanks go to my co-editor Anu Lähteenmäki-Uutela, and co-authors, Peter Dawson, Alessandra Telch, Vandana Gulati, Elham Ghaffarian, and Mark Perry. These heartfelt thanks are also extended to the other co-authors and contributors to this book, and they are Melanie Fillios, Mia Rahim and Abhay Vir Singh Kanwar, Dr Asril Amirul Zakariah, Mohd Lotpi Mohd Yuso, Murshamshul Kamariah Musa.

Abbreviations and Keywords

ACL	Australian Consumer Law
CAP	Common Agricultural Policy
Codex	Codex Alimentarius Commission
CBD	Convention on Biological Diversity
CSR	Corporate Social Responsibility
CSRD	Corporate Sustainability Reporting Directive
CDI	Child Development Index
COVID19	Coronavirus Disease
EFSA	European Food Safety Authority
EEA	European Environment Agency
EU	European Union
FAO	Food and Agriculture Organization
FBAC	Food and Beverages Advertising and Marketing Communications Code
FRSC	Food Regulation Standing Committee
FSANZ	Food Standard Australia New Zealand
FDA	USA Food and Drug Administration
Food Standards Code	Australia New Zealand Food Standard Code
GATT	General Agreement on Tariffs and Trade
GATS	General Agreement on Trade in Services
GRAS	Generally Recognised as Safe
GMOs	Genetically Modified Organisms
IFCO	International Food Container Organization
IFAD	International Fund for Agricultural Development
ICRAF	World Agroforestry Centre
IAASTD	International Assessment of Agriculture Knowledge, Science and Technology for Development
IPCC	Intergovernmental Panel on Climate Change
IFAD	International Fund for Agricultural Development
JAKIM	Department of Islamic Development Malaysia
NGTs	New Genomic Techniques
NFRD	Non-Financial Reporting Directive

OECD	Organization for Economic Cooperation and Development
QSRI	Quick Service Restaurant Initiative for Responsible and Marketing
REFIT	Regulatory fitness and performance programme
RCMI	Responsible Children's Marketing Initiative
SDG	Sustainable Development Goal
SASB	Sustainability Accounting Standards Board
SME	Small- and Medium-Sized Enterprises
TRIPS	Trade-Related Aspects of Intellectual Property Rights
USDA-FSIS	United States Department of Agriculture's Food Safety and Inspection Service
UCPD	Unfair Commercial Practices Directive
UNICEF	United Nations International Children's Emergency Fund
WHO	World Health Organization
WFP	World Food Programme
WTO	World Trade Organization

Keywords

Food security, Information Sharing, Food Law, Climate Change, Corporate Social Responsibility, Human Rights, Food Anthropology, Halal Food.

1 Introduction

Future Food Landscape – Towards Sustainable Food Systems Through Innovations, Cultural Shifts, and Transformative Law

Siva Barathi (Sharl) Marimuthu and Anu Lähteenmäki-Uutela

1.1 Introduction: Sustainable Food Systems as a Target and Duty for Humanity

The motivation for writing this book arises from the growing concern of the unsustainability of current food systems, as highlighted in the UNEP (2022), FAO (2014), IPES-Food (2021, 2015), and the Lancet (Willett et al. 2019) reports. To date, food systems worldwide are utilising too much land and water, destroying biodiversity, causing eutrophication, and warming the planet. The environmental problems will worsen as the global population grows. At the same time, children and adults suffer from malnutrition, small farmers and workers in primary production or food manufacturing do not earn a decent living, and indigenous cultures and livelihoods are affected due to environmental change. Hence, a transition to more sustainable food systems is required.

We need food systems that address the socio-ecological issues yet provide food and nutrition security as well as decent jobs and livelihoods without transgressing the planetary boundaries (Hinrichs 2014; McDermid et al. 2023; Puupponen et al. 2023).

The first step towards these initiatives is to define sustainability itself. Scientists of all disciplines agree on the vision and goal of sustainability transformation, where we should realise the UN Sustainable Development Goals (SDGs) and target a 'safe and just space' for humanity (Duncan et al. 2022). Sustainable development was first proposed in the UN Brundtland Report, highlighting the 'development that meets the needs of the present without compromising the ability of future generations to meet their own needs' (United Nations General Assembly 1987: 43).

Today, the UN has 17 SDGs that have been recognised since 2015 which represent goals to be reached by 2030 for humanity. The development aspects shall balance social, economic, and environmental sustainability. The 17 goals are 1) no poverty; 2) zero hunger; 3) good health and wellbeing; 4) quality

DOI: 10.4324/9781003392279-1

education; 5) gender equality; 6) clean water and sanitation; 7) affordable and clean energy; 8) decent work and economic growth; 9) industry, innovation and infrastructure; 10) reduced inequalities; 11) sustainable cities and communities; 12) responsible consumption and production; 13) climate action; 14) life below water; 15) life on land; 16) peace, justice and strong institutions; and 17) partnerships for the goals. Such goals have interconnections, in which action in one area will affect outcomes in others.

The realisation of SDG2 'zero hunger' depends on the condition of biodiversity (SDG 14 'life below water' and SDF15 'life on land') and SDG13 'climate action', as well as SDG1 'no poverty' and SDG6 'decent work'. There are also trade-offs between the goals, for example bringing people out of poverty may increase their consumption once their life is better, which may lead to pollution, or the need to build more dams for energy security may threaten food production downstream (Renaud et al. 2022). The Doughnut economy model (Raworth 2012) is a well-known model to define 'a safe and just space' for humanity. In fact, the European Environmental Bureau (EEB) has used the Doughnut model as a basis for its sustainable food system vision (EEB 2022). Nevertheless, Raworth's model sets environmental and social justice as equally important building blocks for humanity to thrive.

Planetary boundaries are set as the ecological limits for humanity. The planetary boundaries are planetary subsystems or processes with associated biophysical boundaries and together form a 'safe operating space' in which humanity can thrive and develop (Rockström et al. 2009a, 2009b; Steffen et al. 2015; Rockström et al. 2021). Transgressing the planetary boundaries leads to abrupt and undesirable environmental change. According to the Doughnut model, the nine planetary boundaries involve climate change, ocean acidification, chemical pollution, freshwater withdrawal, nitrogen and phosphorus loading, land conversion, biodiversity loss, air pollution, and ozone layer depletion.

By setting the ecological limits as the outer boundary of the economy, the Doughnut model acknowledges the dependence of humanity on nature, thereby contributing to a deep-rooted shift in worldviews, which is part of sustainability transitions. Social justice forms the Doughnut model's inner boundary, which refers to everyone having energy, water, food, housing, health, education, income and work, peace and justice, political voice, gender equality, social equity, and networks (Raworth 2012). Together, the environmental and social boundaries define a 'safe and just operating space', where 'safe' means that the economic system shall respect the planetary boundaries, and 'just' means it should satisfy basic human needs and promote social justice.

The global Doughnut model has been revised to define a safe and just operating space for states and cities (see Turner and Wills 2022). No state is yet to be in a safe and just space (O'Neill et al. 2018). Even though the poorest countries cannot fulfill the basic needs (due to not reaching the social foundation that forms the inner boundary of the Doughnut model), rich and middle-income countries have huge ecological footprints too large for the planet (Fanning et al. 2022; O'Neill et al. 2018). Countries exceeding the ecological ceiling are in fact threatening the possibility of everyone reaching a just space in the future (see Hoekstra and Wiedmann 2014; WHO 2017). According to EEB (2022), a Doughnut food system utilises a circular food system based on *regenerative practices* rather than excessive production and consumption.

Animal-based food systems raise a concern when it comes to food sustainability and justice as they take up a large share of land, impact the climate and biodiversity of global food systems, and their overconsumption is also harmful for consumer health (Morris et al. 2021). The de-marketing against animal-based food thus has multiple societal benefits and sustainable dietary change requires the support of policy measures implemented throughout the food system. Current agricultural and food policies, climate policies, economic development policies, health policies, and trade policies must be re-evaluated (Morris et al. 2021). Lonkila and Kaljonen (2021) call for research on how to reduce animal-based protein consumption while supporting alternative proteins.

New food sources such as algae or insects may be used to produce ecological, healthy, and interesting products, or new methods and processes such as cellular agriculture can be employed. Society should not focus on novelty for its own sake but on the sustainability agenda. States should steer the innovation system towards sustainable alternatives, both low- and high-tech. A move towards more sustainable food systems is not merely a target but a *duty*. The legal duty to move towards the realisation of the SDGs and a Doughnut-shaped safe and just space is driven from *human rights law* that is binding on states. The duties of states concerning the inner boundary of the Doughnut's model, referring to a just space, are defined by human rights such as the right to food, the right to health, and the right to education.

Most international human rights agreements defining such rights include the UN International Covenant on Civil and Political Rights and the UN International Covenant on Economic, Social and Cultural Rights. The UN Convention on the Rights of the Child takes the children's perspective to human rights. Food system sustainability is central for human rights and becomes prerequisites for good life in general. The outer boundary of the Doughnut model, the safe space, is defined by environmental rights. The universal right of all humans to a clean, healthy, and sustainable environment is getting stronger with UN resolutions, constitutional amendments, and court verdicts. The UN Human Rights Committee (2019) has defined how the right to life includes environmental rights.

The climate crisis has been recognised as one of the worst threats to the right to life (UN Human Rights Council 2018). To fulfil the climate obligations, countries 'must adopt and implement policies aimed at reducing emissions' (UN Joint Statement 2020). Paris Agreement (2015) is a major yardstick in defining the rights-based duties of governments concerning climate change (Council of Europe Commissioner for Human Rights 2019). The human rights agreements and the Paris Agreement shall be read together to define the content of climate rights. In addition to UN guidelines, constitutions, and national laws, climate rights are now defined via lawsuits.

The same rights-based legal developments that we have witnessed with climate are now taking place when it comes to ecosystems, biodiversity, and waters. Citizens and NGOs are embracing the rights-based approach, suing both countries and companies and demanding the realisation of their rights. Some countries are granting rights to nature itself. Food systems will have to be developed that consider all the elements of human rights to a clean, healthy, and sustainable environment. Alternatively, or in addition, species and ecosystems and nature itself are deemed as having the right to exist.

1.2 The Contents of This Book

Agriculture and agricultural practices are both significant areas of concern in ensuring food sustainability. The way we approach, conduct, and manage agriculture, to a certain extent, influences the ability to produce food sustainably. This book encompasses chapters that are designed in a way to enhance our understanding on the role of law and regulation as the institutional framework that shapes food systems and to be used purposefully for driving the transition towards sustainability. The perspectives of science, economics, business, and society are central to planning for transformative food system governance. Hence, the authors are those from varied backgrounds, from the fields of agriculture, law, anthropology, nutrition, economics, and business to discuss transformation in the food system.

We explore the underlying systemic and planetary factors leading to the conclusion that the existing approaches to food governance are inadequate. The most salient aspects of the current, unsustainable situation are discussed. The discussion about the required legal reforms is framed by referencing two (2) distinct legal systems; European Union (EU) and Australia. Some references are also made to Italy and Malaysia. Chapters 2, 3, and 4 set the stage for understanding the sustainability and ethical issues in the global food system. The food system continues to cause severe environmental issues, and it has become critical to address these issues. Food scarcity, price rises, monoculture farming, mainstream farming, logistical issues, and many other problems in subsystems show that both short and long-term solutions need to be carefully considered.

In Chapter 2, Alessandra Telch and Siva Barathi (Sharl) Marimuthu raises and discusses several key points about the unsustainability of the food system caused by the colonising force. They analyse the connection between capitalism and the commodification of food and discuss the role of the General Agreement on Tariffs and Trade (GATT) in shaping the global food chain. Chapter 2 emphasising the need for sustainable food system governance.

Drawing on examples from the European counterparts, Chapter 2 offers recommendations for a legal framework that incorporates sustainable objectives and principles into an 'integrated food system approach'.

To achieve global sustainable food security goals, it is essential to comprehend the links between environmental and economic sustainability. Agriculture is crucial for the sustainability of our food supply, and climate change is a critical factor in this respect. In Chapter 3, Alessandra Telch and Siva Barathi (Sharl) Marimuthu examine the Sustainable Development Goals (SDG) outlined in the UN Agenda 2023 against food sustainability goals. They reiterate that the principle of food sustainability can be found in all the goals. However, for this global strategy to be effective, it is necessary to have the cooperation of all actors involved in the food systems including those in agrobusiness. They argue that the involvement of all stakeholders is required to implement strategies to achieve those goals. For example, the implementation of ethical and sustainable practices in the food systems could significantly enhance environmental sustainability by preserving natural resources. Social sustainability can be improved by promoting fair practices and thereby supporting the community. Economic sustainability is also enhanced by ensuring a resilient food system is in place for both producers and consumers.

In Chapter 4, the author examines the impact of food production and consumption continues to have on the environment and nutrition. In this chapter, Melanie Fillios examines the historical impact of human food choices on the environment. She uses archaeological evidence to show how domestication of plants and animals changed biomes and led to social and environmental degradation. She illustrated these by using case studies of the introduction of sheep to Australia. Other studies also include cattle grazing in the United States and wheat farming in the ancient Near East and Mediterranean. The chapter brings across the valuable point that historical insights can improve future sustainability.

The next three chapters, namely Chapters 5, 6, and 7 investigate the modern changes taking place, namely how human tastes have evolved, how new food products have entered the market, and how health claim efforts influence people's decisions to buy certain foods. A healthy diet not only provides nourishment to the body but also a sense of satisfaction, joy, and pleasure. However, globalisation and industrialisation, directly and indirectly, affect the ability to provide nutritious food for consumption.

Industrialisation threatens the existence of nutritious, traditional, and cultural food choices. Food culture consists of food consumption patterns that keep rapidly changing and evolving. The traditional food system was an essential part of ancient civilisation, which was devoid of synthetic hormones, pesticides, antibiotics, heavy metals, colourants, preservatives, and additives. However, it was noted that during COVID-19, people consumed more home-cooked meals. There is no doubt that the COVID-19 pandemic has impacted the food systems and security worldwide, but it has also impacted the health and resilience of the population. It altered food systems in terms of logistics, lockdowns, and food supply issues, causing people to start cooking with regional ingredients and prefer to buy food from local producers. In Chapter 5 Vandana Gulati and Siva Barathi (Sharl) Marimuthu review and explore the impacts of COVID-19 in terms of the changes it brought to the consumption and production patterns and as drivers of economic change.

People's choices expand as novel food, namely alternative protein products, are introduced to the markets to replace animal-based products. Anu Lähteenmäki-Uutela, Annika Lonkila, and Siva Barathi (Sharl) Marimuthu provide us with an insight into the legal rules on Novel Food such as the alternative protein products in Chapter 6. To provide us with an in-depth understanding of the best practices, the authors compare the legal rules on novel protein products as regulated in selected jurisdictions. Regulatory landscape of novel food is still developing in most areas with regulations expected to be coherent in the coming years in the European Union, United States, and Australia. Currently, however, novel protein innovations face many regulatory hurdles before getting access into the market, and these regulatory challenges are highlighted succinctly in this chapter.

People's choices are also expanded by health claims. Health claims on functional foods are powerful communication tools. If justified, they can help facilitate informed food choices. Often, these claims are related to maintaining health and explaining the health effects of a food ingredient such as plant sterols and stanols but there are instances where these claims are exaggerated, misleading, and even 'medicalised with claims' to prevent or cure disease. In the event of inaccurate marketing, food consumers who rely on that marketing are at risk. In the meantime, enabling misleading claims makes the playing field uneven for entrepreneurs. In Chapter 7, Siva Barathi (Sharl) Marimuthu and Anu Lähteenmäki-Uutela discuss health claims as competing demands between regulatory scrutiny and consumer wants and needs. In a broader sense, sustainability and a long-term commitment and trust-based relationship with the government and consumers should be a priority for businesses, from the planning phase to the point of sale. Two (2) regulatory systems, namely Australia and European Union are compared to analyse the regulatory strategies and solutions that could be effective, efficient as well as fair in regulating food health claims, are provided.

People's perspectives, preferences, and relationships with food continue to evolve. At the same time, food science and technology are developing fast. We examine some possible legal approaches and remedies for sustainable futures where the health of both people and the environment are central. Alessandra Telch, Siva Barathi (Sharl) Marimuthu, and Anu Lähteenmäki-Uutela explore the feasibility of the concept of 'right to nature' to natural entities like landscape and ecosystem and beyond in Chapter 8. They have asked the question, 'Can acknowledging human rights, in particular, the right to food and the right to a healthy environment alongside granting legal personality and rights to natural entities like landscape and ecosystem, bring about a viable solution to food insecurity and its related concerns'? The view that climate change is primarily an environmental concern no longer stands entirely true. It may be true to some degree as the climate crisis encompasses global-scale environmental issues such as global warming, biodiversity loss, desertification, and rising oceans, however, it is inaccurate to confine them solely within environmentalism alone. Ecosystems are seen as highly valuable and as having intrinsic value and rights; worthy of their own protection beyond being mere resources for human use in food production and trade.

An interdisciplinary analysis is incomplete unless a discussion of intellectual property rights is also considered. In Chapter 9, Elham Ghaffarian, Mark Perry, and Siva Barathi (Sharl) Marimuthu discuss the downsides of the restriction of intellectual property rights on new technologies to the least developing countries (LDC). The restriction brings severe impact on LDC countries as these countries are denied benefits from the advancement in technology. Access to modern, smart technologies and biotechnologies are essential for food security. The root problem of this unequal accessibility is influenced by multiple factors including political, legal, economic, and social factors. In this chapter, the authors hope to provide a way forward by suggesting several solutions to accelerate technology flows into the agrifood sector for food security.

In Chapter 10, Siva Barathi (Sharl) Marimuthu and Mr Peter Dawson note Corporate Social responsibility (CSR) as a key element for delivering social good and creating wealth. In other words, doing good for society is good for business. Companies are increasingly understanding that acting sustainably and being sensitive to the needs of stakeholders and the environment, rather than acting outside those parameters, are fast becoming the expected norms. A business setting that is geared toward sustainable practices, including a profitable bottom line and the promotion of societal good, is becoming expected. These aspects are also noted as priorities by the UN in its Sustainable Development Goal (SDG) proclamation and the authors incorporate these aspects in this chapter, albeit in a business framework. Further, a major change is that countries are now looking to adopt mandatory reporting for CSR. This is in line with the latest EU directive which has introduced specific reporting regulations as part of a business's annual reporting obligations. Australia is now taking specific steps to incorporate aspects of CSR in its annual accounts. Thus, a legal position is now established, and this change is also covered in this chapter. Thus, it is recognised that businesses producing goods and services in a sustainable manner experience growth exponentially, which carries benefits for all stakeholders ranging from consumers, employees and staff, investors, the executive, and management as well as supply chain linked businesses. In fact, stakeholders are becoming more circumspect when assessing the merits of an entity's CSR credentials, and decisions on whether to engage and transact business are increasingly being made based on evidence of positive CSR embedding within the strategic planning framework of the business. While CSR has a broader business focus as part of the machinery of producing many economy-wide goods and services for the benefit of a broad range of stakeholders, issues of food security and the production of nutritionally sound food are reflected as both a primary thread overall in this book and as an element of CSR.

Associate Prof Mia Rahim and Mr Abhay Vir Singh Kanwar offer us a new theoretical perspective in Chapter 11. The chapter's key argument is that lack of essential capabilities such as access to education and healthcare, which are necessary for basic biological survival, are the root cause of malnutrition. However, the chapter also highlights that not only access to education and health are essential but also nutritious food are critical for overall wellbeing. In other words, access to nutritious food is equally important to promote optimal conditions for survival. Without the presence of these three capabilities, it is unlikely that a person will enjoy a holistic health.

Chapter 12 is the last chapter in the book, exploring food security and its sustainability. The authors, Dr Asril Amirul Zakariah, Dr Mohd Lotpi Mohd Yuso, Ms Murshamshul Kamariah Musa, focus on the Muslim community and broader audience, aim to enhance the understanding of food security, sustainability, and ethical consumption of new food in the Malaysian Muslim context. The authors examine the interconnectedness of Islamic dietary laws, halal certification procedures, and emerging food technologies in Malaysia. They highlight the complexities that future food brings and the impact they have on the regulatory framework for halal certification in Malaysia. They provide insights into the changing nature of future food and they emphasise that upholding the principles of halal and *ṭayyib* consumption is important in this period of time.

1.3 Conclusion

Although this initiative was a work in progress for several years, the actual drafting of the chapters was between 2023 and July 2024. Food systems continue to face growing pressure to change. Six planetary boundaries have been transgressed, with increased transgression levels since 2015, and the ocean acidification boundary is almost being transgressed (Richardson et al. 2023). Transforming the way food is produced and consumed can leave a truly major impact in bringing the economy within the boundaries. The new EU legislation, including the Corporate Sustainability Reporting Directive EU/2022/2464, the recently accepted Corporate Sustainability Due Diligence Directive, and the Deforestation Regulation EU 2023/1115, paves the way for similar legislation in other countries. Attention to supply chains and footprints is rising due to the CSR and human rights agendas.

People across the world are increasingly aware of and demanding the realisation of their human rights to a clean, safe, healthy, and sustainable environment. The value of ecosystems and biodiversity to provide vital ecosystem services is increasingly understood. Human rights of children and adults concerning nutritious food is still lacking, as heavy marketing efforts focusing on unhealthy food and drink products keep taking place. Regulatory and economic instruments such as taxation, subsidies, or emission trade to regulate and govern food production and consumption are yet to be fully employed.

Food manufacturing and food trade deserve more regulatory attention, as their market power sets them as gatekeepers for change.

References

Council of Europe Commissioner for Human Rights (Dunja Mijatović) 2019, 'Living in a clean environment: A neglected human rights concern', *Human Rights Comment*, 4 June, accessed 20 June 2024, www.coe.int/pl/web/commissioner/-/living-in-a-clean-environment-a-neglected-human-rights-concern-for-all-of-us.

Duncan, J, DeClerck, F, Báldi, A, Treyer S, Aschemann-Witzel, CK, Ahrné, L, Bisoffi, S, Grando, S, Goubys, L, Kohl, J, Hanson, HO, Hudson, R, Lutzeyer, HJ, Nielsen, VH, Ruiz, B, Saggau, E, Valceschini, E, Siebieclec, G & Brunori, G 2022, 'Democratic directionality for transformative food systems research', *Nature Food*, *3*, pp.183–186, https://doi.org/10.1038/s43016-022-00479-x.

European Environmental Bureau EEB 2022, 'Hungry for change: An EU sustainable food systems law for people and nature', accessed 20 June 2024, https://eeb.org/wp-content/uploads/2022/10/EEB-Sustainable-Food-Systems-Law-report.pdf.

Fanning, AL, O'Neill, DW, Hickel, J & Roux, N 2022, 'The social shortfall and ecological overshoot of nations', *Nature Sustainability*, *5*, pp.26–36, https://doi.org/10.1038/s41893-021-00799-z.

FAO 2014, 'Building a common vision for sustainable food and agriculture: Principles and approaches', *Rome*, accessed 20 June 2024, www.fao.org/3/a-i3940e.pdf.

Hinrichs, CC 2014, 'Transitions to sustainability: A change in thinking about food systems change?', *Agriculture and Human Values*, *31*(1), pp.143–155, https://doi.org/10.1007/s10460-014-9479-5.

Hoekstra, AY & Wiedmann, TO 2014, 'Humanity's unsustainable environmental footprint', *Science*, *344*, pp.1114–1117, https://doi.org/10.1126/science.1248365.

International Panel of Experts on Sustainable Food Systems, IPES-Food 2015, 'The new science of sustainable food systems: Overcoming barriers to food system reform', accessed 20 June 2024, https://ipes-food.org/_img/upload/files/NewScienceofSusFood.pdf.

International Panel of Experts on Sustainable Food Systems, IPES-Food 2021, 'A unifying framework for food systems transformation', accessed 20 June 2024, www.ipes-food.org/_img/upload/files/sfsENhq.pdf.

Lonkila, A & Kaljonen, M 2021, 'Promises of meat and milk alternatives: An integrative literature review on emergent research themes', *Agriculture and Human Values*, *38*, pp.625–639, https://doi.org/10.1007/s10460-020-10184-9.

McDermid, SS, Hayek, M, Jamieson, DW, Hale, G & Kanter, D 2023, 'Research needs for a food system transition', *Climatic Change*, *176*(41), https://doi.org/10.1007/s10584-023-03507-2.

Morris, C, Kaljonen, M, Aavik, K, Balázs, B, Cole, M, Coles, B, Efstathiu, S, Fallon, T, Foden, M, Giraud, EH & Goodman, M 2021, 'Priorities for social science and humanities research on the challenges of moving beyond animal-based food systems', *Humanities and Social Sciences Communications*, *8*(1), p.3, https://doi.org/10.1057/s41599-021-00714-z.

O'Neill, DW, Fanning, AL & Lamb, WF 2018, 'A good life for all within planetary boundaries', *Nature Sustainability*, *1*(2), pp.88–95, https://doi.org/10.1038/s41893-018-0021-4.

Puupponen, A, Huttunen, S, Kortetmäki, T, Lähteenmäki-Uutela, A & Kaljonen, M 2023, 'Justice in finnish food policies', *Food Ethics*, *8*(6), https://doi.org/10.1007/s41055-022-00117-z.

Raworth, K 2012, 'A safe and just space for humanity; Can we live within the doughnut?', *Oxfam*, https://doi.org/10.1163/2210-7975_hrd-9824-0069.

Renaud, FG, Zhou, X, Bosher, L, Barrett, B & Huang, S 2022, 'Synergies and trade-offs between sustainable development goals and targets: innovative approaches and new perspectives', *Sustainability Science*, *17*, 1317–1322. https://doi.org/10.1007/s11625-022-01209-9

Richardson, K, Steffen, W, Lucht, W, Bendtsen, J, Cornell, SE, Donges, JF, Drüke, M, Fetzer, I, Bala, G, Von Bloh, W & Feulner, G 2023, 'Earth beyond six of nine planetary boundaries', *Science Advances*, *9*(37), p.eadh2458.

Rockström, J, Gupta, J, Lenton, TM, Qin, D, Lade, SJ, Abrams, JF, Jacobson, L, Rocha, JC, Zimm, C, Bai, X & Bala, G 2021, 'Identifying a safe and just corridor for people and the planet', *Earth's Future*, *9*(4), p.e 2020EF001866, https://doi.org/10.1029/2020EF001866.

Rockström, J, Steffen, W, Noone, K, Persson, Å, Chapin III, FS, Lambin, E, Lenton, TM, Scheffer, M, Folke, C, Schellnhuber, HJ & Nykvist, B 2009a, 'Planetary boundaries: Exploring the safe operating space for humanity', *Ecology and Society*, *14*(2), issue 32, www.ecologyandsociety.org/vol14/iss2/art32/.

Rockström, J, Steffen, W, Noone, K, Persson, Å, Chapin, FS, Lambin, EF, Lenton, TM, Scheffer, M, Folke, C, Schellnhuber, HJ & Nykvist 2009b, 'A safe operating space for humanity', *Nature*, *461*(7263), pp.472–475, https://doi.org/10.1038/461472a.

Steffen, W, Richardson, K, Rockström, J, Cornell, SE, Fetzer, I, Bennett, EM, Biggs, R, Carpenter, SR, De Vries, W, De Wit, CA & Folke, C 2015, 'Planetary boundaries: Guiding human development on a changing planet', *Science*, *347*(6223), p.1259855.

Turner, RA & Wills, J 2022, 'Downscaling doughnut economics for sustainability governance', *Current Opinion in Environmental Sustainability*, *56*, pp.1–10, https://doi.org/10.1016/j.cosust.2022.101180.

United Nations Environment Programme UNEP 2022, 'Emissions gap report 2022: The closing window – Climate crisis calls for rapid transformation of societies', *Nairobi*, accessed 20 June 2024, www.unep.org/emissions-gap-report-2022.

United Nations General Assembly 1987, 'Our common future', *Report of the World Commission on Environment and Development*, accessed 20 June 2024, un-documents.net/our-common-future.pdf.

United Nations Human Rights Committee 2019, 'General comment no. 36: Article 6, right to life', CCPR/C/GC/36, accessed 20 June 2024, Microsoft Word – CCPR C GC 36 formatted.docx (ohchr.org).

United Nations Human Rights Council 2018, 'Human rights and climate change', A/HRC/RES/38/4, accessed 20 June 2024, https://ap.ohchr.org/documents/dpage_e.aspx?si=A/HRC/RES/38/4.

United Nations Joint Statement 2020, 'Joint statement of UN entities on climate change and human rights', HRI/2019/1, 14 May, accessed 20 June 2024, https://documents-dds-ny.un.org/doc/UNDOC/GEN/G20/113/08/PDF/G2011308.pdf?OpenElement.

WHO 2017, 'Don't pollute my future! The impact of the environment on children's health', accessed 20 June 2024, www.who.int/publications/i/item/WHO-FWC-IHE-17.01.

Willett, W, Rockström, J, Loken, B, Springmann, M, Lang, T, Vermeulen, S, Garnett, T, Tilman, D, DeClerck, F, Wood, A & Jonell, M 2019, 'Food in the anthropocene: The EAT-lancet commission on healthy diets from sustainable food systems', *The Lancet*, *393*(10170), pp.447–492, https://doi.org/10.1016/S0140-6736(18)31788-4.

2 From Colonialism to the Commodification of Food

The Criticality of a Globalised Food System

Alessandra Telch and Siva Barathi (Sharl) Marimuthu

2.1 Introduction

The current food system(s) poses a myriad of challenges to be dealt with by humankind. These challenges include environmental degradation to human rights violations, and they trace the roots of the exploitation of ecosystems and disputes arising from the allocation of water and land resources. Understanding the food system structure helps in gaining insight into these challenges. Indeed, our food system(s) does not stand on its own, indeed it is interwoven with environmental, social, and economic threads. The current food systems have evolved due to systemic and human factors; influencing the way we produce, distribute, and consume food. Such influences, deliberate and unintentional, have shaped how we feed and nourish ourselves. Even though there are variations across the globe, there are common traits that can be identified in today's global food network. First, our food production relies on agriculture and livestock farming, a practice that replaces hunting and gathering as the primary method of securing food for human sustenance. Research and studies examining land use reveal a trend – agriculture has become a significant driver of land utilisation in several centuries. According to the UN Food and Agriculture Organization, half of all habitable land today is dedicated to agriculture, influenced by the need for food supply.

The breakdown of land uses on a global map helps to visualise the magnitude of the phenomenon. In fact, the land allocated to livestock, including grazing areas and cropland for animal feed worldwide, covers an area equivalent to the entire Americas (North, Central, and South America combined), whereas cropland (without considering the land used to produce animal feed) is equivalent to the area of East Asia-Pacific, extending as far south as Thailand (Ritchie and Roser 2013). For instance, it is found that ruminant pastures cover more than 25% of the global land surface and about 70% of the agricultural area worldwide (Stehfest et al. 2009). Furthermore, livestock farming occupies 30% of the world's ice-free area and occupies a third of the world's arable land for animal feed (Herrero et al. 2013). Nevertheless, 50% of the agricultural land currently used for livestock feed

DOI: 10.4324/9781003392279-2

production worldwide is not suitable for cultivation and is used exclusively as grassland for grazing livestock such as ruminants (Rivero et al. 2021). We aim to investigate the distribution of resources within food production via data analysis. When we combine the pastures used for grazing with the land used to grow crops for animal feed, livestock occupies around 77% of the world's agricultural land. Taking up most of the world's agricultural land, it produces only 18% of the world's calories and 37% of total protein (Poore and Nemecek 2018).

When resources are limited and there is a need to fulfil the demand of the growing population, the utilisation of cropland per capita is significantly considered in regional policy development and international discussion on sustainable development. Indeed, when we compare the agricultural land per capita in North America to that in Europe, it was found that North America utilises double the area of cropland and pastures for grazing livestock compared to Europe. In Australia, a country with extensive arid and semi-arid land, a significant portion of its land is dedicated to pastures and cropland for grazing livestock (Thackway 2018).

Second, the food trade has expanded to an unprecedented level, to a point that no entity or system, whether at the national or federal level, can function with no external inputs. The agricultural sector generates substantial value, so effective marketing is important for its ongoing sustainability. Four (4) crops, namely sugarcane, maize, wheat, and rice collectively make up about half of the world's primary crop production (Kastner et al. 2012). These crops significantly contribute to global food production.

International trade is projected to expand the global food availability even in the face of many challenges, such as population growth and climate change that threaten the food systems (Bailey and Wellesley 2017). However, the growing reliance on the trade network infrastructure brings about environmental, social, and political consequences that are complex, difficult to identify, and seldom align with economic viability. The recent tension in the Black Sea involving Russia and Ukraine illustrates how international political events impact the grain market worldwide. The entire nations rely on food resources from other countries, making it challenging for them to guarantee supply by the third countries, thus unable to guarantee food security (Grassia et al. 2022).

Third, our food systems are closely connected to the global value chains (Robinson 2018). The food we consume comes from multiple countries and such resources from various regions. In many cases, countries rely on resources originating from other territories (Khoury et al. 2016). The value chains often leave concentrated power in the hands of specific companies, extending their influence from land ownership and seed production to water supply and food retail.

According to Forbes, the leading 25 companies in the food and beverage (F and B) industry had amassed $1.8 trillion in revenue in the last year, which is led by the Swiss Nestle with more than $98 billion in sales, followed by AB InBev, Pepsi, Danone, General Mills, Mondelez, Tyson Foods, JBS, and Kraft-Heinz (Sorvino 2023). In fact, the economic power held by these companies reinforces their presence in the political landscape, resulting in unequal distribution of access to land, seeds, and agricultural services. As highlighted by Heinrich Böll Stiftung in a recent report, international investors are acquiring huge areas of land to secure food and water resources.

Between 2000 and 2016, 10 million hectares of African land were acquired for large-scale agriculture, but only about half are now productive farms, yet hunger and poverty are more prevalent around the large farms than in areas operated by small holdings (Heinrich Böll 2023). Despite efforts to understand the factors driving the financial success of big corporations, experts and researchers often overlook the significant influence of environmental, social, and cultural aspects (Clapp and Scrinis 2017).

2.2 Colonialism, Capitalism, and Commodification of Food

Today's food systems are the result of a series of revolutions that have followed over time. Two major events are always mentioned in literature since there is common agreement about their global relevance. First, the transition from a nomadic lifestyle to sedentary living was linked to the gradual replacement of foraging to agriculture and pastoral practices as the primary food sources. Second, the Green Revolution was primarily driven by the political and business interests of the developed countries. The main objective of this revolution was to enhance global food production by introducing industry practices, such as chemicals and fertilisers into agricultural chains (Pimentel 1996; Evenson and Gollin 2003; Jain 2010).

The same can't be said for the shift in power dynamics and distribution of resources between the New and the Old World as well as between the global South and global North, which have been overlooked. However, it is imperative to grasp the emergence of food system structures and the distinctive traits to comprehend the development of the food system. Such attributes can be traced back to the historical global legal framework prior to the 19th century, during which international law began to form as in the professional setting and state interaction plays a central role in shaping it. In the quest to uncover the political, legal, and sociocultural factors that lead to the establishment of the present-day globalised food systems, the significant influence of colonialism is considered.

Throughout history, wars have ravaged lands, yet hunger and disease have been even more devastating. In acquiring natural resources including food, often nations were driven to expand their territory. In a way, food was also used to assert colonial authority over the occupied population. Within this complex framework, food has evolved into a commodity to be traded in the market. Unfortunately, this commodification has been stressed in the modern era, sidelining the social, cultural, and environmental factors. Indeed, with the rise of capitalism, the division between society and nature is further reinforced, leading to a flawed narrative that suggests humans inhabit a world abundant with limitless commodities.

Today, agriculture is the world's largest industry, wielding significant political and corporate power. It influences and directs people's food choices while becoming the determinant of the nation's fortune and decline. To safeguard their profits, the giant food and farming corporations actively promote the commodification of food. Through lobbying efforts and establishing a monopoly by controlling resources such as soil, water, and biological resources, they solidify their grip on the global food supply chain. The primary food and farming players are financing and advocating for ongoing dominance in international and local policies. Meanwhile, small- and medium-sized farms, which often represent social and environmental aspects of the food supply chain, are inadequately represented in the discussions.

This kind of narrative obscures and devalues the lives and labour of most of the global population. It also downplays the cost associated with the depletion of natural resources and the disruption of ecosystemic services. The outcome is concerning, considering the loss of biodiversity and the diminishing capacity of the ecosystem to regenerate and accommodate human wellbeing. Viewing food solely as a commodity for sale represents the primary cost in accounting and the expansion of alternative markets for agricultural practice. These two (2) aspects are key milestones in our endeavour to revolutionise the methods by which we produce and consume food.

2.3 Food as the Colonising Force in the Past and the Present

Colonialism is defined as a practice in which "a country directly controls less powerful countries and uses their resources to increase its own power and wealth" in the Collins English Dictionary. Certain colonial experiences hold importance in grasping food's dual role as a colonising force and a political tool to analyse the historical experiences in providing valuable insights into today's food systems and challenges. As discussed in the literature, modernisation plays a vital role in facilitating the movement and spread of people, plants, seeds, animals, and various foods across boundaries. The imperial nation, driven by the desire to exploit indigenous land and people, consistently introduces the coloniser's plants and animals. Such transportation leads to profound alteration in the local landscape, ecosystems, and dietary customs (Cinotto 2023).

One of the most prominent instances occurs following the first arrival of Europeans in the American lands. This marks the birth of a globalised market built upon the utilisation of local ecosystems to produce commodities such as coffee, banana, and cocoa, intended for consumption by the more privileged residents of the imperial capitals. The European monarch's charters illustrated the underlying logic of conquest in the series of colonialism, justifying their right to "discover and settle" areas of the New World. These charters acknowledge ownership rights and claim sovereignty over local politics and indigenous communities.

One of the earliest episodes is when the Spanish royal granted Juan Ponce de Leon the rights to a territory that is now known as Florida. He was "adelantado" – a position that bestows civil and criminal jurisdiction over the expedition of any lands the person may discover and settle (Benton 2017). Likewise, in the 16th and 17th centuries, the French and English colonial powers asserted sovereignty over the American territories that they explored, disregarding any pre-existing rights of the Native people residing there (Slattery 2005). Therefore, this legal interpretation of rights. The colonisation process aims to reshape the colonised societies to resemble that of the coloniser, which is achieved by forced exploitation of the local resources. This has broader implications. Not only the colonised countries are profoundly influenced by the changes set in motion by the colonisers, but the colonisers themselves are also influenced by the capitalist land and labour systems they have advocated. This transformation extends to various aspects of the societies, including dietary habits.

In this sense, colonialism goes beyond imposing laws, it represents an interconnection of practices and regulations involving the colonisers and the colonised, resulting in new paradigms and connections that we now recognise as "globalisation." In a way, food plays a role in various ways. Upon the arrival of colonists in the New World, the Europeans introduced the concept of cultural and class-based segregation founded on dietary requirements, adhering to the socio-natural ideology of the Middle Ages, which implements strict guidelines to take care of health (Sangiorgi 2011). Food from the New World was only considered as the last resort during times of famine. Colonisers, firm on their belief and fear that the consumption of local indigenous foods compromise their wellbeing, refuse to incorporate local staple foods such as beans and maize. Instead, they cultivate their own crops by transforming local agriculture to suit their requirements. More importantly, they introduced livestock farming, which thrive in the absence of predators and are equipped with abundant food resources. This has laid the foundation for the emergence of a formidable player in the food supply chain – the meat industry.

Over the years, global meat production has experienced a significant surge. Since 1962, the total meat production has quadrupled, and this trend is anticipated to continue, driven by both the increasing global population and rapid growth in total meal production. Even though the meat consumption rate per capita varies between countries, the rate is inclined to increase when individuals experience rising affluence.

Between 1935 and 1936, the Italian fascist regime conquered Ethiopia, which used to unite with Eritrea and Somalia, forming the "Africa Orientale Italiana." Such action was driven by the ambition to create a "Food Empire" in the region. These characteristics of the endeavour set the Italian imperialist apart from the European imperialist counterparts. One of the intriguing aspects is the innovative relationship between food and empire, laying the groundwork for what we now know to be as *'the supermodernity of global food and its geopolitics,'* or the globalised Food Systems. Today, we are witnessing the resurgence of similar power relations that repropose post-colonial temporalities, legitimising the new colonial ties.

In the last decades, industrial agriculture and food processing have reproduced colonial dynamics in the "modern" context, affecting both countries of the global North and the global South at different impacts. The full extent of this ongoing process does not come into focus until the last few years when the multiple environmental, social, and health consequences stemming from the widespread consumption of highly processed food become evident. The effects include a concerning decrease in biodiversity and the loss of natural resources, a surge in diet-related diseases, as well as the erosion of local culinary traditions and agricultural practices.

2.4 Capitalism and the Commodification of Food

As highlighted before, the governance of the food system played a role in the colonial dynamics in the previous centuries. This influence was first evident during the European country's dominion in the New World. Later, the global North starts to prosper by exploiting the natural resources of the countries in the Southern Hemisphere. Today, the concern for food availability continues to shape all nations' political and market strategies, which is exemplified by Europe's Common Agricultural Policy.

However, the current approach in creating and implementing these policies is restricted because it overlooks a series of negative externalities, as previously discussed. The search for a global response to concerns about food availability, allocation of agrifood resources, and management of the surplus food produced is not new. Indeed, the past decades have witnessed the creation and expansion of a globally recognised system, the General Agreement on Tariffs and Trade (GATT). GATT was established in 1947, as the international community's attempt to create unified rules of conduct in managing the operations of multinational enterprises.

Its purpose is to boost the global trade volume by setting guidelines for the international import and export of goods besides overseeing government involvement in international trade. The Agreement seeks to reduce barriers to international trade by eliminating or reducing quotas, tariffs, and subsidies. Among these, quantitative restrictions are deemed the most distorting and undesirable for trade and the prohibition stands as one of the fundamental principles of GATT. With respect to food systems, the GATT goals and principles lead to a decrease in local food self-reliance in favour of global interdependence.

Right from the outset, questions are raised about whether the provisions of the free trade systems address the concerns of agriculture and food security needs. As stated by Mark Ritchie in his speech at the International Symposium on Food Self-Sufficiency held in Japan, Tokyo in 1988, USDA negotiators are contending the issue of the absence of authority in regulating imports.

> Nations tending towards underproduction would not be able to build up their own food producing capacity, while those nations who tend towards overproduction would be unable to balance supply with demand. Without import controls, they argued, 'overproducing' countries would build up ever larger surplus stocks, which would eventually have to be dumped onto world markets either as food aid or as heavily subsidised exports. The disastrous impacts of this food dumping, especially on food self-reliance in the Third World, has been documented for over a hundred years.
>
> (Ritchie 1988)

In response to the statement by Ritchie, special provisions are incorporated into the original GATT granting each nation the right to limit the number of imports of agricultural products. The proposal by the United States highlights the "Suggested Charter for an International Trade Organization of the United Nations" dated 1946. The proposal remained unchanged throughout the negotiations of GATT and the Charter except for some refinement and the inclusion of "fisheries products".

Article XI on the General Elimination of Quantitative Restrictions reads as follows:

1. No prohibitions or restrictions other than duties, taxes or other charges, whether made effective through quotas, import or export licences, or other measures, shall be instituted or maintained by any contracting party on the importation of any product of the territory of any other contracting party or on the exportation or sale for export of any product destined for the territory of any other contracting party.
2. The provisions of paragraph 1 of this Article shall not extend to the following:

   (a) Export prohibitions or restrictions temporarily applied to prevent or relieve critical shortage of foodstuffs or other products essential to the exporting contracting party;
   (b) Import and export prohibitions or restrictions necessary to the application of standards or regulations for the classification, grading or marketing of commodities in international trade;
   (c) Import restrictions on any agricultural or fisheries product, imported in any form, necessary to the enforcement of governmental

> measures which operate: (i) to restrict the quantities of the like domestic product permitted to be marketed or produced, or, if there is no substantial domestic production of the like product, of a domestic product for which the imported product can be directly substituted; or (ii) to remove a temporary surplus of the like domestic product, or, if there is no substantial domestic production of the like product of a domestic product for which the imported product can be directly substituted, by making the surplus available to certain groups of domestic consumers free of charge or at prices below the current market level; or (iii) to restrict the quantities permitted to be produced of any animal product, the production of which is directly dependent, wholly or mainly, on the imported commodity, if the domestic production of that commodity is relatively negligible.
>
> Any contracting party applying restrictions on the importation of any product pursuant to subparagraph (c) of this paragraph shall give public notice of the total quantity or value of the product permitted to be imported during a specified future period and of any change in such quantity or value. Moreover, any restrictions applied under (i) shall not be such as will reduce the total of imports relative to the total of domestic production, as compared with the proportion which might reasonably be expected to rule between the two in the absence of restrictions. In determining this proportion, the contracting party shall pay due regard to the proportion prevailing during a previous representative period and to any special factors which may have affected or may be affecting the trade in the product concerned.
>
> (Article XI on the General Elimination of Quantitative Restrictions)

The exclusion of agriculture from the general principles of GATT is deemed as an obstacle to establishing a fair and market-oriented agricultural trading system. GATT members are allowed to employ export subsidies on primary agricultural products and to impose import restrictions under certain conditions, resulting in barriers to the trade of primary agricultural commodities on a scale uncommon in other merchandise sectors (Healy et al. 1998). The signing of the Agreement establishing the World Trade Organisation (WTO) in 1994 led to the incorporation of the legal agreement and its principles.

This move empowers WTO to play a more significant role in serving the evolving international trade landscape. Furthermore, GATT (herein referred to as the agreement since GATT as an organisation has been replaced) is complemented by the new General Agreement on Trade in Services (GATS) and the Agreement on Trade-Related Aspects of Intellectual Property Rights (TRIPS). Such additions reflect the transition of international commerce from focusing on exchanging goods to encompassing the trade of services and ideas (World Trade Organisation 2023). In this context, agriculture acquires a special status in the WTO's Agreements and Memorandum of Understanding on trade (signed in 1994 and entered into force on 1 January 1995). This has arisen from the adoption of the Agreement on Agriculture (AoA) negotiated during the Uruguay Round (1986–1994). Under this agreement, WTO Member States are committed to the reform agenda for agricultural policies that lays down specific mandatory commitments in three (3) areas, market access, domestic support, and export subsidies.

Acknowledging a special status for agriculture is crucial to address food systems. However, both GATT and WTO fail to understand the vital relations between food and human physical, social, health, and cultural reproduction, confining the role of food to marketable commodities. Prominent figures in the scientific community concur that this is attributed to the strong influence of the agrifood lobby in shaping and advancing both international market and national agricultural policies. To explain this, we can examine the management of natural resources, focusing on access and equitable sharing of genetic resources.

2.5 Management of Natural Resources

Access and equitable sharing of genetic resources systems, often referred to as "ABS," aim to fairly distribute the benefits deriving from research and development involving biogenetic resources between providers (often biodiversity-rich countries) and users (such as private companies, universities, and gene banks). These systems were developed under the Convention on Biological Diversity (CBD) to address the needs of an ever-evolving field, pertaining to the progress in research and exploitation activities as well as issues associated with fairness and equity (Secretariat of the Convention on Biological Diversity 2000).

ABS shares some common features with GATT, which are the reasons why both systems face challenges in gaining universal recognition among the member countries and in accomplishing their stated objectives or, at the very least, achieving them without significant downsides. The common features shall be discussed.

First, both ABS and GATT are rooted in the idea of state sovereignty over natural resources within the territories. This concept is closely tied to colonial and post-colonial dynamics, significantly impacted by the global North-South divide. Developing countries are introduced to the international legal system through the Convention on Biological Diversity, to assert control over their natural resources and to break free from the economic constraints imposed during the colonial era. However, plant genetic resources are not managed as "a common heritage of mankind." In fact, farmers are prevented from reaping the benefits deriving from these resources; where breeders in the global North control due to the expansion of patent law, set of costs as well as payments for accessing genetic resources (Sirakaya 2022).

Second, the systems are proposed to respond to the food security concerns, driven by rapid global population growth following the Second World War. Soil, water, and genetic resources are exploited to obtain the maximum amount of food possible. Governments, often with financial backing from emerging agrifood industry enterprises, launch extensive research and development efforts aimed at discovering new varieties that ensure higher yields. This leads to the dominance of industrial agriculture via the mainstream farming technique; as well as companies involved in producing and commercialising pesticides and fertilisers to control pests and diseases to enhance productivity in the monoculture fields.

These attributes lead to the challenges encountered in the establishment of GATT and the global food commercialisation system. Simile issues were observed in the context of ABS systems:

- Insufficient acknowledgement of the negative externalities associated with the exploitation of natural resources;
- Tendency to view natural resources as marketable goods, disregarding their role in the restoration and conservation of nature and the prevention of biodiversity loss;
- The impact of agricultural lobbying efforts.

Federal and local agriculture and livestock policies mirror these shortcomings, which have become more evident among the European Member States, often viewed as the leaders when it comes to the development of food policies (European Commission, Directorate-General for Research and Innovation 2020). On the one hand, these countries claim to be the custodian of rich culinary heritage deserving of reverence, with a commitment to adopt foods and farming practices regulated by procedural standards to guarantee their quality:

> European food is already a global standard for food that is safe, plentiful, nutritious, and of high quality. This is the result of years of EU policy-making to protect human, animal and plant health, and of the efforts of farmers, fishers, and aquaculture producers.
>
> (Sirakaya 2022: 4)

However, on the other hand, issues such as land and ecosystem degradation, loss of biodiversity, the spread of NCDs due to unhealthy eating habits, and the impoverishment of local economic networks in favour of global structures are the challenges that affect the European territory.

2.6 Criticalities of the Current Food Systems and the Call for Sustainable Food Systems Governance

Recently, the European food programmes and policies are focused on achieving food security and safety. The guiding principle is to secure sufficient food for all while reducing rural poverty. With this aim in mind, national and regional food networks are developed under the Common Agricultural Policy (CAP) framework. As a result of this production-focused approach, the European food system today ensures a high level of food availability, food safety, and offers a wide range of choices, yet evidence has shown that this approach is not sustainable from the environmental, social, and economic aspects. Over time, this strategy has failed; leading to the threat of the foundation where the food system is based, such as water, soil, and climate. In fact, it has overlooked other crucial areas contributing to the underperformance of the food system, including health, social, and environmental sustainability, which are going to be discussed.

2.6.1 Health Sustainability

Despite the success in terms of the amount of food produced by the Member States, the population grapples with health issues linked to dietary patterns and the food environment. Malnutrition affects many people, with nearly half of the population suffering from micronutrient deficiency, while the prevalence of overweight and obesity is increasing rapidly (European Commission, Directorate-General for Research and Innovation 2020). There is evidence that the calories we consume are not only essential for constructing, supporting, and repairing our bodies but they are also a critical factor in determining our overall health.

The type of food and the quantity of calories we consume play a pivotal role in shaping our wellbeing, encompassing our susceptibility to chronic ailments. The conditions span from cardiovascular disorders such as stroke and heart disease to metabolic disorders like diabetes, osteoporosis, and cancer (WHO 2018). The onset and spread of these illnesses are linked to the food environment where people live. This environment is influenced by affordability, preference, convenience, and cultural norms. These aspects are manipulated by the key stakeholders of the agrifood industry, leading to the overproduction of ultra-processed foods (Downs et al. 2020).

Such foods offer convenience such as being ready to consume and having long shelf-life, they are also appealing due to their hyper-palatability nature. In addition, they yield substantial profit to the manufacturers due to the low cost of ingredients and labour. However, they often lack nutritional balance and consumers are prone to overconsumption, displacing other unprocessed or minimally processed foods and processed culinary ingredients, which, according to research based on the NOVA framework, would have no such negative impact on human health (Monteiro et al. 2009). Consequently, individuals who experience hunger tend to have greater access to ultra-processed foods, placing them at the highest risk of diet-related diseases.

This shows the close connection between food insecurity and poor nutrition. In fact, food insecurity is defined as the state of being without reliable access to affordable and nutritious food (Food and Agricultural Organization of United Nations 2023). To promote accessibility and affordability of fresh and minimally processed foods that offer superior nutritional value, a combination of public health policies and market incentives is crucial. These policies shall encompass all phases of the food supply chain, "from the farm to the fork."

Despite evidence by the global scientific community, that replacing ultra-processed foods with non-ultra-processed foods decreases the risk of obesity and other diet-related non-communicable chronic diseases and premature mortality, the agrifood lobby still impedes the overcoming of this, hindering further obstacles to the drafting and implementation of sound food policies. Another aspect that is important in ensuring health sustainability is the impact of labelling. In fact, consumer understanding of food labelling is important.

Many studies highlight the impact of labelling on consumer attitudes, intentions, and decision-making. For example, Aliaga-Ortega et al. (2019) analysed the effect of nutritional warnings on the labels of processed food on consumers. The analysis looks at the demographic and physiological factors and is based on the theory of planned behaviour. It was found that nutritional warnings influence the choices of processed food purchased by consumers (Aliaga-Ortega et al. 2019).

2.6.2 Social Sustainability

The Secretary General of the United Nations Antonio Guterres in his forward in the seventh edition of the Global Report on Food Crises, emphasised the need for collective action and unwavering commitment. It highlights the struggle to progress towards Sustainable Development Goal 2 to end global hunger (Food Security Information Network 2023). Despite the vast annual food production, which could theoretically feed one and a half times the current world population, food security and improved nutrition remain a distant goal. The number of individuals facing acute food insecurity increased from 112.7 million in 53 countries in 2018 to 257.8 million in 58 countries in 2022.

The escalating food insecurity is linked to factors such as conflicts, mass displacement due to political instability, climate crisis, and natural disasters. The soaring food prices significantly restrict access to food, especially for the local communities. Price increases and extreme climate events affect crop production and livestock, which are important for livelihood, resulting in lower income.

In a survey conducted on people from 69 communities of 14 countries in East and South Asia; Eastern, Central, and Western Africa; and the Caribbean, it was found that most households resort to low-quality food, and females in the house (mothers and girls) often sacrifice their meal portion to prioritise children and males. Meanwhile, men migrate to urban areas in search of higher income, leaving wives and children behind. This situation reflects a systemic crisis within the food chain, resulting in social consequences and an unequal burden on females (ActionAid 2023).

While Europe may not be experiencing a food crisis to the same extent as other regions, it is crucial to keep an eye on the social sustainability of the agri-food systems. The food system is a significant component of Europe's production and consumption landscape. A comprehensive and holistic assessment, such as the life cycle assessment (LCA) promoted within the SDGs policy, can shed some light on the social externalities of food production and consumption patterns.

In the European food systems, small- and medium-sized firms contribute significantly to the total revenue generated. They are responsible for nearly half of the turnover in the industry. However, the smaller firms lack the level of control and coordination in the supply chain that larger companies have. In other words, they may not have as much control over the various stages of food production and distribution as larger companies do, which affects their efficiency and competitiveness. This limitation hinders their ability to engage with policymakers and influence consumers' choices, resulting in imbalanced power dynamics.

As a result, major retailers exploit this situation to increase their profit margins to the detriment of smaller producers. Adopting a life-cycle perspective enables us to assess not only the social dimension of food products and services but also their environmental and economic sustainability. This assessment considers indicators related to fundamental rights, gender equality and societal challenges in general, labour market, as well as investment in human capital and community wellbeing. These aspects can be analysed at different levels, including product and company level, economic sector and region level, or country and state level (Mancini et al. 2023).

Creating a positive social balance for food systems entails creating viable and fair livelihood for farmers, fishers, and workers in the food sector. This involves investing in rural areas to stimulate economic growth and employment opportunities. It also means empowering farmers' role in the food supply chain, to a certain extent, empowering female farmers. Currently, many rural jobs are characterised by low pay and job insecurity, often in peripheral areas. Despite the presence in the food sector, few female farmers have a leadership role and/or own their own land or farm.

2.6.3 *Environmental Sustainability*

Food sustainability challenges require a reconsideration of agriculture and food production. It is essential that nature restoration and food security goals are not opposing each other as they are interdependent. The food industry has a dual impact, it contributes to food security while causing environmental damage such as air, water, and soil pollution at the same time. It also leads to biodiversity loss, soil erosion, climate change, and overconsumption of natural resources, including water and energy, while wasting significant food.

Scientific evidence highlights the environmental impact of food supply chains in Europe – a complex and multifaceted issue emerging from multiple sources. We do not aim to cover all aspects, but we would like to present some key data points to underline the importance of agricultural and food policy in achieving sustainability goals (Donald 2004; Chaudhary and Kastner 2016; Notarnicola et al. 2017; Scherhaufer et al. 2018). According to the Business and Sustainable Development Commission Report, food and agriculture are one of the four economic systems with market opportunities that can be identified in the UN Sustainable Development Goals.

Indeed, a global food and agriculture system in line with the SDGs would deliver nutritious, affordable food for the growing world population, generate higher income, and promote reforestation, freshwater resources, and vital ecosystems, including the world's oceans. It would create a new economic value of more than US$2 trillion by 2030 and would be more resilient to climate risk (United Nations 2023). Agriculture and food production supply chains contribute significantly to greenhouse gas emissions.

According to the European Environment Agency (EEA), the agricultural sector alone is responsible for around 10% of the EU's total greenhouse gas emissions (European Environment Agency 2023). These include emissions from animal husbandry, enteric fermentation, and synthetic fertilisers. Furthermore, Europe's appetite for agricultural products to sustain current consumption patterns and increasing food demand has implications on land use and deforestation rate within and beyond the European borders (Mirazo 2022).

Changes in land use and environmental pollution are the key important factors that damage biodiversity. In addition, the overexploitation of species and the spread of invasive species leave harmful effects. The use of pesticides and fertilisers also has a negative impact on the environment, leading to water pollution and damage to non-target species in the European ecosystems where they are used, and where they are produced in the region. It is crucial to recognise the critical role of biodiversity in agriculture as it supports vital functions and services in the food system. We urgently need to address and reverse the concerning decline in biodiversity. Current data shows that 94% of the biomass of non-human mammals consists of livestock. This rises to 97% if we focus on land mammals alone (Hannah and Max 2020). Also, the agricultural sector significantly impacts our freshwater resources, particularly in regions with scarcity.

According to the EEA, agriculture is the largest freshwater consumer in the EU-28, accounting for up to 60% of total freshwater consumption across Europe. It accounts for 24% of all water from natural sources in the EU-28 area (European Environment Agency 2018). Spain, Italy, Greece, France, and Portugal alone are responsible for 96% of water consumption for agriculture in the EU-28 between 2008 and 2017 (Christiansen 2021). Industrial farming practices, including intensive monocultures, can pollute rivers, lakes, and oceans by releasing excess nutrients into the ecosystems.

In discussing the environmental impact of food production and distribution, addressing the issue of food and packaging waste is also crucial. Our global food system is not as efficient as it could be in handling waste associated with food and its packaging and there is room for improvement of how we manage and reduce waste within the food supply chain. To put it in perspective, in 2011, a report by the Food and Agriculture Organization (FAO) estimated that around one-third of food produced globally was lost or wasted, amounting to a total of 1.3 billion tonnes each year (Food and Agriculture Organization of the United Nations 2011).

The United Nations reports that a country that causes global food loss and waste would be the world's third-largest emitter of greenhouse gases, after the United States and China (Environment 2017; SDG Progress report 2022 n.d). This issue has received global recognition as an urgent matter that requires immediate action. Various institutions, including the European Parliament, national governments, and international organisations, have set ambitious targets to halve food loss and waste by 2025 or 2030.

The European Union is committed to achieving the global Sustainable Development Goal (SDG) Target 12.3 to halve per capita food waste at the retail and consumer level by 2030 and reduce food loss along the food production and supply chains. To accelerate the EU's progress towards this goal, the Commission proposes that, by 2030, Member States reduce food waste by 10% in the processing and manufacturing sector, and by 30% (per capita) at retail and consumption (restaurants, food services, and households (Frequently asked questions: Reducing food waste in the EU, no date).

Due to the system inefficiency, the impact of excess food and food waste is significant and has a profound impact on our climate and environment. Even if the food is not consumed, it still requires resources throughout its life cycle, from cultivation and harvesting to transport and preparation, before being thrown away. In addition, the environmental impact of food supply chains varies significantly, depending on consumer nutritional choices. Furthermore, not all food has the same impact in terms of greenhouse gas emissions, land use, and water consumption.

Poore and Nemecek (2018) provide data that illustrates the environmental impact per kilogram of food product in terms of both greenhouse gas emissions and land use. Predictably, livestock production is at the higher end of both emissions and land use while plant-based production is at the lower end.

Of course, not all production methods produce a similar amount of emission. Life cycle assessment reports can provide valuable insights into the carbon footprint of different production systems. For example, beef produced from local farms that adopt sustainable practices such as grazing on natural pastures, from their own feed, and using manure for fertilisation, all these contribute to significant CO_2 savings compared to beef raised intensively on large farms in a conventional manner (Neri et al. 2018). By identifying food with a lower carbon footprint we can make more conscious and environmentally friendlier choices.

The statistics highlight the impact that agricultural and food production supply chains have on the environment in Europe. They underline the importance of adopting sustainable and responsible practices in these sectors to transform to a more environmentally conscious food system. It is important that food policies, such as the Common Agricultural Policy and the Common Fisheries Policy, are consistent with the European policies and objectives related to environmental sustainability. These include the European Green Deal, the EU's Zero Pollution Action Plan, the Farm to Fork Strategy, the European Climate Pact, and the Food 2030 initiatives (European Commission 2020).

2.7 Conclusion

Food systems involve interconnected components that render isolated interventions ineffective and potentially cause problems elsewhere. To provide safe, nutritious, and healthy food for the current and future generations, a holistic approach is required. Hence, the entire design, governance, and evaluation of food systems must be viewed as interconnected and interdependent. Food policies should incorporate a deeper recognition of how food systems impact the environment, society, and the economy. To achieve this, our legal framework should be further developed to incorporate sustainable goals and principles, leading to a more "integrated approach to our food system."

The current practices in Europe present challenges in achieving a comprehensive understanding of the larger context. It compartmentalised various components, treating them as isolated issues without considering the interconnectedness of their actions and inactions. Segregated departments and policies often lead to divergent objectives that make it hard to plan, execute, and report the initiatives. To encounter this, a more balanced approach that is characterised by well-defined aspects of environmental protection, people's wellbeing, and economic stability are crucial.

Such an approach is essential for the development of an effective strategy, which necessitates change at the global level. According to the Centre for Food Policy Research Brief (Caleffi et al. 2023), there are 45 actions that policymakers can take into consideration to reorient food systems towards environmental sustainability. Moreover, the authors draw attention to the fact that the transition to more environmentally sustainable food systems is viable, with benefits for human health and other positive impacts as well as trade-offs, but the recommended actions require consistent, systematic, and intentional efforts.

Such actions are associated with five main areas of intervention, which demonstrates the complexity of food systems:

- Actions to reorient land use in agriculture (#1 to #7);
- Actions to improve the environmental impact of agriculture and farming (#8 to #22);
- Actions to improve the sustainability of wild fisheries and aquaculture (#23 to #28);

- Actions to reduce food loss and waste (#29 to #36);
- Actions to reorient diet and overall food demand (#37 to #45).

When it comes to the premises, three (3) recommendations are provided to address the problems and issues discussed in this chapter. First, it is prudent to adopt cost accounting and life cycle assessment practices as a foundation in policy formulation before implementing any policies. Such practices will offer a comprehensive understanding of the potential consequences of policies prior to their implementation. This enables an understanding of how choices and actions can harm or benefit the environment. Importantly, the practices will enable policymakers to ensure vital services provided by nature such as clean water and fertile soil are preserved.

In fact, it encourages a more holistic and environmentally responsible approach to policymaking, where a wide range of consequences is considered. Second, it is imperative that we shift our focus from prioritising profits and concentrate on upholding fundamental human rights to nutritious food. It is more that hidden costs associated with food systems have been ignored for an extended period, and costs directly impact our ability to access and enjoy fundamental rights such as adequate food supply, clean water, optimal health, and secured housing.

Finally, a comprehensive approach that considers the impacts of food policies on ecosystems, human health, and people's livelihood is essential. So, this approach requires involvement of the governments, businesses, and society in its entirety. The primary challenge lies in the perception that food is a mere commodity, prioritising quantity over quality while overlooking the complex food systems and their significant impact on the planet. However, food is much more than that, it plays a crucial role in our wellbeing and health, besides empowering societies and protecting natural and urban environments, being linked to the indigenous and traditional knowledge, culture, and cuisine. Indeed, food is a common heritage of humanity and sustains life itself.

References

ActionAid 2023, 'The human costs of the food crisis: How price spikes are wreaking havoc across the globe', 27 June, accessed 29 March 2024, https://actionaid.org/publications/2023/human-costs-food-crisis-how-price-spikes-are-wreaking-havoc-across-globe.

Aliaga-Ortega, L, Adasme-Berríos, C, Méndez, C, Soto, C & Schnettler, B 2019, 'Processed food choice based on the theory of planned behavior in the context of nutritional warning labels', *British Food Journal*, *121*(12), pp.3266–3280.

'Article XI on the General Elimination of Quantitative Restrictions' no date, accessed 29 March 2024, www.wto.org/english/res_e/publications_e/ai17_e/gatt1994_art11_gatt47.pdf.

Bailey, R & Wellesley, L 2017, *Chokepoints and vulnerabilities in global food trade*, Chatham House, London, p.111.

Benton, L 2017, 'The legal logic of wars of conquest: Truces and betrayal in the early modern world', *Duke Journal of Comparative and International Law*, *28*, p.425.

Caleffi, S, Hawkes, C & Walton, S 2023, *45 actions to orient food systems towards environmental sustainability: Co-benefits and trade-offs*, Centre for Food Policy, City, University of London, London.
Chaudhary, A & Kastner, T 2016, 'Land use biodiversity impacts embodied in international food trade', *Global Environmental Change*, *38*, pp.195–204.
Clapp, J & Scrinis, G 2017, 'Big food, nutritionism, and corporate power', *Globalizations*, *14*(4), pp.578–595.
Cinotto, S 2023, *Gastrofascismo e Impero: Il cibo nell'Africa orientale Italiana, 1935–1941*, Mimesis.
Christiansen, T 2021, 'Water and agriculture: Towards sustainable solutions', accessed 1 April, https://forum.eionet.europa.eu/nrc-eionet-freshwater/library/2020-water-agriculture-consultation/2020-water-agriculture-report-consultation/.
Donald, PF 2004, 'Biodiversity impacts of some agricultural commodity production systems', *Conservation Biology*, *18*(1), pp.17–37.
Downs, SM, Ahmed, S, Fanzo, J & Herforth, A 2020, 'Food environment typology: Advancing an expanded definition, framework, and methodological approach for improved characterization of wild, cultivated, and built food environments toward sustainable diets', *Foods*, *9*(4), p.532.
Environment, U.N. 2017, *Promoting sustainable lifestyles*, *UNEP – UN environment programme*, accessed 8 January 2024, www.unep.org/regions/north-america/regional-initiatives/promoting-sustainable-lifestyles.
European Commission 2020, 'Farm to fork strategy: For a fair, healthy and environmentally friendly food system', *Communication from the Commission to the European Parliament, the Council, the European Economic and Social Committee and the Committee of the Regions*, *381*, pp.1–9, https://food.ec.europa.eu/system/files/2020-05/f2f_action-plan_2020_strategy-info_en.pdf.
European Commission, Directorate-General for Research and Innovation, Group of Chief Scientific Advisors 2020, 'Towards a sustainable food system: Moving from food as a commodity to food as more of a common good: Independent expert report, Publications Office', accessed 1 April 2024, https://doi.org/10.26356/sustainablefood.
European Environment Agency 2018, 'Water use in Europe – Quantity and quality face big challenges', https://www.eea.europa.eu/signals-archived/signals-2018-content-list/articles/water-use-in-europe-2014#:~:text=Agriculture%20accounts%20for%20the%20largest,to%20water%20stress%20in%20Europe.
European Environment Agency 2023, 'EEA greenhouse gases-data viewer', 18 April, www.eea.europa.eu/publications/data-and-maps/data/data-viewers/greenhouse-gases-viewer.
Evenson, RE & Gollin, D 2003, 'Assessing the impact of the Green Revolution, 1960 to 2000', *Science*, *300*(5620), pp.758–762.
Food and Agriculture Organization of the United Nations 2011, 'Global food losses and food waste – Extent, causes and prevention', Food and Agricultural Organisation of the United Nations.
Food and Agricultural Organization of United Nations 2023, 'Hunger and food security', *Food and Agricultural Organisation of the United Nations*, US Government, accessed 29 March 2024, www.fao.org/hunger/en/#:~:text=What%20is%20food%20insecurity%3F,of%20resources%20to%20obtain%20food.
Food Security Information Network 2023, 'Global report on food crisis', accessed 1 April 2024, www.fsinplatform.org/global-report-food-crises-2023.
Frequently Asked Questions: Reducing Food Waste in the EU, no date, *European commission – European commission*, accessed 8 January 2024, https://ec.europa.eu/commission/presscorner/detail/en/qanda_19_6706.

Grassia, M, Mangioni, G, Schiavo, S & Traverso, S 2022, 'Insights into countries' exposure and vulnerability to food trade shocks from network-based simulations', *Scientific Reports*, *12*(1), p.4644.

Hannah, R & Max, R 2020, 'Environmental impacts of food production', accessed 11 April 2024, https://ourworldindata.org/environmental-impacts-of-food.

Healy, S, Pearce, R & Stockbridge, M 1998, 'The implications of the Uruguay Round agreement on agriculture for developing countries: A training manual', *United Nations Food & Agriculture Organisation*, *41*.

Heinrich Böll, S 2023, 'The green political foundation, power: Food business, big business – Power: Food business, big business |', accessed 1 April 2024, www.boell.de/en/power-food-business-big-business.

Herrero, M, Havlík, P, Valin, H, Notenbaert, A, Rufino, MC, Thornton, PK, Blümmel, M, Weiss, F, Grace, D & Obersteiner, M 2013, 'Biomass use, production, feed efficiencies, and greenhouse gas emissions from global livestock systems', *Proceedings of the National Academy of Sciences*, *110*(52), pp.20888–20893.

Jain, HK 2010, *Green revolution: History, impact and future*, Studium Press LLC..

Kastner, T, Rivas, MJI, Koch, W & Nonhebel, S 2012, 'Global changes in diets and the consequences for land requirements for food', *Proceedings of the National Academy of Sciences*, *109*(18), pp.6868–6872.

Khoury, CK, Achicanoy, HA, Bjorkman, AD, Navarro-Racines, C, Guarino, L, Flores-Palacios, X, Engels, JM, Wiersema, JH, Dempewolf, H, Sotelo, S & Ramírez-Villegas, J 2016, 'Origins of food crops connect countries worldwide', *Proceedings of the Royal Society B: Biological Sciences*, *283*(1832), p.20160792.

Mancini, L, Valente, A, Vignola, GB, Mengual, ES & Sala, S 2023, 'Social footprint of European food production and consumption', *Sustainable Production and Consumption*, *35*, pp.287–299.

Mirazo, JR 2022, 'Europe eats the world: How the EU's food production and consumption impact the planet', *Worldwide Fund for Nature (WWF)*, https://wwfeu.awsassets.panda.org/downloads/europe_eats_the_world_report_ws.pdf.

Monteiro, C, Cannon, G, Lawrence, M, Louzada, M & Machado, P 2019, *Ultra-processed foods, diet quality, and health using the NOVA classification system*, FAO.

Neri, E, Pulselli, RM & Marchi, M 2018, *Analysis of the life cycle and carbon footprint of slow food presidium products*, www.slowfood.com/wp-content/uploads/2023/12/Report_INDACO_EN.pdf.

Notarnicola, B, Tassielli, G, Renzulli, PA, Castellani, V & Sala, S 2017, 'Environmental impacts of food consumption in Europe', *Journal of Cleaner Production*, *140*, pp.753–765.

Pimentel, D 1996, 'Green revolution agriculture and chemical hazards', *Science of the Total Environment*, *188*, pp. S86–S98.

Poore, J & Nemecek, T 2018, 'Reducing food's environmental impacts through producers and consumers', *Science*, *360*(6392), pp.987–992.

Ritchie, M 1988, 'Impact of GATT on world hunger', Institute for Agriculture and Trade Policy.

Ritchie, H & Roser, M 2013, 'Land use', Our World in Data.

Rivero, MJ, Lopez-Villalobos, N, Evans, A, Berndt, A, Cartmill, A, Neal, AL, McLaren, A, Farruggia, A, Mignolet, C, Chadwick, D & Styles, D 2021, 'Key traits for ruminant livestock across diverse production systems in the context of climate change: Perspectives from a global platform of research farms', *Reproduction, Fertility and Development*, *33*(2), pp.1–19.

Robinson, GM 2018, 'Globalization of agriculture', *Annual Review of Resource Economics*, *10*, pp.133–160.

Sangiorgi, S 2011, *L'invenzione della gioia: educarsi al vino: sogno, civiltà, linguaggio*, Porthos.
Scherhaufer, S, Moates, G, Hartikainen, H, Waldron, K & Obersteiner, G 2018, 'Environmental impacts of food waste in Europe', *Waste Management*, *77*, pp.98–113.
SDG Progress Report 2022, no date, www.fao.org, accessed 1April 2024, https://doi.org/10.4060/cc1403en.
Secretariat of the Convention on Biological Diversity 2000, 'Sustaining life on Earth: How the convention on biological diversity promotes nature and human well-being', Secretariat of the Convention on Biological Diversity.
Sirakaya, A 2022, 'Where access and benefit-sharing comes from: A historical overview', *Genetic Resources*, November, *3*(6), pp.74–88.
Slattery, B 2005, 'Paper empires: The legal dimensions of French and English ventures in North America', in *Despotic dominion: Property rights in British settler societies*, University of British Columbia Press, Vancouver, pp.50–78.
Sorvino, C 2023, 'What's the world's largest food company?', *Forbes*, 8 June, www.forbes.com/sites/chloesorvino/2023/06/08/whats-the-worlds-largest-food-company/?sh=11739bdb7979.
Stehfest, E, Bouwman, L, Van Vuuren, DP, Den Elzen, MG, Eickhout, B & Kabat, P 2009, 'Climate benefits of changing diet', *Climatic Change*, *95*(1), pp.83–102.
United Nation Department of Economic and Social Affairs Sustainable Development 2023, *Better Business Better World*, accessed 1 April 2024, https://sdgs.un.org/publications/better-business-better-world-18049.
World Health Organization 2018, *Noncommunicable diseases country profiles 2018*, www.who.int/publications/i/item/9789241514620.
World Trade Organisation 2023, *GATT – introduction – fact and dictions*, accessed 1 April 2024, www.wto.org/english/tratop_e/serv_e/gats_factfiction1_e.htm.

3 The Role of Regenerative Agricultural Practices in Balancing Food Security Concerns and Natural Resources Management

Alessandra Telch and Siva Barathi (Sharl) Marimuthu

3.1 Introduction

In Chapter 2, we discussed the impact agricultural practices and food production systems have on the environment and its ecosystem. Agriculture is a significant contributor to climate change, accounting for substantial greenhouse gas emissions, deforestation, biodiversity loss, and land degradation. However, agriculture is necessary for human survival as well as for the functioning of the ecosystem. Sustainable Development Goals (SDGs), as outlined under the UN Agenda 2030, are in many ways intertwined with food sustainability. Indeed, the relationship between food and sustainability is embedded in all the goals, as shall be discussed further (United Nation Sustainable Development Goals 2023). In Chapter 3, we explore the intricate relationship between environmental sustainability and economic viability. Our aim is to acquire a comprehensive understanding of the relationship, essential to provide a thorough appreciation of the SDG goals related to sustainable food security. Understanding the relationship is crucial in guaranteeing a reliable and sustainable food supply in the context of the challenges posed by climate change. The chapter will then shed light on practical and actionable strategies for ensuring sustainability in the face of increasing demand for food. In this regard, the chapter proposes a holistic approach that combines sustainable agricultural practices with a new perspective, namely defining human's role in natural resource management.

3.2 Food at the Centre of Sustainable Development Goals (SDGs)

Sustainable Development Goals (SDGs), established in 2015 by the United Nations, are the targets set to "secure rights and wellbeing of everyone on a healthy planet". The SDGs were set with the aim to achieve a better and more sustainable future for all by 2030. They comprise 17 interconnected goals that are broad in scope, which aim to address global challenges related

DOI: 10.4324/9781003392279-3

to poverty, inequality, climate change, environmental degradation, peace, and justice. While these goals are not legally binding, the governments of member states are expected to establish a national framework to achieve them.

SDGs 1 and 2 are about eradicating poverty and hunger, addressing food security, improving nutrition, and sustainable agriculture. These goals are connected to food security; however, food security is not an isolated goal. Rather, it is an outcome to be achieved from all SDGs. Food security is the driver that threads through the entire SDGs. Each SDG influences or is influenced by food sustainability, accessibility, availability, affordability, and utilisation, as outlined in Table 3.1. The integration of sustainable practices to enhance food security within the SDG framework is crucial for the pursuit of a holistic well-being and ecological health.

3.3 Importance of Food Systems and SDGs

Several matters continue to receive global attention: first, the importance of food systems in achieving the SDGs second, a transition towards innovative agricultural practices, and third, recognition of ecologically sustainable food supply chains; however, these desired outcomes have yet to materialise.

There is a lack of a universally accepted definition of what constitutes sustainable agricultural practices. There is also a lack of comprehensive strategy for the implementation of these practices on a large scale. In fact, there are doubts about their ability to meet humanity's food needs (in terms of quantity) when applied on a large scale. These are due to the complexities and challenges involved in redefining agricultural practices in a way that balances sustainability with the need to feed a growing population.

Furthermore, a lack of measures from national and federal legislators as well as government agencies to establish the necessary political, economic, and financial conditions for the sustainable agricultural revolution could be argued as part of the reason for such an outcome. To begin with, large corporations in the food production and distribution sectors position themselves in the marketplace as virtuous. However, they do not distance themselves from the harmful and non-ecological principles that underpin the current production systems.

To overcome the impasse created at the regulatory level and break the dynamics of profit-seeking at the expense of ecological, social, and economic sustainability outcomes that oppress the current food system, this chapter suggests sustainable agricultural practices and new paradigms to define the role of humans in natural resource management.

The aim is to propose a key concept for interpretation which is agroecology. This concept emphasises a harmonious relationship between man and nature, aiming to fulfil both productivity and sustainability needs. It is, therefore, simultaneously prioritising nutrition, health, and environmental sustainability at the heart of food production.

Table 3.1 SDG Goals and Their Relationship to Food Security

SDG Goals	*Objective*	*Relationship with Food Security*
SDG 1	No Poverty	SDG 1 is concerned with eradicating poverty. In essence, in line with food sustainability, fair prices should be ensured for the food grown by small-scale farmers in rural areas. This is because agriculture in rural areas is not just about producing enough food, but it is a form of livelihood, and thus, fair compensation for their produce elevates farmers' standard of living and eradicates hunger and poverty in the meantime.
SDG 2	Zero Hunger	This goal is not merely about eradicating hunger, but also about ensuring nutritious food for everyone. Extreme hunger and malnutrition are interrelated and are a hindrance to economic growth. They lead to a lack of productivity, as individuals are often unable to work when they are prone to diseases, and this leads to costly healthcare as well.
SDG 3	Good Health and Wellbeing	SDG 3 promotes good health and wellbeing as being critical for sustainable development. A sustainable and nutritious diet is critical to achieving this goal. This goal corresponds with SDG 2. In fact, it features the interplay between SGDs 2 and 3. It aims not only to eradicate hunger but also to ensure wellbeing through sustainable diets while fostering environmental sustainability.
SDG 4	Quality Education	SDG 4 promotes quality education as the foundation for improving lives and sustainable development. In the context of sustainable agricultural practices and the overall aims of SDGs, the goal can be interpreted as appropriately relevant in a rural context. In rural areas of low-income countries, children are often required to work in the fields. In some instances, this practice prevents them from even attending school. However, where students access quality education on enhanced agricultural practices, they acquire knowledge and skills that can be applied to sustainable practices. Sound agricultural policies in rural areas that promote quality education can improve family livelihood and ensure appropriate opportunity to receive education is not missed.

(*Continued*)

Table 3.1 (Continued)

SDG Goals	*Objective*	*Relationship with Food Security*
SDG 5	Gender Equality	SDG 5 emphasises the significance of gender equality, and in the context of sustainable food, it is concerned with empowering women who have historically been underrepresented in various sectors, including the agrifood sector. Empowering women in sectors can be seen as enhancing productivity. Women, in some rural areas and low-income countries, are often involved in farming, harvesting, or food processing. However, they are seldom given the decision-making powers or ownership of land or businesses. Providing equal opportunities and recognition that empower women can enhance productivity in the agrifood sectors.
SDG 6	Clean Water and Sanitation	SDG 6 advocates for clean water and sanitation. In the context of a sustainable food production system, this goal highlights the critical relationship between agriculture, water, and environmental sustainability. As noted in Chapter 1, agriculture accounts for a sizable amount of freshwater consumption. Water is used for irrigation, livestock, and crop cultivation, and the heavy water use can lead to water scarcity issues. Furthermore, industry practices can lead to water pollution. The use of chemical fertilisers, which run off into water bodies, can compromise water quality and harm aquatic ecosystems. In this context, regenerative agriculture practices can minimise the negative impact on the environment.
SDG 7	Affordable and Clean Energy	SDG 7 aims to ensure access to affordable, sustainable, and clean energy for all, and it is imperative that innovative solutions to mitigate the environmental impact of the energy-consuming processes involved in the food production systems, are considered. These processes include food processing, storage, and transportation. One of the approaches is to adopt cleaner energy consumption, such as renewable energy (solar, wind, or biomass), to power agricultural machinery. Furthermore, efficient cold storage can assist in reducing food waste.
SDG 8	Decent Work and Economic Growth	SDG 8 emphasises the importance of employment and decent work conditions for an inclusive and sustainable economy. Regarding agricultural practices, this goal aims to address challenges related to working conditions, such as low wages, exposure to environmental hazards,

(*Continued*)

Table 3.1 (Continued)

SDG Goals	*Objective*	*Relationship with Food Security*
		job insecurity, or lack of healthcare and education. Implementing labour laws and policies that protect worker rights and ensuring fair remunerations, protections, and safeguards are integral to these efforts because they will ensure individuals involved in food production sectors are treated fairly.
SDG 9	Industry, Innovation, and Infrastructure	SDG 9 aims to build resilient infrastructure, promote sustainable industrialisation, and foster innovation. Innovation in food production can promote efficiency in food systems in several ways. For example, the use of technology in farming practices, such as precision farming, and data-driven solutions to optimise supply chain logistics, can assist in achieving sustainable development. Further, streamlining food distribution processes can reduce food waste, a significant outcome for sustainable development.
SDG 10	Reduced Inequalities	SDG 10 aims to reduce inequalities within and among countries. Inequalities exist in many aspects of life and affect individuals from all walks of life. In the sustainable food production system, inequality and disparities can exist in the Global North and the Global South in accessing and using genetic resources. Genetic resources are genetic materials of plants, animals, and microorganisms used in agriculture to develop crop varieties and livestock that are resilient. The use of genetic resources will have to be balanced with efforts to conserve biodiversity and preserve ecosystems.
SDG 11	Sustainable Cities and Communities	SDG 11 seeks to create sustainable and resilient cities that are safe for communities. In the context of food sustainability, urban agriculture can serve multiple objectives. Urban food production can reduce travel time long-distance transportation costs, and greenhouse emissions. It can also provide access to fresh produce. Vertical farming and hydroponics are examples of urban agriculture, and such farming methods make efficient use of resources such as water and land. Furthermore, cultivating food within cities also reduces the impact on rural land use. In effect, urban agriculture contributes to community resilience in the face of challenges like limited food supply caused by events such as pandemics and natural disasters.

(*Continued*)

Table 3.1 (Continued)

SDG Goals	*Objective*	*Relationship with Food Security*
SDG 12	Responsible Consumption and Production	SDG 12's primary focus is to encourage responsible consumption and production in various sectors, including agriculture. There are several ways to achieve this. For example, reducing food wastage by consuming a sustainable diet can both ensure food security and minimise environmental harm. Other means include education and awareness programmes. Education can also assist consumers in understanding the impact food production has on the environment and assist in making informed choices.
SDG 13	Climate Action	SDG 13's climate action is closely associated with agricultural practices due to the impact they have on the environment. Agriculture is a major consumer of freshwater resources, and it also contributes to water pollution due to the runoff of pesticides and fertiliser. Unsustainable agriculture practices such as deforestation and monoculture have severe impacts on the environment. In contrast, regenerative agriculture practices can mitigate gas emissions; they focus on carbon sequestration in soils, which offsets emissions. Sustainable farming practices can also aim to reduce the use of harmful chemicals and minimise water pollution. Using diverse crop varieties and resilient farming practices can contribute to minimising the impact farming has on the environment.
SDG 14	Life Below Water	SDG 14 seeks to protect the ocean and sea and conserve marine resources. Like the other goals, this goal is also intricately connected to food sustainability, and it seeks to address responsible management of marine resources and ecosystems. Unsustainable fishing practices such as overfishing and illegal and/or destructive fishing can deplete marine life in the sea, and this can affect the availability of seafood. Sustainable fisheries management, where a balanced and healthy marine ecosystem is maintained, is critical for sustainable food.
SDG 15	Life on Land	SDG 15 is broadly about protecting and restoring terrestrial ecosystems, managing forests, combating desertification, reversing land degradation, and conserving biodiversity. Forests, grasslands, and agricultural lands are essential for sustainable food production. Furthermore, healthy ecosystems provide an avenue for soil

(*Continued*)

Table 3.1 (Continued)

SDG Goals	*Objective*	*Relationship with Food Security*
		fertility and pollination, which are crucial for agriculture. Many communities rely on the forest as a source of livelihood, food, and medicine, and protecting the forest will ensure the availability of local food. The forest also plays a role in regulating water cycles, benefiting agriculture downstream. Sustainable land management can also assist in reversing land degradation, which ensures that land remains suitable for agriculture.
SDG 16	Peace, Justice, and Strong Institutions	SDG 16 promotes peaceful and inclusive societies. It also advocates for access to justice for all and for building effective accountable and inclusive institutions at all levels. Food security, in essence, refers to consistent access to sufficient, safe, and nutritious food. In recent years, many countries have suffered from conflict-induced food insecurity. Armed conflict and displacement disrupt food and water supplies as well as sustainable food production, leading to food shortages and malnutrition among affected populations. Achieving peace and stability is key to sustainable development, including sustainable food production.
SDG 17	Partnership for the Goals	SDG 17 advocates a holistic approach to tackling issues broadly arising in finance, technology, capacity building, trade, and systemic issues. This approach recognises the interconnectedness of various fields, including agriculture, environment, and health. It acknowledges the need for inclusiveness and equitable solutions, which include empowering smallholders, women, and indigenous people.

3.4 Balancing Food Security Concerns with Fair Natural Resource Management

Understanding the importance of food within the 2030 Agenda for Sustainable Development highlights the need to intervene on the negative externalities connected with its current production and consumption patterns, in order to reverse the trajectory in terms of trespassing the "planetary boundaries" (Richardson et al. 2023) and restore us to a safe operating area.

Certainly, organic agriculture aims to reach optimal agroecosystems in terms of social, ecological, and economic sustainability. There are potential policy targets to improve organic performance and match this objective, including:

- Targeted research programmes to develop environmental best practices in organic regulations.
- Enhanced research on crop varieties for conditions specific to organic management.
- Development of domestic organic markets (especially in low-income countries).
- Regional relational certification, and standard systems.
- Establishment of ethical and fair-trade practices to couple with organic certification.
- Subsidies for organic farmers to alleviate the costs of the transition period from conventional to organic farming (Seufert and Ramankutty 2017).

However, being primarily a production system, organic agriculture encounters some limits in its capacity to transform the whole food system. In fact, it faces similar challenges as conventional agriculture. There is a crucial shortcoming as far as both agricultural models are concerned; namely changes to the current food system, such as reducing food waste and changing dietary patterns. These changes (or challenges) are not taken into consideration despite their huge potential to contribute to the cause.

According to recent studies, organic agriculture can contribute to improving environmental impacts while providing sufficient food only if it is implemented in an adequately designed food system in which the issues of food production, food consumption, and food waste are addressed altogether (Muller et al. 2017). These matters cannot be substantially resolved individually, however they can be partially resolved when addressed in combination.

In this context, agroecology, which is both a scientific discipline and an integrated approach to sustainable farming, is deemed as one of the favourable ways to shape the future of food production and consumption. A proper question is not whether agriculture alone could play a role in creating a sustainable food system. The question is whether organic agriculture, integrated in an alternative vision of the food system and conceived as part of the agroecological movement (rather than a mere production practice), could promote a more sustainable and just food system.

The word "agroecology" emerged at the beginning of the 20th century to indicate the application of ecology to agriculture. Since then, both its definition and scope as a scientific discipline have evolved significantly. Over the past 80 years, there has been a change of focus in terms of scales and dimensions, witnessing agroecology's great capacity for adaptation and improvement (Wezel and Soldat 2009).

Agroecology changes from the plot or field scale, which was widespread between the 1930s and 1960s, to the farm or agroecosystem scale. The agroecosystem was preferred between the 1970s and 2000s, although the smaller-scale approaches are still relevant to the present time.

In some publications, the farm is deemed equivalent to an agroecosystem; in others, the agroecosystem is at the broader scope of a local or regional agricultural landscape. From the 1980s, representatives of the agroecological paradigm such as Altieri and Gliessman started to define it as an approach to protect natural resources and to design and manage sustainable agroecosystems (Altieri 1995; Gliessman 1990).

Gradually, agroecology contributes to the promotion of sustainability applied to agriculture, biodiversity, and rural development themes emerged, and the words "soil" and "landscape" are used frequently (Wezel and Soldat 2009).

In the meantime, agroecology identity has evolved as well, becoming a movement and a practice. In fact, the term started to be used to define a new way to look at agriculture, considering its deep relationships with society. In addition, it was recognised as a set of farming and breeding practices aimed at providing solutions for an eco-friendlier agriculture. Today, agroecology is a scientific paradigm. It is useful to respond to the new sustainability challenges of the agrifood system. According to the IAASTD,

> Agroecology is the science and practice of applying ecological concepts and principles to the study, design and management of sustainable agroecosystems. It includes social, political, cultural and economic dimensions and integrates state-of-the-art formal science with traditional and community-based knowledge; local food system experiences; and innovations that are low-cost, readily adaptable by small and medium-scale farmers, and likely to advance social equity while conserving biodiversity, natural resources and ecosystem function.
>
> (IAASTD 2009)

Agroecology in its many versions focuses on the interaction between plants, animals, humans, and the environment. It is today supported by an increasing part of the scientific community and deemed by many global leaders as a successful approach to promote a sustainability revolution in the face of current global climate trends (FAO 2015; De Schutter 2014; Frison 2016; Elver and Tuncak 2017).

Fostering sustainable agriculture ensures food security and nutrition as well as a healthy environment. As highlighted in Chapter 1, most of the negative outcomes of modern food and farming systems are linked to industrial agriculture due to intensive crop monocultures, industrial-scale feedlots, reliance on chemical fertilisers and pesticides, and preventive use of antibiotics. All these factors trigger devastating effects. Agroecology aims at replacing this uniformity with an innovative approach to diversifying farms and farming species, as part of the holistic strategies to build long-term fertility and maintain healthy rural landscapes and vibrant livelihoods. There is widespread agreement as to the advantages of enabling an environment supportive of agroecology, food sovereignty, and ecologically based production systems.

According to the UN Special Rapporteur on the Right to Food Hilal Elver, "Agroecology will [increasingly] be the only way. When everyone understands this maybe it will be too late. We need to push now to make it an acceptable alternative" (Elver 2015).

The microcosms of traditional agriculture, threatened by the growing pressure of industrial agriculture and globalisation, need to be supported by new transitional policies that favour family agriculture and introduce substantial payment for environmental services. For centuries, agricultural systems have been built upon the local resources of land, water, and genetics according to the local knowledge. This enables the nurturing of robust and resilient farms, which held the minimisation of environmental "bads" as an essential principle. Agrobiodiversity plays a key role in resilience, enabling their long-term survival. To reach the goal of sustainable intensification, modern agriculture needs to be more "ecological, biodiverse, local, sustainable, and socially just" (Altieri 2009).

In modern times, the concept of regenerative agriculture has emerged in the discussions on sustainable agriculture. It stands in contrast to the industrial agricultural practices that leave an adverse impact to the environment. Regenerative agriculture is a field with many definitions. Two (2) main schools of thought that can be identified are:

a. Process-oriented approach, seeing regenerative agriculture as a set of practices such as a combination of animals and crops in production systems, no-tillage agriculture, and, more broadly, conservation agriculture and several practices that enhance biodiversity and promote the sustainability of the system.
b. Regenerative agriculture as a goal, improving the status of environment and forests while enabling the provision of ecosystem services, without focusing on how the aim is achieved. That leaves space for a broader interpretation, according to which also industrial agriculture could be regenerative – since the need to expand agriculture in new areas is reduced through intensification of land use, the needs to contaminate and deforest further areas are lessened.

Likewise, there are many definitions of agroecology, each highlighting various ecological and social aspects that need to be taken into consideration for a sustainable and fair food system. According to some authors, agroecology is perceived as a community-driven approach, focusing on specific territories. This approach is seen as a "peasant" agriculture; in other words, it means bringing back farming practices that are rooted in traditional knowledge (Marcelo et al. 2016).

To achieve this, it requires a deep respect for wisdom passed down from farmers which establishes a symbiotic relationship with nature. Working with an understanding of the natural process and ecosystem will bring the right balance. Other definitions highlight the environmental benefits and impacts, while still taking into consideration the social aspects that characterise a holistic approach (Lampkin et al. 2015).

As of today, there is neither a prevailing interpretation nor an agreement on what regenerative agriculture, and agroecology in particular, are. However, both terms are used by both the scientific community and various players in the food supply chain including the private sector. Around 60 percent of all International Fund for Agricultural Development (IFAD) projects completed between 2018 and 2023, implement agroecological practices at the farm, landscape, market, and policy levels (IFAD 2023).

There exists a certification programme associated with regenerative agriculture, complete with a set of standards defining its principles. However, this initiative lacks global consensus. In many instances, the term "regenerative agriculture" is used without a universally accepted definition, rendering it ambiguous. As previously mentioned, regenerative agriculture is just one of several terms implying the necessity for a transformative and sustainable shift in agriculture. Other terms include sustainable intensification, agroecology or agroecological practices, permaculture, and in a broader sense, climate-smart agriculture. Each of these signifies distinct approaches to infusing sustainability into agriculture.

Agroecology is one of the most diffused, it being the object of a rich development in the last decades (Wezel et al. 2009). Often, it is defined by contrast to conventional agriculture. Looking at this comparison, conventional agriculture is depicted as high-tech and profit-driven agriculture, controlled by big corporations. Nevertheless, agroecology is instead described as a prerogative of smallholders, lacking technological input, and driven by environmental protection efforts. This polarisation hinders the potential of agroecology to become mainstream agriculture and promotes unfair practices when it comes to marketing and promotion of agroecological farming. If it is widely accepted that agroecology can benefit from high-technology solutions and is economically viable for both smallholders and big corporations, there would be less interest in faking bucolic and idyllic agricultural landscapes when promoting the benefits of agroecological farming practices.

According to Marcela Quintero, the Associate Director General, Research Strategy and Innovation for the Alliance of Biodiversity International and CIAT, there are three (3) main prior needs in agroecology:

a. To understand if those practices that are depicted as agroecological are indeed such, and what the enabling conditions are;
b. Collective action is needed for agroecological transformation; the focus shall not be only on farmers but on consumers and policymakers as well;
c. There is an urgent scientific need to gain tools for a better assessment of evidence on agroecology's impact on the field and, more in general, in the food system(s) (Marcela 2023).

These requirements contribute to a central challenge; the redefinition of the role played by farmers and farming. The farm should be perceived as a living organism dedicated to nurturing the territory, fostering fertility, striving for self-sufficiency, and contributing to landscape formation. This stands in stark contrast to the prevailing concept of conventional farms today where there is a lack of commitment to territory care, leading to the depletion and contamination of land and soil through external chemical inputs, ultimately ruining the landscape. Farmers are no longer mere producers of goods for market exchange, rather, they are integral resources essential for the provision of ecosystem services.

3.5 Agroforestry to Reconcile Conservation with Social and Economic Benefits

Agroforestry systems are promoted among many farming paradigms associated with sustainable land-use practices, as a valid tool to mitigate numerous environmental issues associated with modern food production systems.

The term was first used in the 1990s to describe the practical experience and scientific knowledge acquired during years of agricultural management of tropical environments, often witnessing the frustration of agroeconomists trying to implement the modern land-use technologies and concepts to ecologically and socially sensitive areas. It has progressively evolved to gain a broader significance, as pointed out by Lundgren and Raintree:

> (Agroforestry is) a collective name for land-use systems and technologies where woody perennials (trees, shrubs, palms, bamboos, etc.) are deliberately used on the same land management unit as agricultural crops and/or animals, either on the same form of spatial arrangement or temporal sequence. In agroforestry systems there are both ecological and economical interactions between the different components.
>
> (Lundgren & Raintree 1982)

More recently, it has been a widespread practice in tropical and developing countries and also relevant in Europe (Den Herder et al. 2017). An estimated one point two billion people worldwide are considered depending on agroforestry farming systems (The World Bank 2004). According to the World Agroforestry Centre (ICRAF), the number of people engaged in agroforestry increased between 2000 and 2010, revealing that 43 percent of agricultural lands include some form of agroforestry, with the greatest coverage in Central and South America.

In 2010, agroforestry covered over one billion hectares and was practised by more than 900 million people (Zomer et al. 2014). Agroforestry systems can therefore be defined as a set of practices designed to satisfy not only production targets but also environmental protection functions within the same ecosystem. This is achievable because of the optimised interactions between trees and shrubs and crops and livestock through man's intervention.

In this chapter, we investigate their ecological and economic sustainability, in particular, the capacity of agroforestry systems to generate a diverse array of commodities. Beyond addressing the biophysical and socioeconomic aspects of traditional food production, agroforestry practices also leave space for the integration of botanicals and ornamental plants, shelter, and pastures for livestock, wood, high-value medicinal properties, and even more complex services that contribute to local economies. These benefit long-term carbon sequestration, soil enrichment, biodiversity conservation, and air- and water-quality improvements.

3.5.1 Chestnut Groves as An Excellent Example

Traditional chestnut groves present an interesting potential because of their multifunctionality. They are a crop that can be an economic resource and at the same time guarantee services for the community (nutritious food, carbon storage, preservation of the environment, preservation of the territory, maintenance of historical memory, tourist-recreational offer, and more)

This is particularly true in Italy, where chestnut groves are deemed as monumental, and the management approach is focused on the whole array of ecosystem services, rather than on fruit production only. Even though to date, there is no legally valid definition of what a monumental tree is, ancient chestnut trees are certainly among them and are consequently often granted protection and respect throughout the nation. This status is essential for guaranteeing a fair and univocal preservation of these old trees; they are often identified based on their size, age, shape of crown, location, and historic and cultural value (Lisa 2011).

There is growing interest in these entities, considering aspects related to cultural heritage, biodiversity, landscape, and secondary products. Many of the ecosystemic functions identified, particularly those linked to environmental and naturalistic values, are lacking in modern orchard-like plantations. They are managed predominantly, if not exclusively, for direct production purposes (Mariotti et al. 2019).

In fact, the history of Italian chestnut cultivation is characterised by balanced management of the resource represented by the chestnut grove, through which the necessary resource for family subsistence is obtained from the territory, without compromising the underlying ecosystem.

To date, chestnut production, including both traditional and modern production systems in Europe is around 170,000 tonnes. This corresponds to 8 percent of world production, with China, Turkey, South Korea, Japan, and North Korea as significant contributors. Italy is still the European leader, with a production of about 50,000 tonnes; the most prolific region is Campania, where about half of Italian chestnuts are produced, followed in order by Latium, Calabria, Piedmont, and Tuscany. In all other regions, except for Apulia where no chestnuts are grown, production is below 1,000 tonnes.

Chestnuts, the species of the genus *Castanea* spread in conjunction with coniferous forests before glaciation and were present throughout the Northern Hemisphere as early as 40 million years ago. From 8000 B.C. onwards there was evidence of their presence in the western Mediterranean area, and around 2000 B.C. Chestnuts were found in Italy, brought mainly by man via the Black Sea and Greece. It is only from the 1st century A.D. Onwards, references to the chestnut trees were found in Roman literature, for their valuable wood for example, they were used for poles in vineyards and for their fruit. With the conquest of Western and Central Europe by the Romans, their definitive spread into today's cultivation areas began (Scartezzini et al. 2023).

For centuries, the lives of entire communities in Italy have revolved around the care and cultivation of the chestnut tree. Its presence has been central to the daily survival of entire populations, so much so that it has been referred to as the "bread tree". It has been the main economic resource, and populations have handed down cultivation techniques, traditions, and harvesting and consumption practices from generation to generation. In this sense, the chestnut and its fruits have been an important element in the subsistence of mountain communities.

The orchards for staple food consisted of a mix of varieties with different ripening periods. The edible fruits can be consumed in different ways: roasted, candied, boiled, dried, or transformed into flour. Chestnuts are an extraordinary fruit, due to their nutritional qualities, gastronomic versatility, and capacity. Orchards also provided several secondary products such as pasture, hay, mushrooms, and berries. In some cases, orchards were also intercropped with cereals (Conedera and Krebs 2007). Flowers are rich in pollen and nectar and, therefore, really appreciated for honey production.

There are living testimonies of the importance of chestnut cultivation as a livelihood for Italian families in the 20th century, such as that of Ugo Bugelli, owner of a farm in the Tuscan Apennines, a chestnut grower and expert connoisseur of the Pistoian mountains. Below is a translated version of his comments.

> Currently, the estimated area under chestnut cultivation in Italy, which certainly includes new intensive plantations and probably also abandoned chestnut groves, amounts to 36,000 hectares. According to a 1939 census, the municipalities of Cutigliano, San Marcello pistoiese, Piteglio and Sambuca pistoiese had almost 9,000 hectares of cultivated chestnut groves. Adding the other mountain territories in the province of Pistoia – especially the municipalities of Pistoia, Marliana, Pescia and Montale – this figure doubled to almost 20,000 hectares. In those years, when sharecropping was in force, mountain farmers – like my grandparents and great-grandparents – were able to reduce or wipe out their debts to their landowners by working around the chestnut tree. The chestnut grove was the most important piece of real estate they owned. Each medium-sized chestnut tree yielded timber worth half the wages of a metalworker.
>
> (Ugo Bugelli 2023, pers. comm, 1 November 2023)

In addition to the purely productive function derived from the trade of the fruit, chestnut groves represented, and continue to represent today, an important element of the culture and the rural landscape. Chestnut orchards play a central role in community rituals, and they are the most significant plants for safeguarding, enhancing, and maintaining the landscapes within the territories. This aspect has been at the core of the advocacy activities of the recently born Slow Food Chestnut Growers Network; aiming at the regeneration of the Italian mountains through the valorisation of their biodiversity, landscape protection, and support to local communities. Chestnuts are essential in this restoration process, being a collective environmental, social, economic, and cultural heritage (Slow Food Rete dei Castanicoltori 2021).

Each year, festivals and markets are organised around the ritual of chestnut harvesting, drying, and flour production in many locations all over Italy. To name a few examples, the feast dedicated to Saint Ursula in the village of Pochi di Salorno, South Tyrol, which takes place each October and foresees the selling of roasted chestnuts to be eaten with new wines; and the festival celebrated in Piteglio on Easter Monday, with the selling and tasting of chestnut flours and products based on chestnut flour (also known as "sweet flour"). This celebration, in particular, dates to the 15th century and is linked to the cult of the Virgin, of which a relic was carried in procession. These examples reinforce the concept that chestnut groves can fulfil a multiplicity of direct or indirect functions, many of which are important and promote beneficial economic benefits (Maltoni et al. 2009).

Supplying complementary products alongside the fruit and providing materials for handicraft activities, these trees reflect the identity of a given territory. In addition, they serve as an indirect or additional income source for rural and mountain populations. In the traditional silo-pastoral management of Alpine regions, chestnut groves were exploited for temporary grazing of small livestock. This practice also extended to the production of fodder and typical cheeses.

The exploitation of wood facilitated growth of the local economy. They relied on this raw material as a natural fuel or for the supply of solid wood used to manufacture furniture, fixtures, basketry, and tools. From 1850 onwards, the forest also supplied tannin for extraction and raw materials for the factories that sprung up in the valleys. The gradual growth of these industries supported the preservation of chestnut groves as relied on efficient forest management. In addition to the aforementioned functions, chestnut ecosystems provide for a rich biodiversity and soil quality. Frequent symbiotic associations exist between chestnut trees and numerous fungal species, some of which are edible and highly esteemed, for example, porcini. Mushrooms are a beloved food; the sale of which can be considered as a secondary valuable income. But, most importantly, they have a high potential in restoring soil health and support plant-fungus relationships and therefore plants' resilience and productivity.

What makes chestnut groves such a favourable environment for the growth of porcini mushrooms is likely the combination of an ample dose of humidity (due to the sparse density of the trees allowing optimal soil moisture), combined with equally good solar irradiation. Here, the undergrowth rich in grass and moss, devoid of brambles and other shrubs, also generally prevents water stagnation and the formation of mud, which is not favoured by porcini mushrooms.

In the meantime, it prevents excessive soil erosion in case of intense precipitation. These elements promote both early births, starting from the late spring season, and late births, extending the porcini season, compared to other habitats that are less bright and experience early cold. This very particular habitat can allow all four species of porcini to thrive Undoubtedly the type that can provide impressive yields in such environments is the summer porcini also known as *Boletus recticulatus* or *B.aestivalis.*

In addition, protective functions are provided: the robust root system and the presence of the herbaceous mantle help in the fight against soil degradation and hydrogeological instability. Furthermore, the maintenance of activities in the chestnut grove also involves the care of any supporting structures (dry stone walls) and small infrastructures to regulate water runoff and limit erosion.

Further tourist, recreational, and educational functions are linked to the high environmental and naturalistic value of chestnut groves, mainly via observation and environmental education, and from a socio-cultural point of view, through the dissemination of knowledge on local history, customs, and traditions. A relevant example is the didactic-experimental "Castagneto di Granaglione" covering an area of around ten hectares, the Chestnut Grove is in Granaglione, on the Tuscan-Emilian Apennines.

It boasts an exceptional collection of chestnut germplasm, represented by the variety of fourteen types of chestnut for fruit and four for wood. This is unique at a national level and it is further enriched by the monumental part of the grove. The chestnut grove ensures the production of flour and dried chestnuts processed into granulate for beer production. This activity is complemented by the production of chestnut honey and the products of the undergrowth that grow wild. In the meantime, it is a place that conveys culture and memory through projects, workshops, events, and school and tourist visits.

Protecting traditional chestnut cultivation means protecting local cultivation techniques, enhancing sustainable and fair management of the supply chain, safeguarding the rural architecture linked to the processing of chestnuts (for example, stone dryers), spreading, and innovating the gastronomic uses of the chestnut and its derivatives, with their important nutritional properties. The recovery of chestnut groves goes hand in hand with the development of slow tourism and support for the economy linked to the cultivation and processing of the chestnut, which can then be offered in local gastronomy.

It therefore represents a huge opportunity for communities of the mountain areas, which are currently subject to depopulation and abandonment. As a result, despite its rich history and leading role in chestnut production and exportation, Italy suffers from a slow and inexorable decay of this agroforestry practice combining the maintenance of the chestnut areas with mushroom picking, animal grazing, and wood cutting.

The analysis of the residual Italian chestnut sector shows extremely differentiated realities in terms of resource endowment, structural and economic characteristics of the supply chain, and the degree of integration between its components. One of the major constraints to its survival and development is the absence of established relationships between these various components. In fact, the Italian chestnut supply chain counts on a few operators who process and market the product on domestic and foreign markets. The supply chain consists of small companies and numerous intermediaries between production and consumption.

This structure is reflected in terms of both the production price (unprofitable) and the consumption price (too high). It also affects the consistency of supplies, both in terms of quality and quantity, and the processability of the fresh product. To this end, traders import foreign products to stabilise supply capacity in both quantity and quality. Successful cases show the need for policies that lead to a redistribution of added value among the supply chain operators that allows producers to be adequately remunerated for the factors of production (Tatiana and Giorgio 2011).

3.6 Conclusion

In conclusion, agroforestry practices are amongst the regenerative agricultural practices with the potential of balancing food security concerns and natural resource management. However, the recognition of the multiple benefits (economic, social, environmental, and cultural) of such practices needs to be emphasised by policymakers and recognised by local governments. In particular, as far as chestnut cultivation is concerned:

- Regulatory simplification is needed for the start-up of new plantations, the recovery of old orchards, and the use of traditional facilities (chestnut dryers).
- Mapping of local existing varieties and matching with analysis on supply (production, cultivated areas, types of chestnut growers) and demand (quantities and types demanded by the industry) on the market.
- Education programmes on sustainable forest management must be developed: knowledge of good traditional chestnut practices is being lost due to the lack of generational change; new skills are also needed to mitigate the effects of climate change.
- Actions for the support and valorisation of producers through local events and the promotion of short supply chains are needed to raise awareness among consumers.
- Support for small-scale chestnut farmers by providing them incentives, technical assistance, and access to the market. This will ensure the viability

of small-scale chestnut businesses and contribute to rural and regional development.

- Creating robust market linkages for chestnut producers is also critical. This can be done by establishing farmer co-operatives facilitating direct marketing channels and promoting local chestnut festivals.
- Investing in research and development in the field of chestnut including funding studies on improving cultivation is also important.

Some considerations have been highlighted at the beginning of the 20th century in detail in a publication entitled *Chestnut Monograph* by Dr Lodovico Piccoli, Professor of Silviculture and Wood Technology at the Forestry Institute of Florence, on behalf of the Italian chestnut extract manufacturers (Piccioli 1922). According to him, the education of both operators in the sector and consumers, combined with the economic support for those engaged in continuing traditional chestnut cultivation, would bring economic and social wealth.

These summarise the first answers to the many questions related to the challenges in the identification of regenerative agricultural practices, their promotion, and the development and sharing of scientific knowledge. In fact, they are specific to many agroforestry management systems (Xavier and Rafael 2024) and shall be central for their thriving.

This chapter focused on the importance of regenerative practices in achieving the SDGs. We used chestnut cultivation as an example. SDGs are established primarily to promote holistic wellbeing while protecting the environment. Regenerative agriculture, namely farming methods that restore and enhance the health of the ecosystem, fulfils most of the goals. For example, adopting regenerative agriculture improves soil health and fertility, leading to higher yields and better-quality chestnuts. It can also contribute to climate change mitigations by sequestering carbon dioxide from tree growths. Furthermore, the adoption of fair-trade practice is yet another contribution to SDGs. Farmers receiving a fair price in chestnut cultivation achieve the SDGs.

References

Altieri, MA 1995, *Agroecology: The science of sustainable agriculture*, Westview Press.

Altieri, MA 2009, 'Agroecology, small farms, and food sovereignty', *Monthly Review*, *61*(3), pp.102–113.

Conedera, M & Krebs, P 2007, 'History, present situation and perspective of chestnut cultivation in Europe', II Iberian Congress on Chestnut 784, June, pp.23–28.

De Schutter, O 2014, 'Final report: The transformative potential of the right to food', Report to the 25th Session of the Human Rights Council HRC/25/57, January.

Den Herder, M, Moreno, G, Mosquera-Losada, RM, Palma, JH, Sidiropoulou, A, Freijanes, JJS, Crous-Duran, J, Paulo, JA, Tomé, M, Pantera, A & Papanastasis, VP 2017, 'Current extent and stratification of agroforestry in the European Union', *Agriculture, Ecosystems & Environment*, *241*, pp.121–132.

Elver, H 2015, 'Special Rapporteur on the right to food', Critical Perspective on Food Systems, Food Crises and the Future of the Right to Food 2020.

Elver, H & Tuncak, B 2017, 'Report of the special rapporteur on the right to food', *UN Human Rights Council*, Geneva, Switzerland, http://daccessods.un.org/access.nsf/Get.

FAO 2015, 'Final report for the international symposium on agroecology for food security and nutrition', 18 and 19 September 2014, Rome, Italy, https://openknowledge.fao.org/server/api/core/bitstreams/35028cbc-6980-4ce3-b155-2f5044170a4f/content.

Frison, EA, IPES-Food 2016, *From uniformity to diversity: A paradigm shift from industrial agriculture to diversified agroecological systems*, Louvain-la-Neuve, Belgium, https://cgspace.cgiar.org/items/9d25f7b8-fbb6-4e81-b0bd-08342706d4ff.

Gliessman, SR 1990, 'Agroecology: Researching the ecological basis for sustainable agriculture', in *Agroecology: Researching the ecological basis for sustainable agriculture*, Springer, New York, NY, pp.3–10.

IAASTD 2009 'Feeding the world greening the planet', *Summary of Findings of the International Assessment of Agriculture Knowledge, Science and Technology for Development* (Fact Sheet, Global Report of IAASTD), accessed 1 April 2024, https://navdanyainternational.org/wp-content/uploads/2016/07/IAASTD-Fact-Sheet.pdf.

IFAD 2023, *Agroecology for sustainable food systems*, accessed 1 April 2024, ifad.org.

Lampkin, NH, Pearce, BD, Leake, AR, Creissen, H, Gerrard, CL, Girling, R, Lloyd, S, Padel, S, Smith, J, Smith, LG, Vieweger, A & Wolfe, MS 2015, 'The role of agroecology in sustainable intensification', Report for the Land Use Policy Group. Organic Research Centre, Elm Farm and Game & Wildlife Conservation Trust.

Lisa, C 2011, 'Gli alberi monumentali: normative, conoscenza e tutela', *L'Italia Forestale e Montana*, *66*(6), pp.509–519, http://dx.doi.org/10.4129/ifm.2011.6.03.

Lundgren, BO & Raintree, JB 1982, 'Agricultural research for development: Potentials and challenges in Asia', *ISNAR, the Hague, the Netherlands*, pp.37–49.

Maltoni, A, Mariotti, B, Jacobs, DF & Tani, A 2019, Pruning methods to restore Castanea sativa stands attacked by Dryocosmus kuriphilus.

Marcelo, M, Adriano, R & Ricardo, J 2016, 'A look at agroecology and popular cooperation in Mozambican savannahs', *The International Policy Centre for Inclusive Growth, UN Development Programme 'Policy in Focus*, pp.43–49, https://ipcig.org/sites/default/files/pub/en/PIF36_Food_and_nutrition_security.pdf.

Mariotti, B, Castellotti, T, Conedera, M, Corona, P, Manetti, MC, Romano, R, Tani, A & Maltoni, A 2019, 'Linee guida per la gestione selvicolturale dei castagneti da frutto', Rete Rurale Nazionale 2014-2020, Scheda n. 22.2 – Foreste, Consiglio per la ricerca in agricoltura e l'analisi dell'economia agraria, Roma, ISBN 978-88-3385-017-7.

Muller, A, Schader, C, El-Hage Scialabba, N, Brüggemann, J, Isensee, A, Erb, KH, Smith, P, Klocke, P, Leiber, F, Stolze, M & Niggli, U 2017, 'Strategies for feeding the world more sustainably with organic agriculture', *Nature Communications*, *8*(1), pp.1–13.

Piccioli, L 1922, *Monografia del castagno: suoi caratteri morfologici, varietà, coltivazione, prodotti e nemici*, 2nd edn, Stab. Tipo Litografico G. Spinelli & C, pp.105–109.

Quintero, M. 2023, Online Speech for European Institute for Innovation and Sustainability (EIIS), "Food & Sustainability" course, 6th edn.

Richardson, K, Steffen, W, Lucht, W, Bendtsen, J, Cornell, SE, Donges, JF, Drüke, M, Fetzer, I, Bala, G, von Bloh, W & Feulner, G 2023, 'Earth beyond six of nine planetary boundaries', *Science Advances*, *9*(37), p. eadh2458.

Scartezzini, HV, Bossi Fedrigotti, V, Eccli, I, Perli, G, Gatti, J, Laimer, M, Zago, B & Borzaga, RP 2023, *La castagna: Origine, lavorazione e significato in Alto Adige*, Effekt.

Seufert, V & Ramankutty, N 2017, 'Many shades of gray – The context-dependent performance of organic agriculture', *Science Advances*, *3*(3), p.e1602638, 1–14, 11.

Slow Food Rete dei Castanicoltori 2021, 'IL MANIFESTO', Presented at the International Event "Oltreterra", Manifesto della Rete Slow Food dei Castanicoltori – Slow Food – Buono, Pulito e Giusto.

Tatiana, C & Giorgio, G 2011, 'Situazione e prospettive della castanicoltura da frutto in Italia', *Agriregionieuropa anno*, *7*(24).

Ugo Bugelli 2023, Pers Comm – Testimony given to the author by Ugo Bugelli in November 2023, on the occasion of a visit to the chestnut grove in Piteglio during the period when chestnuts were being harvested to be taken to the "metato" and dried for milling: *"Attualmente la superficie stimata a castagneto da frutto in Italia, che sicuramente include anche i nuovi impianti intensivi e probabilmente anche castagneti abbandonati, ammonta a 36,000 ettari. Secondo un censimento del 1939 i soli comuni di Cutigliano, San marcello pistoiese, Piteglio e Sambuca pistoiese contavano quasi 9,000 ettari di castagneto da frutto coltivato. Aggiungendo gli altri territori montani della provincia di Pistoia – soprattutto dei comuni di Pistoia, Marliana, Pescia e Montale – questa cifra raddoppiava, raggiungendo quasi i 20,000 ettari. In quegli anni ove vigeva la mezzadria, i contadini montanari – come i miei nonni e bisnonni – riuscivano a diminuire o azzerare i debiti contratti con i padroni, proprietari terrieri, con il lavoro fatto intorno al castagno. Il castagneto era il bene immobile più importante che possedessero. Ogni castagno di media taglia dava legname per un valore corrispondente a metà salario di un operaio metalmeccanico."*

United Nation Sustainable Development Goals, www.un.org/sustainabledevelopment/sustainable-development-goals/.

Wezel, A, Bellon, S, Doré, T, Francis, C, Vallod, D & David, C 2009, 'Agroecology as a science, a movement and a practice: A review', *Agronomy for Sustainable Development*, *29*, pp.503–515.

Wezel, A & Soldat, V 2009, 'A quantitative and qualitative historical analysis of the scientific discipline of agroecology', *International Journal of Agricultural Sustainability*, *7*(1), pp.3–18.

World Bank 2004, 'Sustaining forests: A development strategy', *The World Bank*. Appendix 2, p. A-3. Washington, DC, https://documents1.worldbank.org/curated/en/424531468781760578/pdf/Sustaining-forests-a-development-strategy.pdf.

Xavier, B & Rafael, M 2024, 'In Brazil's Caatinga, adapted agroforests are producing food from dry lands', mongabay.com.

Zomer, RJ, Trabucco, A, Coe, R, Place, F, Van Noordwijk, M & Xu, JC 2014, 'Trees on farms: An update and reanalysis of agroforestry's global extent and socio-ecological characteristics', Working Paper 179, (ed WACISARPD WP14064.PDF), Bogor, Indonesia, p.33.

4 The Human-Food-Environmental Nexus

Anthropological Perspectives on the Impact of Human Food Choices Through Time

Melanie Fillios

4.1 Introduction

Human history is entangled with the history of plants and animals. The 'Neolithic revolution', was coined by V. Gordon Childe (1936) for the raft of changes to ushered in by the widespread adoption of agriculture and the domestication of animals. Childe and others envisioned that humanity progressed along a hypothetical ladder of civilisation – starting with what were thought to be the 'simplest' cultures – mobile hunter-gatherers and progressing to the most complex – hierarchical states – characterised by sedentism, craft specialisation, and intensive agriculture. Increasing social complexity was viewed as the hallmark of these great, commonly 'western' civilisations – with intensive agricultural systems and animal husbandry as integral parts. The prevailing theory hypothesised that the ability to farm and raise livestock enabled people to remain in one place; eventually living in higher-density settlements characterised by larger populations, higher levels of formal education, and complex social and economic systems. These trademark trappings of 'civilisation' eventually ushered in the age of industrialisation leading to what we now conceptualise as the Western model of modern society. Food sits at the very core of this story and is a basic human need that undeniably drove the rise of complex civilisations.

Until recently, we did not pause to consider the secondary effects this raft of swift changes had on the delicate human-animal-environmental nexus that pre-dated these human systems. Today, however, focus is increasingly shifting to address the impacts of human decision-making around food on the environment. Understanding the historical impacts of human food choice on natural ecosystems provides a deeper understanding of the likely future impacts of our decisions – and none is more important, more far-reaching, or more relevant, than food.

4.2 In Brief: The Impact of Human Food Choice on the Present

Given food is necessary for the survival of all species, and the world's population is on a fast track toward ten billion people (two billion more mouths to

DOI: 10.4324/9781003392279-4

feed by 2050), it follows that food production systems have become complex, and heavily industrialised around a handful of main crops. Added to this large-scale system is the drive for profit. Moving food production into the hands of large corporations, like Monsanto/Bayer, Nestle, or Tyson, has resulted in a disconnect between most humans and their environment. In the developed world, most food is harvested, processed, and shipped a fair distance from where it was grown. Global supply chains mean that a family in the United States can consume a sheep reared in New Zealand. In our 24/7 global economy, consumers can have whatever they want, whenever they desire, driving the expansion of big agriculture and factory farming. One factory alone in Brazil houses 8 million chickens which produce 5.5 million eggs *each* day. Accepting the interconnectedness of food necessitates accepting the global and interconnectedness of its effects on the environment – and by extension, humanity. The United Nations has addressed food security and sustainable agriculture as one of its 17 Sustainable Development Goals (sdgs.un.org/goals), underscoring the importance of the food-environment nexus.

In the modern world, and arguably across time and space, food production has been focused on output. The nineteenth and twentieth centuries were characterised by agricultural innovations that allowed global food production to soar. While famines struck countries like Ethiopia, the developed world grew grain for livestock and produced a huge food surplus. In 2023 alone, the world produced more food than it consumed; with one point three billion tonnes going to waste and generating 8–10% of the world's greenhouse gas emissions (IFCO.com). Food waste is an environmental challenge, just as much as water security and increases in temperature – and global food production depends on both good soil, sufficient water, and stable, predictable weather. The great conundrum is that while food production depends on these variables, it also affects them by causing environmental degradation through erosion from land clearing, increased greenhouse gases, and loss of topsoil – accompanied by associated climatic extremes of drought and flood. In short, the human desire to feed itself – and to turn a profit in doing so, has contributed to the climate catastrophe we now face.

Livestock production is also responsible for the worrying state of global food production. Demand for meat has tripled in the developing world in four decades, while egg consumption has increased sevenfold, driving a huge expansion of large-scale animal operations. Providing grain to the large feed lots scattered around the globe is yet another worrying factor. Corn is grown mainly to feed the big three animal domesticates – cattle, pigs, and chickens. A significant portion of the world's grain production is sent to China and South Korea to feed their pigs and chickens. The demand for more crops to feed livestock is likely to result in the need to double crop production by 2050.

Added to the environmental consequences of intensive food production systems, is the global burden of disease that originates with animals and livestock. Zoonotic diseases cause harm to both animal and human health, and COVID-19 was an all too stark warning of the precarious situation in which the world finds itself with respect to food.

Climate change both exacerbates and is exacerbated by food production. Global average temperatures have been setting new records with each successive year, while rainfall has become less predictable. Extreme weather events that destroy crops – whether floods, droughts, heat, or violent storms – have become more common. Pests, weeds, viruses, and diseases move to new areas and affect crops, livestock, and aquaculture production. Climate change is also altering the productivity of capture fisheries and the distribution of fish stocks, making future harvests less certain.

> The conditions in which food are produced vary tremendously across the world. In advanced countries, technological innovations are bringing high-tech solutions to many farms. At the same time, small farms with less than two hectares of land represent 84% of farms globally but produce only one-third of global crop production. Farmers and fishers operating on a small scale seldom have either the resources or the education to access the latest technologies, and often hesitate to try new approaches they perceive as too risky to their own food security and livelihoods.
>
> (OECD.org)

What is far more poignant is that the situation in which much of the world now finds itself can be traced back to the start of large-scale food production nearly 8000 years ago.

4.3 The Impact of Human Food Choice on Past Environments

Humans have always impacted their environment. In Australia, First Nations People have used firestick farming to burn patches of vegetation for at least 60,000 years (Pascoe 2014). Firing the landscape facilitated the hunting of smaller species by flushing them out of the bush and had the effect of creating and maintaining patches of open grasslands for the cultivation of yams and other bush foods. Regular anthropogenic burning was also an effective method of mitigating the devastating effects of bushfires which today burn out of control in areas of unmanaged vegetation. The widespread increase in global wildfires has caused catastrophic loss of both human and animal life, with attendant economic loss – $22.8 billion USD in 2018 alone (statista.com). While this increase in wildfires is often pegged to climate change, it is less commonly associated with the effects of the food production systems that have contributed to these larger climatic patterns. It is to this underlying driver of change, to which we now turn.

4.3.1 Food Production as a Driver of Past Climate Change

Human eco-dynamics encompasses the nuanced interplay between humans and their impacts on the natural world (Fitzhugh et al. 2018). Archaeological evidence is commonly used to understand human eco-dynamics, offering unprecedented insight into the consequences of human/environmental interplay. The archaeological record is replete with examples of climate-induced events, most of which appear as human abandonment of settlements. In both the Near East and Eastern Mediterranean, there was widespread abandonment of villages during the late Bronze Age (c.1000 BC), which many are increasingly examining against the lens of climate change – at least on the surface. Archaeologists suggest that increasing aridification resulted in less water, impacting the ability for sedentary villages to farm at the scale needed to support larger populations. At early Iron Age Zagora on Andros, Greece, the settlement was abandoned without a trace – likely due to the absence of water (Knight and Beaumont 2018). There is no archaeological evidence of invasions or warfare – only a suggested lack of the most basic resource. Aridification meant that people abandoned higher-density settlements in favour of low-density mobile bands based around herding and season horticulture. In the ancient world, risk mitigation meant abandoning higher-density living and returning to an earlier way of life.

While climate change has been directly blamed for the demise of the most notable civilisations of the American southwest, including the Chacoan phenomenon, c.1000 AD (Judge 1989), this may too be an entirely simplistic explanation. Recent research has argued instead that the development of sedentism and agricultural systems are the root causes of civilisation collapse, as these systems render human groups incapable of mitigating climatic risks, such as periods of low rainfall (Nelson and Schachner 2002). The inability to adapt leads to population dispersal, and this is a pattern repeated across time and space in the archaeological record. It is also possible that farming in marginal areas negatively impacted the balance of delicate ecosystems, removing the buffer found in areas of greater environmental diversity, such as along coastal areas. The archaeological record is filled with similar patterns of climate-induced change, and sometimes collapse; suffice it to say, the human-animal-environmental entanglement over the production of food was a driving force in civilisations throughout history.

4.4 Archaeological and Historical Case Studies

In our modern world, it is difficult to find an ecosystem devoid of human impact. Even the polar ice caps now bear scars of human activity. It is undeniable that intensive human food production systems bear much of the responsibility and there is a growing body of research to support this accusation. The relationship between intensive pastoralist systems – be they crops or animals – and natural ecosystems, provides a poignant view of the impact of these systems on the environment. While this relationship is more often than not discussed against the dire effects of these systems on the natural environment, we argue that by examining relevant archaeological and historical case studies, we can foster a greater understanding of these impacts that can in turn be used to alter our current course toward collapse.

Grazing animals have been part of most natural landscapes globally. From herds of buffalo in North America and Africa to horses in Eurasia and kangaroos in Australia, the relationship between grazing species and the environment was a balanced system – with animal population density proportional to a resource base. Human intervention into this natural system via introduction of new domesticates resulted in the intensification of cycles of increased resource exploitation. This was the case with both plants and animals. While anthropologists have studied domestication and the intensification of resource exploitation spatiotemporally as a defining characteristic of complex civilisations, the environmental impacts of this relationship and the disequilibrium caused, have only recently begun to garner scrutiny. Understanding these relationships now holds promise to change future human food systems through an understanding of the impacts of one-sided, intensive exploitation of formerly balanced environments.

> The introduction of ungulates into new ecosystems results in a radically changed biological regime, and where domestic grazing animals are introduced, the process of environmental change associated with the irruption of herbivores into new environments is complicated by other variables that include land clearance methods, systems of range management, stocking rates, patterns of land tenure, and land use. Accommodation between the environment and the new species is eventually achieved but the initial onslaught causes, in Simpson's words, "an ecological revolution of truly vast proportions.
>
> (Melville 1997: 61)

Human-animal interactions provide a window into the historical impacts of the choice to manage a given species which can delineate possible future impacts of this choice, such as the wider global problem of resource security. Population growth combined with changes in climate patterns pose a serious threat to the viability of global food supplies, which are challenges neither independent of each other nor exclusively modern phenomena. Given the water/feed requirements of domestic animals, the livestock industry is a major player in these global issues. As the world faces increasing periods of climate instability, there is an urgent need to understand the potential trade-offs associated with the global food economy and re-evaluate future goals in light of maintaining sustainable industries.

With modern climate research strongly suggesting a future with even greater climatic instability and more frequent global water crises, an increased demand for unreliable natural resources is worsened by the ecological footprint resulting from raising livestock. Mitigating the inevitable changes that accompany this bleak forecast necessitates changes in the way we live, the plants we grow, and the livestock we keep – in short, the food we eat. Understanding the ecological impact of plant and animal domesticates historically can provide a roadmap to navigate this uncertain future.

Foodways provide a new way of looking at human cultural adaptations to a new suite of environmental conditions. The Colonial era (post-eighteenth century) in particular, was one of rapid environmental change, whereby European colonisation spread plants, animals, and diseases around the world (Landon 2005). Ancient and historic foodways illustrate how the climate influenced past peoples as well as how colonists influenced new environments by responding to and changing them (Steele 2015). Indeed, in recent decades there have been a growing number of archaeological studies whose multidisciplinary approaches can act as proxies for information on past climate and environment, and changes in both (Emery 2004, 2007, 2010; Emery and Thornton 2008a, 2008b, 2012a, 2012b; Sandweiss and Kelley 2012). Archaeological evidence can be used as a proxy for climate conditions, and so contribute to understanding local human interactions and responses to environmental changes, such as the economic strategies used to cope with them (Jones and Britton 2019).

Looking to the past has, therefore, become increasingly useful in exploring these human-environmental interactions, on a local, regional, and global scale (Jones and Britton 2019). Domesticates can 'reveal anthropogenic modifications to their environments, diets, physiologies and life histories', as direct results of human activity (Pilaar Birch 2013; Zangrando et al. 2014; Makarewicz 2016; Jones and Britton 2019; Pitt et al. 2019). Part of the domesticate life histories include their management by past human societies and because animal husbandry strategies were influenced by specific environments, these histories can reveal tailored management strategies to suit the specific conditions encountered (Jones and Britton 2019). Adjustment of past animal management strategies to suit local environmental conditions is exemplified by research on the diet of sheep in Prehistoric Britain which reveals they were eating seaweed and grazing in salt marshes (Balasse et al. 2006; Britton et al. 2008). Similarly, zooarchaeological research in Neolithic Scandinavia suggests that cattle were manipulated to have multiple birth seasons (Gron et al. 2016), while research on Neolithic European cattle examined the environmental constraints of seasonal calving, and the resulting impacts on milk availability and cheese making (Balasse et al. 2021).

Foodways provide a better understanding of the past consequences of human decisions, and this understanding should be used to inform present and future food choices. Understanding 'the nature and extent of environmental and climatic changes in the past, and the ways in which societies responded to such changes, may be crucial to being able to predict and adapt to the contemporary climatic challenges' (Jones and Britton 2019: 969). Australia has a vastly different climate to Britain and understanding the environmental and social impacts that European animal husbandry made can provide didactic insights into the very real challenge we currently face in creating a stable food supply in a future of rising global temperatures and climatic extremes.

4.4.1 Australia and the Introduction of Sheep

Sheep were among the first livestock transported to Australia, and quickly became the most important animal domesticate in the new economy. The rich archaeological record from early colonial Australia, coupled with historical stock lists, delineates the pivotal role sheep played in the birth of this new nation, providing the innovation and stability behind one of white Australia's earliest colonial food systems. The intricate relationship between humans and sheep shaped a national dietary and economic mainstay, as well as a nation's character, culture, and physical environment.

Australia provides one of the most salient studies of the impact of food production on the environment. As a relatively 'new' country with respect to the introduction of European plant and animal domesticates, the effects of these species on an ancient and delicately balanced landscape are blatantly visible – and in some cases lie in living memory. The recency of the process also means there is a raft of documentation of associated effects on the natural landscape, which can serve as a proxy for similar effects in areas in which the process is much older and for which written records and documentation are scarce.

Australia is the driest continent on Earth with some of the most ancient landscapes and 'poorest' soils. Millions of years of erosion largely devoid of the volcanic and seismic activity of the European and American continents have resulted in comparatively nutrient-poor soils over much of the continent (Massey 2017). The capacity of these soils to produce traditional, domesticated European cereal crops is significantly reduced in comparison with geologically younger continents. Yet, indigenous peoples expertly exploited this landscape, managing food 'production' in balance with these variables. Indigenous plant cultivation looked much different to European farming, so much so that it seemed absent to European colonisers (Pascoe 2014).

Australia exemplifies what happens when pastoralism is introduced to an environment that knows neither domesticated grazing animals nor the attendant cereal cropping that is its frequent companion. The introduction of hard-hoofed animal domesticates, coupled with widespread land clearing, ploughing, and later repeated pesticide and fertiliser application for cereal cultivation, have resulted in high levels of landscape degradation that have increased its susceptibility to the harsh extremes of floods and droughts that are a constant feature of this continent.

While Australia's natural biome has been and continues to be, affected by both introduced plant and animal domesticates, the most notable and well-studied is the sheep. Sheep grazing was the initial method of colonial land use and provided the mechanism by which much of the hinterland of Australia was settled. However, few are aware of the early research on the environmental effects of the sheep industry. Australian soil scientists examined the environmental changes observed between 1803 and 1854 in the tablelands of NSW associated with sheep, correlating stocking and grazing rates and the onset of deterioration in vegetation, soils, and water resources.

> (They) were among the first to directly address the relationship between grazing and environmental change. . . . (This work) formed the basis for research that has clarified the relationship between grazing and erosion and the deterioration of the water regime.
>
> (Melville 1997: 61)

Prior to the introduction of sheep and other hard-hoofed domesticates (cattle, horses, pigs), soft-footed kangaroos were Australia's largest, and most populous grazing species. These new species over-grazed the delicate vegetation, leading to the erosion of thin soils, resulting in marked land degradation with increased susceptibility to the extremes of drought and flooding rains for which Australia is known. Arguably, their introduction resulted in a disruption to an ecological equilibrium that had lasted for thousands of years and was one on which indigenous people relied.

Sheep were brought to Australia from England on the First Fleet in 1788 and quickly grew from the 29 recorded in the 1788 census to 12 million by 1854 (Australian Bureau of Statistics 2003). During this period of Australia's infancy, sheep served a dual purpose and were used for both their meat and secondary products. The sheep industry changed the economic, psychological, and physical landscape of Australia. In many ways, Australia's iconic sheep industry represents the culmination of over 11,000 years of directed animal domestication. Australia currently has an estimated 111 million sheep, accounting for 9% of the world's flock (www.abs.gov). The intricate relationship between humans and sheep shaped the nation's character and culture, arguably placing Australia on the world stage. Sheep have altered both the physical and economic landscape of Australia. They have single-handedly provided a livelihood for those involved in their care, and to this day continue to provide a nation with an economic benefit, whose importance is aptly illustrated in the contentious issue of live exports. Even Marx recognised the effects of domestication, arguing that the British enclosures of communal agricultural lands to make way for sheep turned peasants into wage labourers, creating the conditions for the emergence of capitalism (Marx 1992).

The Indigenous population of Australia felt the impact of these introductions perhaps even more than the natural ecosystem. At the time of European invasion, Aboriginal people lived a mobile, largely hunter-gatherer existence, predicated on the hunting of large and small macropods, fishing, and regular regime of cultural burning of the landscape to manage the natural world, cultivate bush foods and flush out small game. Mobile bands moved seasonally with food and water sources – without a need for permanent villages or European cultivation systems predicated on a monoculture crop. Sheep grazing, and the attendant introduction of plant domesticates, changed this way of life. European pastoralists privatised and fenced off land, cutting off access to water and food sources, while sheep altered the vegetation on the landscape. The result for Indigenous populations along eastern Australia was devastating. Not only did these practices cause conflict and bring disease, but they negatively impacted long-serving food sources, leading to starvation and death.

Diet and culture are intertwined – and food can mean many things. Diet is a potent symbol of cultural, economic, and national identity. Food preference is much more than subsistence for many people. It is a way to maintain a tie to the past, to differentiate, and to symbolise. British colonisers in Australia worked against starvation to maintain this tie, choosing death before eating kangaroos and bush foods.

In Australia, it can be argued that the need to maintain a largely British cultural preference for sheep meat led to the degradation of the natural environment and the relative demise of the original human inhabitants of the continent. Australia is an interesting case study on many levels, but it is particularly unique in its determination to stick to a British diet, despite the starvation, death, and difficulty this adherence produced. This determination is exemplified in the expedition of Burke and Wills, famous for the tragic end that befell the European explorers who ventured out to cross the Great Dividing Range in search of the mythical Inland Sea, only to succumb to starvation in a land that had sustained Aboriginal People for 60,000 years. Unlike the Pilgrims who settled in what is now the United States, Australian colonists were determined to maintain a British diet – at the cost of many lives.

In colonial Australia, most historical sources suggest that mutton, preferably locally raised, was the preferred meat. Beef and pork were also prevalent, although being more expensive were consumed less often by the working classes. 'English' food was regarded as desirable and thus retained. Mutton was comfort food from home, while native fauna, like kangaroo, was foreign and undesirable. Why English colonists in Australia remained steadfast in their adherence to traditional foods, whereas in the Americas, native food was more readily incorporated into the diet, is an interesting question. Perhaps some of this difference can be traced back to the different socio-economic backgrounds of many of Australia's first European inhabitants, which were initially drawn from the lower classes. Certainly, in rural areas and in periods of scarcity, native fauna was consumed. In the early 19th century Hobart, New South Wales experienced a period of scarcity and so sheep were not exported to the colonists in Hobart, who quickly turned to kangaroo to fill the gap (Fillios 2016). Similar patterns are apparent at Port Arthur in Tasmania (D'Gluyas et al. 2015) and rural Sydney (Blake 2010). Unfortunately, the aversion to eating native species by the early colonists, and subsequent intensive sheep husbandry, resulted in significant environmental consequences and cultural changes, for both Indigenous people and native species – changing an ancient landscape and ancient culture for good.

Sheep pose an ecological conundrum for Australia – a trade-off between their ability to create wealth while at the same time straining a fragile environment. Sheep are resource-intensive and the expansion of pastures necessary for their maintenance has resulted in the destruction of forests, water pollution, and increased greenhouse gas emissions. Despite these global impacts, the development and impact of the sheep industry have yet to be critically evaluated in Australia – currently the world's second-largest producer of sheep products.

It is commonly held that Australia was built on the back of sheep. Sheep shaped the culture and industry of a new country and a new people – creating what would eventually become one of the most iconic images of Australia. Sheep, and other hard-hoofed animals like cattle, also caused widespread environmental degradation of their grazing environments, and with their high-water requirements, were, and still are, difficult to manage sustainably in a country of climatic extremes.

Australia's British colonists likely did not consider the impact their food choices would have on a novel, and very different place – and in particular the way in which the choice to manage one species over another would shape and alter the fragile environment with which colonists came into contact. Environmental change driven by cultural food preference was an unintentional process, but one that has had dire consequences for almost every new environment into which both plant and animal domesticates were introduced.

4.4.2 Cattle Grazing in the Americas

Unlike Australia, early settlement in the Americas was characterised by the arrival of several different European cultures (Dutch, British, French, and Spanish), and diet was initially shaped, especially in rural contexts, by indigenous peoples. Indigenous influence on diet was especially prevalent east of the Mississippi, where archaeological evidence for French subsistence practices in the mid-western United States (Fort Michilimackinac, Fort Ouiatenon, Cahokia wedge) suggest that compared to their English counterparts, the French traders had far greater interaction and trade with Native Americans, significantly altering their diets to incorporate higher rates of wild mammals – with an almost complete dearth of sheep (Cleland 1970; Scott 1991, 1996; Martin 1986, 1988, 1991). Perhaps this plurality of initial cultures was in part responsible for the variability seen in early American diets. Dutch New Amsterdam became the English New York, pigs became less desirable as the popularity of sheep and cattle increased (Greenfield 1989). In the 17th century, New Amsterdam foodways were dominated by the three main domestic taxa (cattle, sheep, pig), but were supplemented by native species, which the Dutch prepared according to their ancestral European methods (Janowitz 1993).

The confluence of European colonists, new environments, and local indigenous peoples produced changes in husbandry, and thereby diet. Archaeological faunal remains from Sarah Boston's Farmstead in Massachusetts established that New England Native Americans incorporated and adapted European animal husbandry strategies into their Native Nipmuc practices (Allard 2015). Zooarchaeological evidence may explain how a change to static husbandry strategies contributed to changes in cattle size (e.g. Reitz and Ruff 1994), with change in land use strategies resulting in access to less forage. These changes resulted in poorer nutrition and thus decreased cattle size (Arbuckle and Bowen 2002). In Ozan township, Arkansas, archaeological research reveals the devastating environmental effects of the combined factors of the rapid rate of settlement and introduction of cotton farming, resulting in drought and soil erosion (Proebsting 2016).

As is clear by the above examples, there is a wealth of archaeological and historical research on early American foodways and so here we will limit the focus to the social and environmental impact of cattle and specifically address their impact on native biomes and human populations during that pivotal 19th century phase of Westward expansion.

Of the three major animal domesticates, cattle have arguably received the most attention in recent years with respect to the significant environmental effects of their intensive husbandry. Cattle have large water requirements, with one cow needing up to 100 litres of water per day, and 16,000 litres of water needed to produce one kilo of beef (Evans 2019). Cattle also contribute to greenhouse gas emissions, global deforestation, topsoil loss, and food shortages. However, are these negative environmental consequences of human entanglements with cattle a result of modern intensive cattle production, or are they implicit in the management and domestication of cattle as a species? Complicating the story is a mass accumulation of wealth that frequently attends large cattle herds, as noted by Engels (2010 [1884]), early symbolic representations of cattle in the palatial feasts of the late Bronze Age Mycenaeans (Wright 2004), and by miniature cattle figurines recovered from wealthy tombs in Ancient Egypt. Throughout human history, livestock has meant wealth, and no other species symbolises this more saliently than cattle. Livestock – domesticated, inheritable animals – were the first private property (Engels 2010 [1884]) – the value of which is still visible in the Masai of Kenya, the vast properties in Australia, and cattle ranches of the Americas.

The Americas are virtually synonymous with cattle ranching. Extending from the American West to Argentina, beef production and intensive cattle husbandry were historically important, and continue to be so. Much like Australia was built on the sheep's back, the Americas were built on the backs of cattle. And as with sheep in Australia historical large-scale cattle grazing had both a human and environmental cost.

Cattle were initially introduced by Spanish conquerors via Santo Domingo in 1493 after crossing the Atlantic with Columbus on his second voyage. This introduction facilitated European expansion by transforming notions of property and destroying the native environments into which they were introduced (Ficek 2019). In Santo Domingo, the cattle grew larger, and as they grazed uncontained, they spread to the grassy savannas that indigenous peoples had formerly maintained with fire and cultivated crops. Cattle kept the forest back by grazing on young trees and shrubs, transforming what had once been agricultural fields into pastures. In the Caribbean cattle began their environmental and human transformation in the Americas.

In the Western United States cattle grazing had similar effects as on Santo Domingo – widespread environmental degradation and an associated cost on traditional indigenous lifeways. Cattle are implicated in the change from timbered open spaces to treeless plains across the western United States coincident with their spread during the 19th century. Archaeological evidence also abounds for environmental and cultural degradation of indigenous agricultural systems associated with intensive grazing. Cattle extended their range up the Americas, via Mesoamerica, and into the southwestern United States, ultimately resulting in land claims by Spanish colonists, once again at the expense of native indigenous peoples (Ficek 2019).

Degradation of indigenous agricultural systems was accompanied by economic and cultural exploitation of native peoples on the Spanish missions in Southern Arizona and Northern Mexico. In these places, as in many others, Spanish colonists exploited indigenous communities as a labour force to initiate and support extensive cattle ranching (e.g. Pavão-zuckerman and LaMotta 2007; Pavão-Zuckerman 2011, 2017; Pavão-Zuckerman and Martínez-ramírez 2020). Without the labour force, large-scale production would not have been possible – and this eventually gave rise to a global, industrialised beef economy, feuding a capitalist expansion across the Americas.

Herds continued to grow in the American Southwest as the transition from Spain occurred, and by the middle of the 18th century in South America and the 19th in the United States, cattle numbered in the millions and had permanently altered the ecology and culture of all with whom they came into contact. The introduction of cattle resulted in ecological and cultural loss – exterminating native plants and bison and leading to the displacement of Native Americans onto reservations 'where they were fed government beef purchased from ranchers who occupied their land' (Ficek 2019: 264).

The interplay between culture, economics, and the environment, alongside the biological needs of the species also influenced the spread of cattle in other parts of the Americas. For example, cattle were better suited than sheep to the hot and humid environment of the Chesapeake Bay colony. In this case, the environment drove change such that despite the traditional importance of sheep in the British diet, there was a switch to cattle, which were better suited to the environment (Cheek 1998). American dietary flexibility and adaptation are also evident in the archaeological evidence from the early colonists at Plymouth, Massachusetts Bay, and Newfoundland, Canada. In both cases, traditional 'English' meats – primarily sheep and pork, were replaced by cattle and pig, which were both better suited to the sandy and forested environment (Fischer et al. 1997; Hodgetts 2006).

4.4.3 Cereal Agriculture in the Near East and Mediterranean

Thus far we have focused on the impacts of animal domesticates on human food choice and the environment. However, the domestication of plants, and cereal grains in particular, also brought a raft of changes. Like animal domestication, most grains (with the notable exception of corn) were initially domesticated in the Near East around 8000 years ago. Research suggests there were likely multiple centres of domestication over a short period of time in multiple locations. Plant cultivation changed the course of humankind. It allowed people to remain in one place on a semi-permanent permanent basis and facilitated the growth of villages and towns, leading to the 'agricultural revolution', aptly named for the raft of changes it produced. Initially, agriculture provided food security for growing populations and led to the formation of stable communities. It also facilitated the growth of social differentiation via the ability to accumulate wealth in food. The social stratification that characterised large ancient civilisations, such as Ur and Uruk in Mesopotamia, Mycenae in Late Bronze Age Greece, and the Nile Valley of Dynastic Egypt, was largely predicated on agriculture and animal husbandry. The link between plant and animal domestication is also strong and a key part of the web of human-animal environmental entanglement, especially given that some grain is grown exclusively for use as animal fodder.

Many plants have made a significant and long-lasting impact on human society across a range of uses that include food but also medicines and textiles. Cotton has, and continues to have, a major impact on human ecosystems, as does rice, sugar, tea, coffee, cacao, and most recently sorghum, soy, and canola. Here we focus on cereal cultivation and on wheat in particular because of its cross-cultural popularity as a food staple.

Modern industrial farming is often synonymous with monoculture – a heavy reliance on one crop. Industrial agricultural systems rely on repeated cycles of applications of chemicals for pest control and fertilisers to compensate for nutrient-poor soils used to produce the same crop harvest after harvest. Add to this system, genetically modified plants and it is easy to compare modern agricultural systems to a house of cards teetering on the edge of a large-scale disaster. Modern agricultural systems have forgone risk mitigation in the pursuit of large profits – with dire environmental impact.

The environmental effects of cereal monoculture are surprisingly similar to those of European animal domesticates. These include degraded soils reliant on continual applications of chemical pesticides, herbicides, and fertilisers, which in turn wreak toxic havoc on native species. Large-scale land clearing for cultivation has even wider-reaching environmental impacts, including global warming through the removal of trees, plants, and shrubs that contribute to atmospheric CO_2. In short, industrial cereal cultivation is a cow or sheep by another name – with similar dire effects.

Archaeological research across the Near East and Mediterranean has shown that the need to improve pastures for cereal cultivation followed plant domestication in relatively quick succession. Isotopic evidence for manuring of cultivated areas from the Neolithic (c. 6000 years ago) underscores the transformative effects of agricultural systems on natural environments through time (Bogaard et al. 2013) – and further highlights the necessity of directed, human intervention into a system to produce sufficient yield.

According to Jared Diamond, agriculture was 'the worst thing that ever happened to the human stomach' (1987: 100). One of the greatest misnomers surrounding farming is its role in nutrition, risk mitigation, and leisure time. Many hunter-gatherer groups have been extensively studied by anthropologists, such as the Yanomamo of Brazil and the !Kung San of the Kalahari. Their mobile way of life provided excellent risk mitigation. Following food availability meant they moved seasonally around the landscape, often visiting the same patches on an annual rotation. They had more leisure time than farming communities, consumed a greater number of balanced, nutrient-dense calories per day than farming peoples, and generally worked less hard (Harper and Le Beau 2003).

Human health has also not fared well under intensive cereal agriculture. As discussed at the start of this chapter, grains break down into sugars, which lead to caries and tooth decay that often result in infections which could result in death. Tooth decay is rarely present in hunter-gatherer groups – as is the malnutrition resulting from a reliance on monoculture, or the increased susceptibility to famine. Research on Indigenous human skeletal remains from Dickson (burial) Mounds in Illinois and Ohio River Valleys of the United States show a 50% increase in tooth enamel defects indicative of malnutrition (Goodman 1989), a four-fold increase in iron deficiency anaemia, a three-fold increase in bone lesions and an increase in degenerative spinal conditions resulting from hard, physical labour, in addition to a decrease in life expectancy from 26 to 19 (Goodman et al. 1984). Across the ocean, human remains recovered from Greece and Turkey show similar negative associations, including a decrease in height coincident with the adoption of agriculture 3000 years ago (Diamond 1987).

Farming is not in and of itself detrimental to humans, animals, or the environment. Agriculture allowed human populations to expand, and facilitated craft specialisation, freeing some to pursue other activities in which human creativity shone, resulting in many inventions for which humans are known. Rather, intensive, large-scale agriculture is the bigger issue. Agriculture is a double-edged sword, for it bolstered human inventiveness, supported population growth and sedentism, education, and complex societies – while at the same time exposing humans to risks such as starvation, malnutrition, and disease that were no longer able to be mitigated as they were in more mobile groups.

4.5 Conclusion: Drawing on the Past to Change the Future

Throughout history, food has defined us. Brillat-Savarain once wrote 'Dis-moi ce que tu manges, je te dirai ce que tu es' ('Tell me what you eat, and I will tell you what you are') (1854). This chapter argues that throughout history, food choices have been interwoven with cultural identity and these choices have produced a raft of effects on the natural environment. Whether in reference to the Australian preference for consuming mutton over more readily available native species, such as kangaroo, or to consumption of high-status beef, food choices are a significant way of maintaining ties to heritage and social identity, of differentiating white European colonists from indigenous peoples, and from distinguishing between wealthy and poor.

Historic and modern plant and animal domesticates reflect the interplay between the environment and human innovation, trade, behaviour, and cultural norms. These human-animal-environmental interactions facilitate exploration of the rise and impact of global challenges. Anthropological perspectives offer a unique perspective on human ecodynamics over the *longue durée* which can help better understand how human utilisation of plants and animals has been shaped by the economy and environment – and most importantly, how this relationship may shape both with respect to global food systems in the future.

Repeated research has shown that when people move to new regions where animal husbandry is unknown, they will seek to maintain their original traditions (Bökönyi 1975). This theory and ideas of culture change vs cultural persistence and continuity (e.g. Voss 2005, 2008, 2012, 2015; Voss et al. 2018), characterises much of the more recent movement of peoples to North, Central, and South America, where the British, French, and Spanish had varying degrees of success incorporating their own culture cores.

Ficek (2019) writing specifically with respect to cattle, suggests that they should be considered as more than just commodities caught up in the machinations of industrial production, cattle actively transform environments by entering relations of interdependence with humans and other species. These relations and transformations have consequences for humans and the societies they try to build. As they eat, digest, move, trample, and occupy space, cattle move in and out of expansionist projects in ways that often escape human control' (Ficek 2019: 260). We argue this holds true for almost all domesticated plant and animal species.

4.5.1 *Cultural Change as a Way Forward*

What causes some to adopt new foods and foodways, while others dogmatically cling to the food of their heritage? Why are some cultures open to change, while others starve rather than change? What factor(s) determine whether a new food will be welcomed or shunned, and what is the limit of culture when it comes to subsistence?

The concepts of continuity and change are key aspects of subsistence strategies, particularly in the degree to which humans desire to retain traditional dietary preferences in new environments – however, as the Australian example illustrated, biology and reason do not always trump cultural preference.

These and other questions guide human food choice now, and if we are to move to a future in which other, less traditional foods are welcomed, we must understand human decision-making around food. Perhaps in many respects, food 'choice' is a first-world problem. In areas of food scarcity, malnutrition, and famine, hunger trumps culture. But should it take starvation to move the world to more sustainable foods? What will it take for the sustainability of global food systems to take pride of place in human decision-making?

So many questions, and yet the real value of understanding the interplay between human food choice and the environment may lie in learning to change our cultural preferences in deference to local environmental conditions – especially in the face of a future with an increasingly variable climate. This may mean turning away from lamb, beef, and pork – animals with high water requirements, and massive ecological consequences, toward more sustainable choices, including 'pests' like kangaroo, goat, and insects.

Most areas of European colonisation reflect the same general archaeological trends, suggesting that the recent movement of European peoples spatiotemporally progressed on similar trajectories. Human migration patterns can be roughly separated into an initial phase, in which faunal diversity is high, consisting of a variety of wild and introduced domesticates. As humans move into a new environment, food security and population health are both unstable as people attempt to adapt to a new suite of environmental – and often social – conditions. This initial phase is also characterised by social, economic, and nutritional instability and often results in the depletion of native species (as exemplified by the crash in kangaroo numbers in the Sydney basis shortly following European contact) (Karskens 2009). Subsequent periods show a marked decline in species diversity, with an especially large decrease in the use of native species. Reliance on a handful of introduced European domesticates follows, with an associated growth in population and specialised economic structures, built on the back of these animals, including textile and meat industries. The general trend is then one of decreased species richness and increased intensification of specialised or species-targeted animal husbandry – as aptly exemplified by the growth of the Australian sheep industry.

The human-animal-environmental nexus provides an excellent insight into the development of global and local food systems and their interplay with culture. As Karskens (2009) adeptly illustrates, cities emerge from 'kaleidoscopic complexity'. The early livestock industry was tied to the same geographical constraints and opportunities as the indigenous peoples whose country they claimed – and yet the results could not be more disparate.

Understanding historical foodways offers a way forward. Discussing the drivers behind food choice, coupled with a clear understanding of the environmental impacts of this choice, opens a conversation about future foodways. We need a much broader understanding of the complex interplay between culture, environment, and a burgeoning new economic system, a promising way forward for the future of food that is sustainable and suited to an ever more fragile world. Learning from the past enables us to contextualise present-day situations, increasing our ability to inform current mitigation strategies in response to changing global pressures on the environment – both natural and human-induced.

References

Allard, A 2015, 'Foodways, animal husbandry and nipmuc identity: Faunal analysis from Sarah Boston's Farmstead, Grafton, MA, 1790–1840', *International Journal of Historical Archaeology*, *19*, pp.208–231.

Arbuckle, BS & Bowen, J 2002, 'Zooarchaeology and agricultural colonization: An example from the colonial Chesapeake', in M Mondini, S Muñoz & S Wickler (eds.), *Colonisation, migration, and marginal areas*, Oxbow Books, pp.20–27.

Australian Bureau of Statistics 2003, 'The wool industry – Looking back and forward, Cat', No.1301.0, Australian Bureau of Statistics, Canberra, accessed 1 March 2024, www.abs.gov.au/ausstats/abs@.nsf/featurearticlesbyCatalogue/1476D522EBE22464CA256CAE0015BAD4?OpenDocument.

Balasse, M, Gillis, R, Živaljević, I, Berthon, R, Kovačiková, L, Fiorillo, D, Arbogast, RM, Bălăşescu, A, Bréhard, S, Nyerges, ÉÁ & Dimitrijević, V 2021, 'Seasonal calving in European Prehistoric cattle and its impacts on milk availability and cheese-making', *Scientific Reports*, *11*(1), p.8185.

Balasse, M, Tresset, A & Ambrose, S 2006, 'Stable Isotope evidence (δ13C, δ18O) for winter feeding on seaweed by Neolithic sheep of Scotland', *Journal of Zoology*, *270*, pp.170–176.

Blake, N 2010, 'Diet in urban and rural nineteenth-century New South Wales: The evidence from the faunal remains', *Australasian Historical Archaeology*, *24*, pp.25–34.

Bogaard, A, Fraser, R, Heaton, T, Wallace, M, Vaiglova, P, Charles, M, Jones, G, Evershed, R, Styring, A, Andersen, N, Arbogast, R, Bartosiewicz, L, Gardeisen, A, Kanstrup, M, Maier, U, Marinova, E, Ninov, L, Schaefer, M & Stephan, E 2013, 'Crop manuring and intensive land management by Europe's first famers', *Proceedings of the National Academy of Sciences of the United States of America*, *110*(31), https://doi.org/10.1073/pnas.1305918110.

Bökönyi, S 1975, 'Effects of environmental and cultural changes on prehistoric fauna assemblages', in MC Arnott (ed.), *Gastronomy: The anthropology of food and food habits*, Mouton, The Hague, pp.3–12.

Brillat-savarin, JA 1854, *The physiology of taste: Or transcendental gastronomy*, Translated by F Robinson, Lindsay and Blakistan, Philadelphia.

Britton, K, Müldner, G & Martin, B 2008, 'Stable isotope evidence for salt-marsh grazing in the Bronze Age Severn Estuary, UK: Implications for palaeodietary analysis at coastal sites', *Journal of Archaeological Science*, *35*, pp.2111–2118.

Cheek, CD 1998, 'Massachusetts bay foodways: Regional and class influences', *Historical Archaeology*, *32*(3), pp.153–172.

Childe, VG 1936, *Man makes himself*, Watts & Company, London.

Cleland, C 1970, 'Comparison of the faunal remains from French and British refuse pits at fort michilimackinac: A study in changing subsistence practices', *Canadian Historic Sites Occasional Papers in Archaeology and History*, *3*, pp.8–23.

D'gluyas, C, Gibbs, M Hamilton, C & Roe, D 2015, 'Everyday artefacts: Subsistence and quality of life at the Prisoner Barracks, Port Arthur, Tasmania', *Archaeology in Oceania*, *50*(3), pp.130–137.

Diamond, J 1987, 'The worst mistake in the history of the human race', in A Podolesfsky & P Brown (eds.), *Applying anthropology: An introductory reader*, Manfield Publishing, Mountain View, pp.95–98.

Emery, KF 2004, 'Environments of the Maya Collapse: Zooarchaeological perspective from the Petexbatún, Guatemala', in KF Emery (ed.), *Maya zooarchaeology: New direction in method and theory*, UCLA Press, Los Angeles, CA, pp.81–96.

Emery, KF 2007, 'Assessing the impact of ancient Maya animal use', *Journal of Nature Conservation*, *15*, pp.184–195.

Emery, KF 2010, *Dietary, environmental, and societal implications of ancient Maya animal use in the Petexbatún: A zooarchaeological perspective on the collapse*, Vanderbilt University Press, Nashville, TN.

Emery, KF & Thornton, EK 2008a, 'A regional perspective on biotic change during the classic Maya occupation using Zooarchaeological isotopic chemistry', *Quaternary International*, *191*, pp.131–143.
Emery, KF & Thornton, EK 2008b, 'Zooarchaeological habitat analysis of ancient Maya landscape changes', *Journal of Ethnobiology*, *28*(2), pp.154–179.
Emery, KF & Thornton, EK 2012a, 'Tracking climate change in the ancient Maya world through Zooarchaeological habitat analysis', in G Iannone (ed.), *The great Maya droughts in cultural context*, University Press of Colorado, Boulder, pp.301–325.
Emery, KF & Thornton, EK 2012b, 'Using animal remains to reconstruct landscapes and climate of the ancient Maya world', in C Lefèvre (ed.), *Proceedings of the general session of the 11th ICAZ conference*, Archaeopress, Oxford England, Paris, France.
Engels, F 2010 (1884), *The origin of the family, private property and the State*, Penguin Classics, New York.
Evans, M 2019, *On eating Meat: The truth about its production and the ethics of eating it*, Murdoch Books, Sydney.
Ficek, R 2019, 'Cattle, capital, colonisation: Tracking creatures of the anthropocene in and out of human projects', *Current Anthropology*, *60*(supplement 20), pp.S260–S271, https://doi.org/10.1086/702788.
Fillios, MA 2016, 'The faunal remains from Cottage Green (Monteplier Estate), Hobart', Unpublished report prepared for Austral Archaeology Pty Ltd.
FIscher, JB, McArthur, LH & Petersen, JB 1997, 'Continuity and change in the food habits of the seventeenth-century English colonists in Plymouth and Massachusetts Bay', *Ecology of Food and Nutrition*, *36*, pp.65–93.
Fitzhugh, B, Butler, VL, Bovy, KB, Etnier, MA 2018, 'Human ecodynamics: A perspective for the study of long-term change in socioecological systems', *Journal of Archaeological Science: Reports*, *23*, pp.1077–1094.
Goodman, A 1989, 'Dental enamel hypoplasias in prehistoric populations', *Advanced Dental Research*, September, *3*(2), pp.265–71, https://doi.org/10.1177/08959374890030022801, PMID: 2701160.
Goodman, A, Lallo, J, Armelagos, G & Rose, J 1984, 'Health changes at Dickson Mounds, Illinois (950–1300 A.D.)', in M Cohen & G Armelagos (eds.), *Palaeopathology and the origins of agriculture*, Academic Press, Cambridge.
Greenfield, HJ 1989, 'From Pork to Mutton: A zooarchaeological perspective on colonial New Amsterdam and early New York City', *Northeast Historical Archaeology*, *18*, pp.85–110.
Gron, KJ, Montgomery, J, Nielsen, PO, Nowell, GM, Peterkin, JL, Sørensen, L & Rowley-Conwy, P 2016, 'Strontium isotope evidence of early Funnel Beaker Culture movement of cattle', *Journal of Archaeological Science: Reports*, *6*, pp.248–251.
Harper, C & Le Beau, B 2003, *Food, society, and environment*, Prentice Hall, NJ.
Hodgetts, LM 2006, 'Feast or famine? Seventeenth-century English colonial diet Ferryland, Newfoundland', *Historical Archaeology*, *40*(4), pp.125–138.
Jones, J & Britton, K 2019, 'Multi-scale, integrated approaches to understanding the nature and impact of past environmental and climatic change in the archaeological record, and the role of isotope zooarchaeology', *Journal of Archaeological Science: Reports*, *23*, pp.968–972.
Janowitz, MF 1993, 'Indian corn and Dutch pots: Seventeenth-century foodways in New Amsterdam/New York', *Historical Archaeology*, *27*, pp.6–24.
Judge, WJ 1989, 'Chaco Canyon-San Juan Basin', in LS Cordell & GJ Gumerman (eds.), *Dynamics in Southwest prehistory*, Smithsonian Institution Press, Washington, DC, pp.209–262.
Karskens, G 2009, *The colony: A history of early Sydney*, Allen & Unwin, Sydney.
Knight, MJ & Beaumont, LA 2018, 'Water supply and climate change at Zagora on Andros: New approaches and perspectives on the early iron age cyclades', in E

Angliker & J Tully (eds.), *Cycladic archaeology and research: New approaches and discoveries*, Archaeopress, Oxford, pp.59–71.

Landon, DB 2005, 'Zooarchaeology and historical archaeology: Progress and prospects', *Journal of Archaeological Method and Theory*, *12*, pp.1–35.

Makarewicz, CA 2016, 'Toward an integrated isotope zooarchaeology', in GM Grupe (ed.), *Isotopic landscapes in bioarchaeology*, Springer, Berlin, Heidelberg, pp.189–209.

Martin, TJ 1986, 'A faunal analysis of fort ouiatenon, an eighteenth-century trading post in the Wabash Valley of Indiana', PhD thesis, Michigan State University.

Martin, TJ 1988, 'Animal remains from the Cahokia Wedge Site', in BL Gums (ed.), *Archaeology at French colonial Cahokia*, Illinois Historic Preservation Agency, Springfield, pp.221–234.

Martin, TJ 1991, 'Modified animal remains, subsistence, and cultural interaction at French colonial sites in the Midwestern United States', in JR Purdue, WE Klippel & BW Styles (eds.), *Beamers, Bob whites, and blue points: Tributes to the career of Paul W. Parmalee*, Illinois State Museum, Springfield, pp.409–419.

Marx, K 1992, *Capital: A critique of political economy*, vol. 1, Penguin, NY.

Massey, C 2017, *Call of the Reed Warbler*, University of Queensland Press, Brisbane.

Melville, EGK 1997, *Plague of sheep: Environmental consequences of the conquest of Mexico*, Studies in Environment and History, Cambridge University Press, Cambridge.

Nelson, MC & Schachner, G 2002, 'Understanding abandonments in the North American Southwest', *Journal of Archaeological Research*, *10*, pp.167–206.

Pascoe, B 2014, *Dark Emu: Aboriginal Australia and the birth of agriculture*, Magabala Books, Broome.

Pavão-zuckerman, B 2011, 'Rendering economics: Native American labor and secondary animal products in the eighteenth-century Pimería Alta', *American Antiquity*, *76*(1), pp.3–23.

Pavão-zuckerman, B. 2017, 'Missions, livestock, and economic transformations in the Pimería Alta', in JG Douglass & WM Graves (eds.), *New Mexico and the Pimería Alta*, University Press of Colorado, pp.289–309.

Pavão-zuckerman, B & Lamotta, VM 2007, 'Missionization and economic change in the pimería alta: The zooarchaeology of San Agustín de Tucson', *International Journal of Historical Archaeology*, *11*(3), pp.241–268.

Pavão-zuckerman, B & Martínez-ramírez, J 2020, 'Zooarchaeology of mission Nuestra Señora del Pilar y Santiago de Cocóspera', *International Journal of Historical Archaeology*, *24*, pp.456–482.

Pilaar Birch, S 2013, 'Stable Isotopes in zooarchaeology: An Introduction', *Archaeological and Anthropological Sciences*, *5*, pp.81–83.

Pitt, J, Gillingham, PK, Maltby, M, Stafford, MR & Stewart, JR 2019, 'Changing cultures, changing environments: A novel means of investigating the effects of introducing non-native species into past ecosystems', *Journal of Archaeological Science: Reports*, 23, pp.1066–1075.

Proebsting, E 2016, 'Plowing prairies and raising stock: Historical ecology and community life on the cotton frontier of Southwest Arkansas', *Historical Archaeology*, *50*(1), pp.114–134.

Reitz, EJ & Ruff, B 1994, 'Morphometric data for cattle from North America and the caribbean prior to the 1850s', *Journal of Archaeological Science*, *21*, pp.699–713.

Sandweiss, DH & Kelley, AR 2012, 'Archaeological contributions to climate change research: The archaeological record as a paleoclimatic and paleoenvironmental archive', *Annual Review of Anthropology*, *41*, pp.371–391.

Scott, EM 1991, 'Such diet as befitted his station as clerk: The archaeology of subsistence and cultural diversity at Fort Michilimackinac, 1761–1781', PhD thesis, University of Minnesota.

Scott, EM 1996, 'Who ate what? Archaeological food remains and cultural diversity', in E Reitz, L Newsom & S Scudder (eds.), *Case studies in environmental archaeology*, Plenum Press, New York, pp.339–356.
Steele, TE 2015, 'The contributions of animal bones from archaeological sites: The past and future of zooarchaeology', *Journal of Archaeological Science*, *56*, pp.168–176.
Voss, BL 2005, 'From *Casta* to *Californio*: Social identity and the archaeology of culture contact', *American Anthropologist*, *107*(3), pp.461–474.
Voss, BL 2008, 'Gender, race, and labor in the archaeology of the Spanish colonial Americas', *Current Anthropology*, *49*(5), pp.861–893.
Voss, BL 2012, 'Status and ceramics in Spanish colonial archaeology', *Historical Archaeology*, *46*(2), pp.39–54.
Voss, BL 2015, 'What's new? Rethinking ethnogenesis in the archaeology of colonialism', *American Antiquity*, *80*(4), pp.655–670.
Voss, BL, Kennedy, JR, Tan, JS & NG, LW 2018, 'The archaeology of home: *Qiaoxiang* and nonstate actors in the archaeology of the Chinese diaspora', *American Antiquity*, *83*(3), pp.407–426.
Wright, J 2004, *The Mycenean feast: An introduction*, American School of Classical Studies at Athens, Princeton.
Zangrando, AF, Tessone, A, Ugan, A & Gutierrez, M 2014, 'Applications of stable isotope analysis in zooarchaeology: An introduction', *International Journal of Osteoarchaeology*, 24, pp.127–133.

5 Post-COVID Future

Living and Managing Life After COVID From Food Security Perspective

Vandana Gulati and Siva Barathi (Sharl) Marimuthu

5.1 Introduction: Food as a Necessity

Food is the basic need and foundation of our lives and the main provider of the essential nutrients needed by our body for its growth and maintenance. The Universal Declaration of Human Rights recognises that everyone has the right to a standard of living adequate for the health and wellbeing for themselves and their family including food, clothing, and housing, as stated in Article 25 (Jones et al. 2013). However, many countries are suffering from a food crisis. The Global Report on Food Crises 2018 (Food Security Information Network 2018) shows that about 124 million people across 51 countries and territories faced crisis levels of acute food insecurity in 2017 (El Bilali et al. 2019).

Human population has been grouped into different ethnicities, religions, nationalities, and food cultures (Cao et al. 2020). The essential nutrients that we receive from our foods are macronutrients (carbohydrates, fats, and proteins) and micronutrients (vitamins and minerals). Food provides energy to the body and is important for the immune system; good food is needed to maintain good health (Shabbir et al. 2020). Nutritional science has proven that an imbalance in nutrition and dietary habits is the root cause of various diseases.

Food insecurity arises when the human right to food is compromised and is defined as "when people do not have the economic, social and physical resources to shop, cook or eat in order to ensure a sufficient supply of nutritionally appropriate food" (Purdam et al. 2016). The Food and Agriculture Organization (FAO) mentioned that more than three point one billion people, or 42 percent of the global population, were unable to afford a healthy diet in 2021.

The world is still recovering from the COVID-19 pandemic, and repercussions of the war in Ukraine, the current war in Gaza, rising food prices, agricultural inputs, and energy, along with weather-related events and food insecurity conflicts have had a greater impact on food systems (Burki 2022; Amin et al. 2022). The contributing factors such as poverty, hunger and

DOI: 10.4324/9781003392279-5

malnutrition, inadequate diets, land degradation, water scarcity, social inequalities, biodiversity loss, and climate change are generating negative outcomes in food availability and affordability (Lang and Barling 2012). The demand for food will increase by 50 percent by 2030 and by 80 to 100 percent by 2050 as the world population is forecast to grow to over nine billion by 2050.

This demand can only be effectively met when traditional food cultures are brought back. Furthermore, public policies need to be reformed to coordinate with the agriculture sector and economic development to save natural resources, develop crops that have greater tolerance to pests, and build supply chains to provide better availability and affordability of foods (Expósito 2023).

5.2 Traditional Food Cultures

Traditional foods reflect cultural inheritance and are based on knowledge and beliefs that include practices and values gathered from the experiences of older generations and developed through the ages in ancestral kitchens. Food cultures have evolved over the years to improve the nutritional and social wellbeing of the people. Traditional food cultures are deeply rooted in centuries of culinary traditions and thus hold a special place in the fabric of cultural societies across the globe.

The knowledge of traditional foods has been passed down from one generation to the next and is deeply embedded in community, customs, rituals, and history. Traditional foods are characterised by their diversity, locally adapted ingredients, and unique preparation methods. They are the reflection of culture but also a powerhouse of nutrition, contributing to health and wellbeing. Traditional food cultures include local ingredients and have the potential to enable cultural continuity and the conservation of histories.

Traditional food cultures provide food security, enhance livelihoods, and improve nutritional and social wellbeing as they are specific to regions, environments, and seasons (Daison 2023). They are an expression of culture, history, and lifestyle and may confer health properties that have been tested over time. They also preserve the important ingredients and recipes of the culinary heritage of nations that future generations can get acquainted with (Trichopoulou et al. 2007). Traditional foods encompass local ingredients that are diverse, and mainly obtained from plants and their parts such as roots, flowers, tubers, leaves, stems, nuts, seeds, millets, and fruits.

The traditional food knowledge can promote biocultural diversity, sustainable food production, and a healthy ecosystem; it will not only improve cultural identification but also connect communities to the world. The traditional population was dependent on vegetables, fruits, and fermented foods, and consumed less animal and meat products. Traditional foods were rich sources of fibre, vitamins, and minerals and also provided proteins, carbohydrates, unsaturated fats, antioxidants, carotenoids, and other phytonutrients

(Trichopoulou 2021). Micronutrient deficiencies and chronic conditions were not that common before the colonial era and globalisation.

The diets were sustainable with low environmental impact. Local food production practices were climate resilient, preserved biodiversity, brought a sense of community wellbeing, and provided nutritional security (Marrero and Mattei 2022). The local food system is an integral part of traditional food culture that promotes locally sourced ingredients and seasonal foods, reducing the need for long-distance transportation and minimising food waste. Strengthening local food production and distribution networks can enhance the sustainability and resilience of food systems to contribute to global food and nutrition security.

5.3 Globalisation and Industrialisation: A Threat to Regional and Traditional Cuisines

Food culture has greatly evolved in the past 10,000 to 15,000 thousand years. The hunter-gatherers were replaced by farmers. The domestication of plants and animals has greatly increased the food supply, and new technology and agricultural practices, urbanisation, and globalisation have enormously changed the traditional food systems and cultures (Crittenden and Schnorr 2017). The traditional cuisines were dependent on available foods, seasonal cycles, regions, culture and language, and cooking and eating together.

Industrial revolution in general and giant corporations have caused the loss of many traditional culinary practices while causing adverse health issues (MacLennan and Zhang 2004). The authors argue that traditional food cultures need to be strengthened as they play a crucial role in the construction and maintenance of collective identities deeply rooted in their place of origin. Modern food production is highly mechanised due to developments in technologies used in food production, processing, preservation, transportation, storage, and supply chains and, therefore, there is the increased availability of pre-prepared, unseasonal foods (Benny 2018).

This is an era of the modern world of convenient foods that are more processed, devoid of nutrients, and dependent on global export-oriented agriculture. Dietary patterns have also changed due to the widening of the fast-food chains. Globalisation has eroded traditional food cultures and the intergenerational transmission of cooking practices, food practices, tastes, and meanings based on local ingredients.

Industrialisation is driven by corporations focused on increasing profit margins, power, and influence. Culinary modernism provides processed, preservable, industrial, novel, and fast food that is cheaper and affordable. Earlier, men used to grow crops and do laborious work in the field whereas women used to dry, grind, chop, cook, and make fresh meals for the family every day throughout the year. In modern times, people have an option of ordering their meals through their electronic devices such as mobile phones, laptops, and computers. The importance of home cooking has been diminished (Laudan 2001).

5.4 Impacts of COVID-19: Food Supply Chain Disruptions

COVID-19 was a global tragedy, not only for human lives but also for all industrial sectors, from the automotive and telecom sectors to tourism, aviation, oil construction, and healthcare industries. The unavailability of clinical care and vaccines caused much anxiety and fear across the globe. The lockdowns caused further labour shortages, logistics disruptions, and food supply chain problems. In the meantime, the crisis resulted in panic buying and hoarding (Mishra et al. 2022).

States also started "hoarding" food by imposing trade constraints and putting export bans which further threatened to exacerbate global food supply problems. The negative impacts on the world economy and food security were apparent in the entire cycle, from the field to the companies to the consumers. Moreover, the food production and distribution system are diverse and dependent on weather and season. The different processes and stages are connected to each other and a glitch in one system in one stage or season affects the entire supply chain (Aday and Aday 2020).

Food supply chain disruptions and logistical challenges caused much wastage; perishable food items such as milk, fresh produce, cheese, meat, and meat products were thrown away, causing further food crises (Barman et al. 2021). In the United States of America, 14 million milk cartons were dumped every day due to supply chain issues. Crops and produce were destroyed or left to decay when farmers were unable to sell them. Farmers were left with no choice but to shut down the packaging plant, kill, and dispose of carcasses. In one instance in the United States, a farmer disposed of 300,000 pigs (Marchant and Boyle 2020).

Tea plants were lost in India as cafes were shut down. Food waste mountains created by COVID-19 also harmed the environment as excess supply rotted and created methane (World Economic Forum 2020). On the other hand, it is also argued that lockdowns influenced people's habits and behaviour, leading to a decrease in food wastage compared to the pre-COVID-19 period. In a study by Ismail et al. (2021), a substantial percentage of consumers perceived a decrease in household food waste.

In many countries, the agriculture sector heavily relies on the temporary migrant population that comes, for example, to pick fruit in Australia. Labour crises due to lockdowns forced Australian farmers to dump their crops (Stead 2023). The global agricultural sector was also negatively impacted due to non-availability of seeds and fertilisers (Mardones et al. 2020). COVID-19 made Australia recognise how its food supply chains are vulnerable to geopolitical, environmental, economic, and societal shocks. Australia is an agricultural nation and has the 12th best food security rating in the world, yet 70 percent of Australian produce is exported internationally (Cook et al. 2022).

The local supply chain issues warrant closer attention. According to Kent et al. (2022), the food system can be improved by balancing food exports with local demands, strengthening the local food systems, increasing transparency and consumer awareness of food supply chains, building connections and collaborations in the food system, having clear contingency plans, and supporting community capacity. As a result of COVID-19, many farmers struggled with their direct sales due to the closure of farmers' markets, restaurants, and cafes and had to find other alternatives to sell perishable goods (Mouloudj et al., 2020).

The food processing sector is one of the biggest manufacturing and fastest growing sectors in Australia. This sector also faced challenges during COVID-19 due to labour shortages, longer supply and delivery lead items, increased market complexity, and increased biosecurity regulations. Sustainability challenges are economic, environmental, social and ethical, and operational. Paul et al. (2023) recommends green manufacturing and machine learning, supported by governments, as solutions for sustainability challenges of the food processing sector.

For more reliable and sustainable food trade and marketing, studies have proposed that logistics, transportation, and storage facilities be improved with robotics, decentralisation of food manufacturing, urban distribution centres, internet-based supply chains, click and collect, public distribution systems, fair price shops, and e-farm marketing be employed (Barman et al. 2021; Karunarathna et al. 2022).

The restrictive measures during COVID-19 impacted the daily lives of people, their dietary practices, and their eating habits. It has also impacted the quality of food available. The uncertainty in the cost of living, food prices, job markets, and livelihoods of people caused a global economic downturn (Barman et al. 2022). In Australia, for example, people's purchasing power was impacted and people with socioeconomic and cultural disadvantages became vulnerable to increased food prices. Rural communities in Australia were greatly impacted by not having access to healthy and fresh food items in supermarkets (Whelan et al. 2021).

The lockdowns did enable people to spend more time at home and to cook fresh meals, try new recipes, bake, eat nutritionally dense foods, and make healthier choices overall. A survey conducted in Australia found a positive dietary habit where almost half of the respondents reported cooking meals from scratch, trying new recipes, and being involved in family cooking. This resulted in long-term benefits such as passing on the cooking skills and traditional recipes to the children and other family members, improvement in family bonding, as well as greater health benefits with the consumption of fresh, home-cooked nutritious meals (Margerison et al. 2024).

However, the negative impacts of COVID-19 on social life, anxiety, fear, and financial constraints were high. Many were not able to embrace the new cooking habits (Sarda et al. 2022). Anxiety, stress, depression, and social isolation affected eating habits and led to increased intake of processed food and poor nutritional quality food (Niles et al. 2020). A multi-country survey evaluated the food behaviour and eating motivation during COVID-19 lockdown and found that home cooking increased as no choice of takeaway was available.

Consumption of fresh fruits, vegetables, and olive oil also increased; however, at the same time, higher consumption of guilty pleasure foods such as cakes, cookies, chocolates, snacks, and processed foods also increased as these foods acted as "self-medication" to deal with the stress and anxiety associated with COVID-19 (Lamy et al. 2022). There was also a shift to ultra-processed foods high in salt, sugar, and fats with longer shelf-life products that further increased susceptibility to COVID-19 (Pryor and Dietz 2022).

Studies showed most of the people chose to have healthy, safe, and home-cooked meals as well as fruits and vegetables at the initial stages of the pandemic but as the pandemic progressed, fear of illness, fear of loneliness, and financial distress drastically influenced the consumption and food choice behaviour and people started emotional eating (Skalkos and Kalyva 2023) Another habit adopted by many was home gardening.

People grew their own vegetables, fruits, and other fresh produce that provided a constant supply of a balanced and nutritious diet. It also helps them maintain their physical activity routine and is found to be an economic and secure farming system. Home gardening improves food security, diversity, and nutritious value, helps reduce food waste, and boosts the microenvironment around the family home (Lal 2020). This can help with food insecurity issues as well as positive health wellbeing.

Overall, poor people were globally the most affected by COVID-19 due to the following reasons (Swinnen and McDermott 2020):

- Through rising food prices, falling incomes, or both, people had *less real income* to pay for their food. This led to cutting down on nutrition and buying more grains and staples in bulk at low cost instead of fresh produce and meat.
- Productive assets for poor people are *physical labour* whereas richer people typically have a portfolio of productive assets, such as capital and land, and their labour is non-manual. Even in lockdown, richer people were able to work remotely.
- Disruptions in public programmes that provide food, nutrition, and health services adversely affected lower socioeconomic groups, in particular. Programmes for pregnant and lactating mothers, immunisation programmes for children, and public food relief programmes were discontinued.
- Poor people had less access to health and sanitation facilities, including running water which was crucial for protection against COVID-19.

Among the poor, women were more likely to suffer more adverse impacts from the crisis. COVID-19 caused around 400 million women to suffer from anaemia and 10.5 million children under the age of five from wasting. A further 78 million children presented stunted growth and 17 million were overweight (World Health Organization 2021). Nutrient deficiencies contribute to chronic health conditions, impaired learning, depression, stress, and fatigue and can adversely affect growth and development in children (Mardones et al. 2020; Ahmed et al. 2023).

Environmental stresses such as drought, cold, temperature fluctuations, disease infestations, fluctuations in weather events, and changing climatic conditions are already negatively affecting the crop production and nutritional values of the foods. Resilience of food systems and supply chains needs to be seriously addressed to ensure a sustainable food and nutritional supply in the era of global climate change (Rezvi et al. 2023). Food relief programmes in times of crisis need to focus on the quality as well as the quantity of food to enhance nutrition recovery (Laborde et al. 2020).

5.5 Future Policies for More Resilient Food Systems

The COVID-19 pandemic significantly affected food systems and food security worldwide, impacting the health and resilience of populations and leading to substantial changes in food cultures. In the future, states must support markets in keeping the food supply chains operational so that food is available to all (Montenegro and Young 2020). Moving forward, it is important to reassess current (and establish new) policies. Implementing policies to promote sustainable and resilient food systems including reducing food waste, supporting local food production, and promoting agroecology are critical post-COVID-19. We discuss some policies that should now be continued post-COVID-19.

- Proper hygiene practices
  Governments strengthened the food safety regulations to minimise the risk of contamination and transmission of the virus through food. This included increasing monitoring, inspections, and enforcement of hygienic practices in food outlets (Locas et al. 2022). Assessment of food safety during COVID-19 included examination of potential virus transfer through contaminated packaging or other food chain pathways (Gunduz and Cengiz 2022). Guidelines were widely issued to promote proper hygiene and sanitation practices in food handling and preparation. Regular handwashing, use of personal protective equipment, sanitation of surfaces, and maintaining social distance were amongst those established (Gwenzi 2021; Thakur and Mathur 2022; Adling and Malinao 2022).
- Emergency preparedness
  There is a need to strengthen emergency preparedness plans (EPP) for future pandemics or crises that could affect food security. A multi-stakeholder engagement involving both central and local governments, communities, and NGOs will be required in shaping policies (Amin et al. 2022). The EPP can include enhanced coordination and communication between government agencies, local communities, and international organisations for a rapid response to pandemic crises (Alam and Hoque 2022). It can also incorporate implementation of early warning systems (including tracing and detection) that can detect and mitigate disruptions in the food supply chain swiftly (Zhang et al. 2021). Furthermore, there can also be contingency

plans to manage stockpiling behaviours of the people for essential food items during a crisis. In addition, a collaborative effort at the international level to address global food challenges exacerbated by the pandemic crisis is also imperative (Mardones et al. 2020; Urom et al. 2022). Knowledge exchange and capacity-building programmes between countries, aimed to enhance the food management systems and to respond to future food crises, can be widely encouraged.

- Community-supported agriculture
  Several measures can be put in place to support small-scale food businesses and local food producers including strengthening local food production and distribution networks. In this regard, community-supported agriculture and farmer-direct distribution supported farmers' markets and local food suppliers in regional areas can reduce food distribution channels and increase the access of the food supply to needy families and communities (Godrich et al. 2022). Many small- or medium-sized producers also lack the logistic infrastructure needed to support efficient transportation of produce to meet urban demands. A readiness to respond and the capacity to anticipate and adapt to food supply crises will help reduce vulnerability and food waste (Shah et al. 2022).
- Food waste management strategies
  Implementing strategies for reducing food waste is a critical component in managing food waste, especially when resources are limited. In that regard, several strategies can be adopted, such as improved storage and preservation, enhanced distribution systems to promote food redistribution programmes, and food-recycling infrastructure to facilitate the diversion of food waste from landfills (Sharma et al. 2020). There should also be support for research and development of alternative uses for food waste such as biofuels and animal feed to create additional value from food waste (Nakaishi and Takayabu 2022).
- Crisis management for farmers
  Resilience-promoting policies are critical to mitigate the impacts of the pandemic crisis in agriculture; in particular, there must be a crisis management plan to assist farmers to cope with the disaster and that this may require a development of a crisis management plan (Lioutas and Charatsari 2021).
- Trade agreements
  Promoting trade agreements that prioritise food security and reduce barriers to the movement of essential food commodities across borders is also critical to achieve food security (Friel et al. 2020). However, some countries may be willing to prioritise the protection of domestic production over international trade, hindering efforts to reduce barriers (Koppenberg et al. 2021). Another challenge is harmonising food quality and safety standards across countries to facilitate trade. These challenges have been ongoing for several years (Wilson et al. 2003; Poms et al. 2009). Regulating the quality and safety of food products will require companies to implement quality

and safety management that are harmonised with international standards (Kapustian et al. 2021).

5.6 Conclusion

The insights and lessons from COVID-19 are only helpful if they are applied to future proof and pressure test our responses to further global shocks of a similar nature. By and large, we have identified the structural, logistical, and technical difficulties imposed by COVID-19 and the consequent strangulation of economic activity thereafter through government intervention. Further, as a counterbalance, we have witnessed just how flexible and responsive consumers are to global shocks and how markets respond both locally and internationally. The localised return to our "food roots" in some communities is a good example and this richness is now embedded in those communities. In addition, food security, food insecurity, climate change, and geopolitical issues are all added complications to the mix.

The COVID-19 experience and the changes driven by consumers and markets should help to design better policies and build more resilient and inclusive food systems for the future. Public policies should focus on guaranteeing the human right to adequate food and quality as well as quantity must be improved for the population with the aim of providing food security.

Vertical farming and sky farming strategies are options for adoption based on circular economy strategies, as are aquaponics and hydroponics. Home gardening, community gardening, mulching, composting, reducing indiscriminate use of pesticides, and community cooking clubs can play an important role in advancing food and nutritional security. This will help reduce food wastage, strengthen the resilience among community members, and improve ecosystem services. Prioritising the implementation of specific strategic policies to promote sustainable and resilient food systems, reduce food waste, advocate agroecology, and support local food production is imperative at this juncture.

References

Aday, S & Aday, MS 2020, 'Impact of COVID-19 on the food supply chain', *Food Quality and Safety*, *4*(4), pp.167–180.

Adling, NMJ & Malinao, RJL 2022, 'Knowledge, attitudes, and practices of Filipino BSIT in food technology students toward food hygiene and sanitation', *International Journal of Multidisciplinary: Applied Business and Education Research*, *3*(10), pp.1878–1884.

Ahmed, T, Ilieva, RT, Shane, J, Reader, S, Aleong, C, Wong, HY, Chu, C, Brusche, D, Jiang, K, Lopez, D & Yan, A 2023, 'A developing crisis in hunger: Food insecurity within 3 public colleges before and during the COVID-19 pandemic', *Journal of Hunger & Environmental Nutrition*, *18*(1), pp.1–20.

Alam, A & Hoque, MM 2022, 'Local level collaborative governance for pandemic responses: Unpacking a case in Bangladesh', *Policy & Governance Review*, *6*(3), pp.207–228.

Amin, F, Poespito Hadi, W, Zauhar, S & Santoso Haryono, B 2022, 'Determinants of post COVID-19 food security policy success', *International Journal of Disaster Resilience in the Built Environment*, *13*(4), pp.440–450.
Barman, A, Das, R & De, PK 2021, 'Impact of COVID-19 in food supply chain: Disruptions and recovery strategy', *Current Research in Behavioral Sciences*, *2*, p.100017.
Barman, A, Das, R & De, PK 2022, 'Logistics and supply chain management of food industry during COVID-19: Disruptions and a recovery plan', *Environment Systems and Decisions*, pp.1–12.
Benny, H 2018, 'The fate of culinary traditions in the modern world', Doctoral dissertation, Swinburne University of Technology.
Burki, T 2022, 'Food security and nutrition in the world', *The Lancet Diabetes & Endocrinology*, *10*(9), p.622.
Cao, C, Xiao, Z, Wu, Y & Ge, C 2020, 'Diet and skin aging – From the perspective of food nutrition', *Nutrients*, *12*(3), p.870.
Cook, S, Jackson, EL, Fisher, MJ, Baker, D & Diepeveen, DD 2022, 'Embedding digital agriculture into sustainable Australian food systems: Pathways and pitfalls to value creation', *International Journal of Agricultural Sustainability*, *20*, pp.346–367.
Crittenden, AN & Schnorr, SL 2017, 'Current views on hunter-gatherer nutrition and the evolution of the human diet', *American Journal of Physical Anthropology*, *162*, pp.84–109.
Daison, OK 2023, 'Documentation and nutritive evaluation of traditional foods of Kerala-Ernakulam District', St Teresa's College (Autonomous), Ernakulam.
El Bilali, H, Callenius, C, Strassner, C & Probst, L 2019, 'Food and nutrition security and sustainability transitions in food systems', *Food and Energy Security*, *8*(2), p.e00154.
Expósito, A 2023, 'Exploring the link between irrigated agriculture and food security: Evidence from the case of Spain', En Nourishing Tomorrow: Clean Engineering and Nature-friendly Living.
Friel, S, Schram, A & Townsend, B 2020, 'The nexus between international trade, food systems, malnutrition and climate change', *Nature Food*, *1*(1), pp.51–58.
The Global Report on Food Crises 2018, 'Food Security Information Network' https://www.fsinplatform.org/sites/default/files/resources/files/GRFC_2018_Full_report_EN_Low_resolution.pdf
Gunduz, CPB & Cengiz, MF 2022, 'Assessment of food safety during Covid-19 pandemic', *International Journal of Life Sciences and Biotechnology*, *5*(2), pp.247–269, https://doi.org/10.38001/Ijlsb.1039126.
Godrich, SL, Macau, F, Kent, K, Lo, J & Devine, A 2022, 'Food supply impacts and solutions associated with the COVID-19 pandemic: A regional Australian case study', *International Journal of Environmental Research and Public Health*, *19*(7), p.4116.
Gwenzi, W 2021, 'Leaving no stone unturned in light of the COVID-19 faecal-oral hypothesis? A Water, Sanitation and Hygiene (WASH) perspective targeting low-income countries', *Science of the Total Environment*, *753*, p.141751.
Ismail, HB, Rezgui, M, Jribi, S, Debbabi, H & Dogui, D 2021, 'COVID-19: Impact of service and food quality on student satisfaction and food wastage in a Tunisian Canteen', *Uluslararası Tarım Arastırmalarında Yenilikçi Yaklasımlar Derg*, *5*, pp.52–69, https://doi.org/10.29329/Ijiaar.2021.339.4.
Jones, AD, Ngure, F, Pelto, G & Young, SL 2013, 'What are we assessing when we measure food security? A compendium and review of current metrics', *Advances in Nutrition*, *4*(5), pp.481–505.
Karunarathna, N, Siriwardhane, DRJ & Jayarathne, PGSA 2022, 'Extraordinary strains in food supply chains: A literature review on COVID-19 induced food supply chain disruptions and resilience', Proceedings of the First Australian International Conference on Industrial Engineering and Operations Management, December, Sydney, Australia.
Kapustian, A, Cherno, N, Antipina, O, Gural, L, Naumenko, K, Malinka, O & Stepanova, G 2021, 'Technological expertise, quality and safety management systems

of food products, validation of the technological processes control measures', *Scientific Works*, *85*(2).
Kent, K, Gale, F, Penrose, B, Auckland, S, Lester, E & Murray, S 2022, 'Consumer-driven strategies towards a resilient and sustainable food system following the COVID-19 pandemic in Australia', *BMC Public Health*, *22*(1), p.1539.
Koppenberg, M, Bozzola, M, Dalhaus, T & Hirsch, S 2021, 'Mapping potential implications of temporary COVID-19 export bans for the food supply in importing countries using pre crisis trade flows', *Agribusiness*, *37*(1), pp.25–43.
Laborde, D, Martin, W & Vos, R 2020, 'Poverty and food insecurity could grow dramatically as COVID-19 spreads', International Food Policy Research Institute (IFPRI), Washington, DC.
Lal, R 2020, 'Home gardening and urban agriculture for advancing food and nutritional security in response to the COVID-19 pandemic', *Food Security*, *12*(4), pp.871–876.
Lamy, E, Viegas, C, Rocha, A, Raquel Lucas, M, Tavares, S, Capela E Silva, F, Guedes, D, Laureati, M, Zian, Z, Salles Machado, A, Ellssel, P, Freyer, B, González-Rodrigo, E, Calzadilla, J, Majewski, E, Prazeres, I, Silva, V, Juračak, J, Platilová Vorlíčková, L, Kamutali, A, Regina Tschá, E, Villalobos, K, Želvytė, R, Monkeviciene, I, Elati, J, De Souza Pinto, AM, Midori Castelo, P & Anzman-Frasca, S 2022, 'Changes in food behavior during the first lockdown of COVID-19 pandemic: A multi-country study about changes in eating habits, motivations, and food-related behaviors', *Food Quality and Preference*, *99*, p.104559.
Lang, T & Barling, D 2012, 'Food security and food sustainability: Reformulating the debate', *The Geographical Journal*, *178*(4), pp.313–326.
Laudan, R 2001, 'A plea for culinary modernism: Why we should love new, fast, processed food', *Gastronomica*, *1*(1), pp.36–44.
Lioutas, ED & Charatsari, C 2021, 'Enhancing the ability of agriculture to cope with major crises or disasters: What the experience of COVID-19 teaches us', *Agricultural Systems*, *187*, p.103023.
Locas, A, Brassard, J, Rose-Martel, M, Lambert, D, Green, A, Deckert, A & Illing, M 2022, 'Comprehensive risk pathway of the qualitative likelihood of human exposure to severe acute respiratory syndrome coronavirus 2 from the food chain', *Journal of Food Protection*, *85*(1), pp.85–97, https://doi.org/10.4315/Jfp-21-218.
Mardones, FO, Rich, KM, Boden, LA, Moreno-Switt, AI, Caipo, ML, Zimin-Veselkoff, N, Alateeqi, AM & Baltenweck, I 2020, 'The COVID-19 pandemic and global food security', *Frontiers in Veterinary Science*, *7*, p.578508, https://doi.org/10.3389/Fvets.2020.578508.
MacLennan, R & Zhang, A 2004, 'Cuisine: The concept and its health and nutrition implications-globa'l', *Asia Pacific Journal of Clinical Nutrition*, *13*(2), pp.131–135.
Margerison, C, Aydin, G, Larsson, C, Booth, A, Worsley, A & Nanayakkara, J 2024, 'Australian adults cooked more and tried new recipes during COVID-19 restrictions and lockdowns', *Appetite*, *193*, p.107122.
Marrero, A & Mattei, J 2022, 'Reclaiming traditional, plant-based, climate-resilient food systems in small islands', *The Lancet Planetary Health*, *6*(2), pp. e171–e179.
Mishra, R, Singh, RK & Subramanian, N 2022, 'Impact of disruptions in agri-food supply chain due to COVID-19 pandemic: Contextualised resilience framework to achieve operational excellence', *The International Journal of Logistics Management*, *33*(3), pp.926–954.
Montenegro, LD & Young, MN 2020, 'Operational challenges in the food industry and supply chain during the COVID-19 pandemic: A literature review', 7th International Conference on Frontiers of Industrial Engineering (ICFIE), September, IEEE, pp.1–5.
Mouloudj, K, Bouarar, AC & Fechit, H 2020, 'The impact of COVID-19 pandemic on food security', *Les cahiers du CREAD*, *36*(3), pp.159–184.

Nakaishi, T & Takayabu, H 2022, 'Production efficiency of animal feed obtained from food waste in Japan', *Environmental Science and Pollution Research*, *29*(40), pp.61187–61203.
Niles, MT, Bertmann, F, Belarmino, EH, Wentworth, T, Biehl, E & Neff, R 2020, 'The early food insecurity impacts of COVID-19', *Nutrients*, *12*(7), p.2096, https://doi.org/10.3390/Nu12072096.
Paul, A, Shukla, N & Trianni, A 2023, 'Modelling supply chain sustainability challenges in the food processing sector amid the COVID-19 outbreak', *Socio-Economic Planning Sciences*, *87*, p.101535.
Poms, R, Thomas, M, Finglas, P, Astley, S, Spichtinger, D, Rose, M, Popping, B, Alldrick, A, Van Egmond, H, Solfrizzo, M & Clare Mills, EN 2009, 'MoniQA (monitoring and quality assurance): An EU-funded network of excellence working towards the harmonization of worldwide food quality and safety monitoring and control strategies – Status report 2008', *Quality Assurance and Safety of Crops & Foods*, *1*(1), pp.9–22, https://doi.org/10.1111/J.1757-837x.2009.00004.X.
Pryor, S & Dietz, W 2022, 'The COVID-19, obesity, and food insecurity syndemic', *Current Obesity Reports*, *11*(3), pp.70–79.
Purdam, K, Garratt, EA & Esmail, A 2016, 'Hungry? Food insecurity, social stigma and embarrassment in the UK', *Sociology*, *50*(6), pp.1072–1088.
Rezvi, HUA, Tahjib-Ul-Arif, M, Azim, MA, Tumpa, TA, Tipu, MMH, Najnine, F, Dawood, MF, Skalicky, M & Brestič, M 2023, 'Rice and food security: Climate change implications and the future prospects for nutritional security', *Food and Energy Security*, *12*(1), p.e430.
Shabbir, H, Shabbir, I, Aslam, M, Sarwar, MF, Sarwar, MH & Sarwar, M 2020, 'Fundamental aspects of vitamin B complex in human nourishment and fitness', *American Journal of Food Science and Health*, *6*(4), pp.109–118.
Shah, JA, Mazlan, NI & Haris, NBM 2022, 'Assessment of farmers' readiness to face challenges of the post-movement control order (Mco) in the central zone of Malaysia', *International Journal Of Academic Research In Business And Social Sciences*, *12*(12), https://doi.org/10.6007/Ijarbss/V12-I12/15795.
Sharma, HB, Vanapalli, KR, Cheela, VS, Ranjan, VP, Jaglan, AK, Dubey, B, Goel, S & Bhattacharya, J 2020, 'Challenges, opportunities, and innovations for effective solid waste management during and post COVID-19 pandemic', *Resources, Conservation and Recycling*, *162*, p.105052, Https://doi.org/10.1016/J.Resconrec.2020.105052.
Skalkos, D & Kalyva, ZC 2023, 'Exploring the impact of Covid-19 pandemic on food choice motives: A systematic review', *Sustainability*, *15*(2), p.1606.
Stead, V 2023, 'Temporariness made interminable: Pacific Islander farmworkers in Australia and the enduring crises of global agricultural production', *Journal of Agrarian Change*, *23*(3), pp.579–589, https://doi.org/10.1111/Joac.12524.
Swinnen, J & McDermott, J 2020, 'COVID-19 and global food security', *EuroChoices*, *19*(3), pp.26–33.
Thakur, S & Mathur, P 2022, 'Food safety knowledge and changes in practices and concerns of Indian families during the COVID-19 pandemic', *Nutrition & Food Science*, *53*(2), pp.319–333.
Trichopoulou, A 2021, 'Mediterranean diet as intangible heritage of humanity: 10 years on', *Nutrition, Metabolism and Cardiovascular Diseases*, *31*(7), pp.1943–1948.
Trichopoulou, A, Soukara, S & Vasilopoulou, E 2007, 'Traditional foods: A science and society perspective', *Trends in Food Science & Technology*, *18*(8), pp.420–427.
Urom, C, Guesmi, K, Abid, I & Enwo-Irem, IN 2022, 'Co-inventions, uncertainties and global food security', *Environmental Economics and Policy Studies*, pp.1–26, https://doi.org/10.1007/S10018-022-00347-9.

Whelan, J, Brown, AD, Coller, L, Strugnell, C, Allender, S, Alston, L, Hayward, J, Brimblecombe, J & Bell, C 2021, 'The impact of COVID-19 on rural food supply and demand in AustraliaUtilising group model building to identify retailer and customer perspectives', *Nutrients*, *13*(2), p.417, https://doi.org/10.3390/Nu13020417.

World Economic Forum 2022, 'Here's how covid 19 creates food waste mountains that threatens the environment', *Nutrition Connect*, https://nutritionconnect.org/resource-center/heres-how-covid-19-creates-food-waste-mountains-threaten-environment.

World Health Organization 2021, *The State of food security and nutrition in the World 2021: Transforming food systems for food security, improved nutrition and affordable healthy diets for all*, Food & Agriculture Org.

Wilson, JS, Otsuki, T & Majumdsar, B 2003, 'Balancing food safety and risk: Do drug residue limits affect international trade in beef?', *Journal of International Trade & Economic Development*, *12*(4), pp.377–402, https://doi.org/10.1080/0963819032000154810.

Zhang, W, He, H, Zhu, L, Liu, G & Wu, L 2021, 'Food safety in Post-COVID-19 pandemic: Challenges and countermeasures', *Biosensors*, *11*(3), p.71.

6 Alternative Protein Products and the Legal Rules on Novel Foods

A Global Comparison

Anu Lähteenmäki-Uutela, Annika Lonkila, and Siva Barathi (Sharl) Marimuthu

6.1 Introduction

Regulation of unconventional food sources such as algae, insects, and other emerging food sources has received increased attention. These sources provide a way to revolutionise the way people nourish themselves and protect the environment. It is worth researching how they are regulated and how regulations may impact food innovation adoption and dissemination.

Animal-based food production is resource-demanding. Carbon intensity and the impact of land use are the main problems. Alternatives are sought to replace ways that make us transgress the planetary boundaries. A shift to alternatives to animal-based food production is deemed as reducing the risk of pandemics (Good Food Institute, n.d.). From a consumer perspective, alternative protein products have appeared in grocery stores and supermarkets to replace meat and dairy products. These include novel plant-based proteins, fungi, algae, insects, and lab meat. Some new foods are genetically modified organisms (GMOs) or produced by utilising GMOs.

The legal system sets the rules for introducing novel protein products. Some legal rules are to ensure the safety of novel foods in daily consumption. For this purpose, several countries have enacted novel food regulations that set the processes and principles for scientific evaluation and administration. Novel products deemed as alternative proteins may also challenge the existing marketing regulations.

This chapter summarises the legal rules on novel foods in the European Union, the United States, Australia, and Singapore, and discusses recent case examples of how alternative protein products are regulated. It is concluded with suggestions of the best practices in regulating novel foods to ensure safety, while not creating too many obstacles for sustainability transformation.

6.2 Novel Food Legislation Across the World with Alternative Protein Cases

6.2.1 European Union

The European Novel Food Regulation (EU 2015/2283) is applicable to foods that have not been consumed to a significant degree in the European Union

DOI: 10.4324/9781003392279-6

(EU) prior to 17 May 1997. Novel foods must receive premarket approval from the European Commission, upon a scientific evaluation by the European Food Safety Authority (EFSA). For foods that have been safely consumed outside the EU but not in the EU, their procedure is more simplified, where the food requires a history of at least 25 years of safe use before being marketed.

There is a consultation process to determine whether the food or ingredient is a novel food (EU Consultation Process on Novel Food, n.d). For example, mung bean (*Vigna radiata*) protein isolate is a novel food as it is different from the mung bean flour (2019). A plant protein concentrate fermented with the shiitake mycelium (*Lentinula edodes*) is also novel (2019). Pea (*Pisum sativum*) protein hydrolysate (2020), soy (*Glycine max*) protein hydrolysate (2020), rice protein (2022), brewer's spent grain protein (2023), and cereal protein concentrate (2023) are not novel. Protein isolate from sunflower seeds (*Helianthus annuus*) is novel (2023).

The EU Novel Food Catalogue includes all information on novel food authorisations and rejections (EU Novel Food Status Catalogue, n.d). For algae, a recent novel food application in the EU is on the microalga *Chlamydomonas reinhardtii* by US company Triton Algae Innovations, Ltd. The single-cell green alga is about 10 micrometres in diameter and swims with two flagella. The company wants to use it as an ingredient in bread, cookies, crackers, cakes, pasta and noodles, breakfast cereals, soups and sauces, smoothies, ready-to-eat meals, and pizzas, and functional/fortified beverages at the maximal use level of 10% (i.e., 10 g/100 g) in the described food products, "as an alternative dietary protein source". The applicant refers to the ingredient status in the United States: the US Food and Drug Administration (FDA) has given it a "no questions" letter under the GRAS (Generally Recognised As Safe) scheme as the replacement for dietary protein, with no percentage limitations (Triton Algae Innovations Ltd 2023).

Several macroalgae are non-novel in Europe, for example, kombu (*Laminaria digitata*), bladderwrack (*Fucus vesiculosus*), sugar kelp (*Saccharina latissima*), Atlantic wakame (*Alaria esculenta*), wakame (*Undaria pinnatifida*), dulse (*Palmaria palmata*), sea lettuce (*Ulva lactuca*), and nori (*Porphyra tenera*) (EABA 2021). Even with the traditionally used species, novel food authorisation may be required when it comes to the extract. Two macroalgae products, fucoidan extracts from wakame (*Undaria pinnatifida)* and bladderwrack (*Fucus vesiculosus)* have been accepted as novel foods for use in foods and food supplements (Lähteenmäki-Uutela et al. 2021).

Insect food has gained business and research interest in Western countries since the United Nations (UN) Food and Agriculture Organization (FAO) report in 2013 (van Huis et al. 2013). Several companies have submitted novel food applications in the EU. After years of EFSA and EU Commission processes, all the main species are authorised at the end of 2023, encompassing mealworm *Tenebrio molitor*, the dried larvae of the yellow mealworm beetle (EU Commission approval 2021), migratory locust *Locusta migratoria*, in the frozen, dried, and powder form (2021), house cricket *Acheta domesticus*, in the frozen, dried, and powder form (2022), house cricket ***Acheta domesticus*** in partially defatted powder (2023), lesser mealworm ***Alphitobius diaperinus*** in the larval form, frozen, dried, paste and powder (2023). Some of the EU insect food approvals are according to the proprietary data in which case the applicant may be granted five years of data protection, which means other companies cannot use the same data to back their applications.

Cultured meat is meat developed from animal cell culture, which means growing animal cell lines in a bioreactor in a growth medium. The EU novel food regulations apply to foods made of cultivated meat even when the cells are from normal farmed animal species. Cultured meat applications have not yet been submitted in the EU. There is some resistance in Europe against cultured meat, cultured meat is prohibited in Italy in 2023 (Reuters 2023), and a similar bill has been suggested in France (European Biotechnology News 2023). Lab-grown food is deemed as threatening to the traditional European food cultures and livelihoods.

Plants, yeasts, fungi, macroalgae, microbes, insects, and larger production animals can be genetically modified to enhance their growth, nutrition content, or pest resistance or disease resistance level. Animal DNA can be modified to make cells produce their own growth hormones, which is promising for lab-grown meat (Stout et al. 2024). To place GM food in the EU market, Regulation 2003/1829/EC on GM food and feed shall apply. Such foods require premarket authorisation and must be labelled. About a dozen GMOs for food and feed use are authorised including soybean, rapeseed, maize, and cotton (see EU GMO Authorisation for Food and Feed, n.d; EU GMO register n.d).

To date, gene editing by CRISPR-Cas9 is currently under the same GMO rules but the new regulatory New Genomic Techniques (NGTs) framework was proposed in 2023. The new law shall apply to the techniques of creating plant varieties faster without adding foreign genes (European Commission 2023). The exemption from general GM laws is limited to "Category 1 NGT plants", stipulated in Annex I of the proposal where "equivalence to conventional plants" is defined as the number of genetic modifications (max 20) and nucleotides inserted or substituted in each modification (max 20). In the future, some genetically modified alternative protein food plants may benefit from the exclusion. Fungi are not excluded under the proposal (preamble 9), and algae are not mentioned. The use of gene scissors in animal DNA is not excluded under the proposal, either. With regards to the cultivated meat that uses GM microbes for fermentation and when the final product does not contain viable cells of the production microorganism or detectable amounts of its DNA, the final product is not deemed as GMO and does not need to be labelled as such.

Finally, novel plant-based products, specifically vegan meat and dairy imitations are not categorised as novel foods but have disrupted the market and continued to challenge the food labelling regulation (EU)1169/2011. This regulation mandates all food products must be labelled with accurate information about the ingredients, nutritional value, and origin. Furthermore, the information on the package cannot mislead consumers. The intention behind the regulation is to prevent food fraud and increase transparency and consumer awareness (Ohm Rørdam 2013).

The existing legislation dates to the establishment of the Common Market and the development of the Common Agricultural Policy, aimed to protect economic interests of important agricultural sectors (Bolton 2017). For example, margarine could not be called butter, so that consumers would not unknowingly buy substitute products. The existing regulatory framework has struggled to accommodate the increasing consumer interest in plant-based products for environmental, ethical, and health reasons.

The market for plant-based products is rapidly increasing, having grown by 21% from 2020 (Good Food Institute 2023). Proponents of strict regulation in relation to plant-based foods suggest that consumers must be protected against confusing plant-based products with animal-based foods (Ridler 2021). Therefore, the EU has ruled that plant-based products cannot use terms such as milk, butter, cream, or yoghurt, which are reserved for animal-based products according to the European Court of Justice (C-422/16) in 2017.

Even stricter regulation was pushed forward via amendments to the Regulations on the common organisation of markets in agricultural products (EU) 1308/2013 with Amendment 171 that sought to ban descriptive dairy-related words such as "creamy" or references to the climate emissions of dairy products. With the new regulation, consumers could not be informed of the purpose of dairy imitation products, which would be difficult for companies, many of whom opposed the regulation vehemently. The ban was later scrapped by the Parliament due to public scrutiny as the consumer petition against Amendment 171 had gained almost half a million signatures across Europe (Proveg.org 2021).

A similar discussion is ongoing in relation to the labelling of "meaty" imitation products, where the regulation on the use of words is not as strict as dairy. Individual EU member states have attempted to set bans on the use of words such as "steak" or "ham". In 2023, France's administrative court Conseil d'État requested the European Court of Justice to rule whether such bans are in line with the EU law. The increasing number of consumers specifically seeking plant-based products on supermarket shelves may lead some parties to rethink misleading consumers.

Indeed, some are deliberating whether strict regulations about plant-based food labelling do fulfil the principle of proportionality. Furthermore, strict labelling regulation may contradict EU's own sustainability targets in relation to dietary changes, as set out in the European Commission's farm-to-fork strategy (COM/2020/381 final) as part of the European Green Deal, with the goal of shifting towards plant-based diets. Overall, changes in food labelling regulation should support regulatory and policy coherence. Furthermore, the plant-based sector has also criticised the legislation for stifling innovation and called for recognition of the new European agricultural markets.

6.2.2 United States

Food law in the United States does not adopt the novel food concept. Under the Federal Food, Drug, and Cosmetic Act, any substance intentionally added to food is a food additive and, as such, requires premarket approval by the FDA, unless the substance is "Generally Recognised as Safe" (GRAS). GRAS status is important for alternative protein products as it clarifies the legality of the food or food ingredient across the country. For novel foods, GRAS is determined based on scientific procedures, according to either self-determination or notification to the FDA with the "No Questions" response.

The GRAS scientific and technical standards are the same for both options and the same for additives (US FDA n.d.a). Science must prove the food or food ingredient is non-pathogenic and non-toxigenic. In general, companies use third-party consultants to build a GRAS dossier. A database list of the recently published GRAS notices and FDA letters is useful for companies (US FDA n.d.b). The "No Questions" remark does not certify that the food is GRAS, it signifies that the FDA has no questions at that time.

There are several plant-based alternative proteins on the US GRAS list that receive the "No Questions" remark. These include rice barley protein by EverGrain (GRAS Notice No. 1031 with amendments, 2021), pea protein by Burcon NutraScience Corporation (GRAS notice No. 804, 2018), soy leghemoglobin protein by Impossible Foods (GRAS notice No. 737, 2017), and hemp seed protein by Fresh Hemp Foods (GRAS notice GRAS Notice No. 771, 2018). Recently, Cargill Inc. submitted a notice for corn protein (GRAS Notice No. 1069, 2022) as well as Tate and Lyle a chickpea protein notice (GRAS Notice No. 1098, 2022). At the moment, these notices have not yet received any responses.

Proteins produced by yeasts is in another category. In 2023, Clara Foods received the "No Questions" remark for its egg white protein produced by yeast, *Komagataella phaffii* (GRAS notice No. 1104 with amendments, 2022; see Bernauer et al. 2021). Cargill has received the "No Questions" remark for its dried *Saccharomyces cerevisiae* yeast fermentate (GRAS No. 928, 2020). Yeast hydrolysate peptide complex manufactured by a Korean company Cremar and distributed by a French company Fytexia Corp under the trade name DNF-10 is another fermentate produced using the *Saccharomyces cerevisiae* (GRAS Notice No. 1033, 2021) yeast. According to the company, the peptide suppresses appetite, and is sold in Korea, Japan, China, United States, and Thailand (Cremar n.d.). A "No Question" remark is not yet published at the time this paper is written.

In September 2022, Better Meat submitted a GRAS notice for its "biomass of a wild type of isolate of *Neurospora crassa* to be used as an enhancer and meat substitute (including pork), poultry, dairy, and seafood ingredients" (GRAS notice No. 1117, 2022). *Neurospora grassa* is a filamentous fungus. Such fungi have attracted increasing interest as alternative proteins, and Bartholomai et al. (2022) deem *Neurospora* as safe. At the time this paper is written, the FDA has not yet published the "No Questions" remark.

Indeed, the company Triton Algae Innovations submitted a GRAS notice to the FDA on the *Chlamydomonas reinhardtii* microalgae (GRAS notice No. 773, 2018) and received "No Questions" remark from the FDA. Spirulina *Arthrospira platensis* has been notified by several companies and received "No Questions" remarks (GRAS Notice No. 127 from 2003 and GRAS Notices No. 394, 417, and 424 from 2012). Other microalgae included in the GRAS list with the "No Questions" remark include *Chlorella sorokiniana* powder and micro powder (GRAS notice No. 986, 2020), *Dunaliella bardawil* (GRAS notice No. 251, 2010) and astaxanthin extracted from *Haematococcus pluvialis* (GRAS notice No. 580, 2015).

Macroalgae/seaweed food is not at the top of the US federal regulatory agenda. Macroalgae do not fall into regulatory categories as they are neither seafood nor vegetables (Maine Public 2022). Since the FDA and the USDA are not involved, macroalgae have not been notified as GRAS. Macroalgae are still used as food in the United States, and there are some state-level regulations to guarantee safe food use. Extracts are another issue. Fucoidan from *Undaria pinnatifida* (GRAS notice No. 565, 2015) and fucoidan from *Fucus vesiculosus* (GRAS notice No. 661, 2017) are authorised.

Insects are not on the GRAS list. Insects such as crickets and mealworms are still sold and consumed in the United States. Industry experts (Future of Edible Insects 2021) suggest that the GRAS dossiers of insect companies would not pass FDA review. Regulatory bodies seem to be using discretion by letting insects be sold when the intake is low and there is no evidence of people being harmed. Another perspective is that insects are safe substances that do not need GRAS. If the intake of insects and business is significant, then the industry shall be able to create a sufficient GRAS dossier (Future of Edible Insects 2021).

With cultured meat, the FDA has completed its safety assessment of two cultivated chicken products by two US companies, UPSIDE Foods and GOOD Meat. This made the United States the second country in the world after Singapore to authorise cultivated meat. The products are currently served at small scale in restaurants. The safety of cultivated chicken products of other companies or cultivated beef, pork, or seafood products must be assessed separately.

The FDA inventory of Human Food Made with Cultured Animal Cells Inventory (fda.gov) aids other companies as it includes all data on previous cultured meat investigations. (US FDA n.d.b). The FDA collaborates with the United States Department of Agriculture's Food Safety and Inspection Service (USDA-FSIS) because these two agencies share jurisdiction over the safety of animal-based products.

The labelling of plant-based products is in flux in the United States. In the United States, the Food and Drug Administration (FDA) has primary jurisdiction over the labelling of plant-based protein products provided by the Federal Food, Drug, and Cosmetics Act (FDCA). Although the current FDA regulations define that the terms of dairy products shall be only used for products derived from dairy animals, the FDA's enforcement of the rule is non-existent (Raciti 2020). However, in 2023, the FDA proposed that plant-based products can be labelled as milk when paired with a descriptive plant-based word, for instance, oat milk.

The FDA states that consumers, in general, understand that plant-based milk alternatives do not contain milk, and indeed purposefully choose to purchase them because it is not milk. Such guidance also suggests that the nutritional value compared to dairy milk should be highlighted on the package. (FDA 2023.) The suggestion of the Plant-Based Foods Association (2019) resembles the FDA's (2023) proposal that the term "milk" shall be coupled with the main ingredient such as oat milk and the terms non-dairy or dairy-free are outlined.

In comparison to these developments, a bipartisan proposal coined by the Dairy Pride Act has been introduced in the United States Congress (National Milk Producers Federation 2021). The Dairy Pride Act calls for enforcement of the existing FDA regulations and scrapping of the new FDA proposal. In relation to "meaty" products, the Real MEAT Act was reintroduced in Congress in 2023 as an attempt to include the term "imitation" to all plant-based products (Fischer 2023).

The lack of enforcement of regulation has called for states to introduce stricter legislation related to plant-based product labels. At least 13 states, such as Missouri, Texas, Arkansas, and Alabama have opted to ban "meaty" term from being used to describe plant-based products. However, plant-based companies have rallied against such restrictive state laws as unconstitutional and restrictions against freedom of speech. In 2022, a federal court permanently prohibited (enjoined) Arkansas from enforcing a law that would prevent the sale of plant-based meat imitation products in the state using any conventional meat term, such as chorizo (*Turtle Island Foods SPC v. Soman*, Case No. 4:19-cv-00514).

The Court highlighted that it is crucial that prominent disclosures are in place to ensure that consumers are not being misled (e.g. vegan chorizo or plant-based hot dogs). However, when proper qualifiers are in place, the enforcement of the Arkansas law is deemed unconstitutional (Drozen et al. 2022). Furthermore, state bans might not take effect due to the impact on regional commerce, unless neighbouring states set similar regulations (Siddiqui et al. 2023). The patchwork of requirements combining state and federal labelling regulations create challenges for plant-based and novel food companies, considering that state regulations have encountered challenges related to the First Amendment's protection of freedom of commercial speech.

*6.2.3 **Australia***

Australia is interested in alternative proteins not only because of the consumers, the country is, in fact, developing its global protein strategy in view of its export market (CSIRO 2022). Under Australian law, novel food means "a non-traditional food that requires an assessment of the public health and safety considerations". Novel foods are regulated under the Australia New Zealand Food Standards Code – Standard 1.5.1 – Novel foods.

The required premarket risk assessment includes toxicological and nutritional issues evaluated in relation to consumption patterns. All novel proteins including algae and insect-based ingredients as well as lab-grown meat go under the definition of novel food in Australia. Companies can ask for recommendations from the Advisory Committee on Novel Foods on whether a food is novel, however, their recommendation is not legally binding. The novel food application is submitted to the Food Standards Australia New Zealand (FSANZ 2023a).

A novel food can be sold either as food or used as a food ingredient only after being listed in Schedule 25 of the Food Standards Code. Schedule 25 lists permitted novel foods along with their conditions for use including use levels, restrictions on use, and labelling requirements, which is available at the Federal Register of Legislation - Australia New Zealand Food Standards Code - Schedule 25 – Permitted novel foods (Compilation No. 7 of Schedule 25 as in force on 19 July 2023 (up to Amendment No. 220)).

FSANZ may grant, upon request, exclusive permission to novel ingredients or food of a specific brand for a period of at most 15 months, which enables market advantage. After the exclusivity period is over, the permission becomes generic and non-brand specific, where the food may be sold under other brands (FSANZ 2023b).

The Australian list of authorised novel foods is shorter than the EU list of authorised novel foods or the US list of GRAS substances. The two authorised novel foods in Schedule 25 that can be used as alternative proteins are dried marine macroalgae (*Schizochytrium sp.*) and rapeseed protein isolate (*Brassica napus*, *Brassica rapa*, or *Brassica juncea)*. Three species of insects are categorised as not requiring novel food authorisation under Australian law, they are (1) super mealworm (*Zophobas morio*), (2) house cricket (*Achetus domesticus*), and (3) mealworm beetle (*Tenebrio molitor*). Even though these three insect species are not traditional foods, no food safety concerns are highlighted by the Advisory Committee of Novel Foods, and the three insects can be sold as food or used as a food ingredient (Department of Agriculture, Fisheries, and Forestry 2023). The New South Wales Food Authority (2021) sees environmental potential in insect foods.

Cultured meat requires novel food authorisation in Australia. FSANZ is following how cultured meat was regulated in the European Union, the United States, Japan, Israel, China, and Singapore (FSANZ 2023c), and has not published its own guidelines on the topic. The first application for animal cell-based food has been submitted to FSANZ recently, and the decision is to be released in 2024. The application is from the company Vow which produces cultured quail (Clean Public – Vow 2023). The Magic Valley company is planning to apply for commercialisation of its minced meat products made by cultivating pork and lamb cells (ABC Rural 2023).

Foods produced using gene technology, including any living organism, are regulated under Standard 1.5.2 of the Food Standards Code. Approved GM foods are listed in Schedule 26 under the Australia New Zealand Food Standards Code. Since 2016, about 30 GMOs for food use have been approved. The first was Monsanto's insect-protected soybean as well as insect-protected and herbicide-tolerant corn, followed by canola, potato, rice, safflower, cotton, and wheat. In 2021, FSANZ authorised *Pichia Pastoris* containing the leghaemoglobin c2 gene from *Glycine max* to be used in meat analogue products. This means the yeast is genetically modified with soy genes to produce soy leghaemoglobin.

In relation to the labelling of plant-based alternative foods, the situation in Australia resembles that of the EU and the US, where the regulatory landscape is still developing. In Australia, there are no regulations to prohibit the use of specific terms to describe plant-based products. However, in 2022, upon an inquiry by the Australian Senate, it is deemed necessary to bring clarity to consumers and create a regulatory framework for plant-based labelling (Rural and Regional Affairs and Transport Legislation Committee 2022).

Following the inquiry, the current government committed to creating guidelines in cooperation with both animal and plant-based industries. The Alternative Proteins Council of Australia also issued industry guidelines for meat labelling (Alternative Protein Council 2023a) and dairy alternative products (Alternative Protein Council 2023b). The use of the term milk for plant-based products such as soymilk (Siddiqui et al. 2023) is allowed. The industry guidelines suggest that common meat and dairy descriptors must be coupled with other qualifiers or suffixes such as oat milk and chicken-style.

6.2.4 Singapore

Under Singaporean rules, novel foods must receive premarket approval from the Singapore Food Agency. Novel foods are food ingredients and foods that have yet to have a history of safe use. Safe use means the food or food ingredient has been consumed as "an ongoing part of the diet by a significant human population (the population of a country) for a period of at least 20 years and without reported adverse human health effects". A food or food ingredient can be regarded as a novel food even if the compounds included are chemically identical to naturally occurring substances if the food or food ingredient is produced through new technologies.

Precision fermentation to produce functional ingredients is mentioned as an example of such technology. To obtain novel food approval, the marketer must present adequate evidence to prove the food is not hazardous or toxic. If an applicant presents a perfect dossier, the Agency will decide in nine to 12 months. (Singapore Food Agency 2023). The Singapore Food Agency introduced Novel Food Virtual Clinics in 2021 where novel food companies can engage with the Agency at earlier stages of their research to minimise compliance costs and delay (Singapore Food Agency n.d.a).

Novel plant-based, microalgae-based, and macroalgae-based proteins are defined as novel foods in Singapore. As microalgae cultivation is possible in urban and compact spaces even without sunlight, it provides an alternative to conventional food for a land-scarce country like Singapore (Wassmann et al. 2024). For instance, a microalgae protein company that was established in Singapore, Sophie's Bionutrients, later moved its headquarters to the Netherlands.

For insects, upon a public consultation held by the Singapore Food Agency in 2022, 16 insect species are authorised to be sold as food in 2023, including house cricket *Acheta domesticus*, the larvae of mealworm *Tenebrio molitor* and lesser mealworm *Alphitobius diaperinus*, the pupa and caterpillar of silkworm *Bombyx mori*, and honeybee *Apis mellifera*. Also, fibroin from silkworm cocoons is regarded as safe, as this protein has been consumed in South Korea and Japan. Black soldier fly *Hermetia illucens* is not among the authorised species so the application for novel food approval is required (Singapore Food Agency n.d.b).

Singapore is a global frontier in authorising cultured meat. The cultured chicken by GOOD Meat was authorised by the Singapore Food Agency in December 2020 and is sold in Singapore grocery stores. GOOD Meat is a subsidiary of the US company EatJust. A French-cultivated chicken start-up Vital Meat has recently submitted their novel food application in Singapore and believes they will be the first European company there to receive authorisation (Vegconomist 2023).

Singapore seems to attract novel food applications due to its reputation in supporting cultured meat innovation. Singapore overviews the regulatory environment for alternative proteins to curb the food security issue because 90% of Singaporean food consumption relies on imports. This is targeted to change by 2030 when Singapore aims to "sustainably produce 30% of the nation's nutritional needs locally" (Singapore Food Agency 2021).

Another type of alternative protein, Solein by Finnish company Solar Foods, has started its commercialisation journey from Singapore. The microbial protein has received a novel food authorisation from the Singapore Food Agency in October 2023. The protein is grown with CO_2 and electricity. Solar Foods with their research partners is also studying the production of beta-lactoglobulin whey protein by feeding their proprietary microbe with hydrogen and CO_2.

In Singapore, plant-based products and other novel food products must be labelled so that consumers can make informed decisions of the different products. This means that qualifying terms such as mock, imitation, and plant-based shall be used if meaty or dairy terms are used. This also applies to restaurants and other food establishments. The misrepresentation of the origin of food products is deemed as an offence under the Sale of Food Act. (Yeung, n.d.).

6.3 Conclusions and Discussion

The compliance with food law is integral for the access of alternative protein products in the market. Companies must put effort into conducting the required studies and to submit the applications to gain the authorisation. Novel food regulation processes delay the entry of novel foods into the market, including alternative protein products that have significant potential for environmental benefits. However, most countries deem legislation, scientific evaluation, and administrative procedures necessary to ensure food safety.

Ideally, the global scientific community could agree on what is deemed safe for use (making the food non-novel) and safety criteria for novel foods. Countries would ideally create an encouraging regulatory environment for innovation with clear rules and swift procedures to attract investment and while dealing with crisis resilience and food security. Regulators are indeed humans, they may get entangled with neophobic or prejudicial emotions and tendencies, making them not so eager to advocate for foods that replace the traditional ones. Novel food products are likely to disrupt vested interests in the food system and, therefore, create different forms of resistance.

In this chapter, the legislation of alternative protein products in different countries and markets was examined, highlighting the recent examples of the legal evaluation of the key alternative protein products. We saw that many innovative novel foods are produced by different companies to tackle the regulations while reaching supermarkets and restaurants in the respective regions. Most innovative food and ingredient companies start from the markets where the regulatory environment is more developed. The market for alternative proteins is exciting for scientists, businesses, and regulators.

Nevertheless, some unnecessary barriers remain such as lengthy and resource-consuming procedures, scientific evidence requirements of different countries, and marketing rules are still unclear. Regulatory clarity is needed for the market to develop and to provide predictability for companies. Traditional concepts such as consumer protection in the case of food fraud may be outdated and poorly suited to a situation where consumers are purposefully searching for alternative products due to several motivations. Regulators must be wary of the strategic use of legal concepts and justifications by incumbents, for example, by the livestock industry, to further their own economic interests.

In fact, food law is not adequate to promote a transition to alternative proteins. Countries should favour food production that is compatible with the planetary boundaries, for instance, foods with low climate, land use, biodiversity, deforestation, and water footprint. Trade law, public procurement law, investment law, marketing law, tax law, and administrative law can be leveraged. Agricultural subsidies have interfered with the market for decades and they must now be turned into strong levers to steer the food system towards a shift to sustainably produced proteins. Government interference with the food marketing system shall be justified by everyone's right to a clean, safe, healthy, and sustainable environment.

References

ABC Rural by Fiona Boom 2023, 'Lab-produced meat could be on Australian supermarket shelves as soon as next year', Lab-Produced Meat Could be on Australian Supermarket Shelves as Soon as Next Year – ABC News, accessed 7 February 2024.

Alternative Protein Council 2023a, 'Industry Guidelines for the Labelling of Meat Alternative Products in Australia and New Zealand 24.4.2023', accessed 10 January 2024, www.alternativeproteinscouncil.org/wp-content/uploads/2023/04/APC_Meat_Alternative_Guideline_24-4-23.pdf.

Alternative Protein Council 2023b, 'Industry Guidelines for Labelling of Plant-Based Dairy Alternative Products in Australia and New Zealand 24.8.2023', accessed 10 January 2024, www.alternativeproteinscouncil.org/industry-guidelines-labelling-of-plant-based-dairy-alternative-products-in-aunz./.

Bartholomai, BM, Ruwe, KM, Thurston, J, Jha, P, Scaife, K, Simon, R, Abdelmoteleb, M, Goodman, RE & Farhi, M 2022, 'Safety evaluation of *Neurospora crassa* mycoprotein for use as a novel meat alternative and enhancer', *Food Chemistry and Toxicology*, *168*, p.113342, https://doi.org/10.1016/j.fct.2022.113342.

Bernauer, L, Rotkohl, A, Lehmayer, LGK & Emmerstorfer-Augustin, A 2021, '*Komagataella phaffii* as emerging model organism in fundamental research', *Frontiers of Microbiology*, *11*, p.607028, https://doi.org/10.3389/fmicb.2020.607028.

Bolton, B 2017, 'Dairy's monopoly on words: The historical context and implications of the tofutown decision', *European Food and Feed Law Review*, *12*, pp.422–430.

Clean Public – Vow 2023, 'Application 1269: Cultured quail as a novel food', Novel Food Dossier Submitted by the Company. https://www.foodstandards.gov.au/food-standards-code/applications/A1269-Cultured-Quail-as-a-Novel-Food, accessed 7 February 2024, foodstandards.gov.au.

Consultation Process, n.d., *European commission*, https://food.ec.europa.eu/safety/novel-food/consultation-process-novel-food-status_en.

Cremar n.d., *Functional protein. Yeast peptide*, accessed 4 February 2024, https://cremar.co.kr/en/products/functional-protein/.

CSIRO 2022, Australia's Protein Roadmap at Australia's Protein Roadmap – CSIRO, accessed 7 February 2024.

Department of Agriculture, Fisheries, and Forestry 2023, *Edible insects – DAFF*, accessed 7 February 2024, agriculture.gov.au.

Drozen, MS, Mann, RF & Pelonis, EC 2022, 'Court enjoins enforcement of arkansas meat labeling law', *The National Law Review*, 18 October, accessed 10 January 2014, www.natlawreview.com/article/court-enjoins-enforcement-arkansas-meat-labeling-law.

EABA 2021, 'Algae as novel food in Europe', EABA information paper https://www.algae-novel-food.com/output/algae-novel-food/download.pdf, Downloaded 8 March 2024.

European Biotechnology News 2023, 'French parliamentarians against cell-based meat – European biotechnology', 18 December, accessed 9 February 2024, european-biotechnology.com.

European Commission 2023, 'Proposal for a Regulation of the European Parliament and of the Council on plants obtained by certain new genomic techniques and their food and feed, and amending Regulation (EU) 2017/625', Brussels, 5 July 2023. COM (2023) 411 final.

EU Consultation Process on Novel Food, n.d., https://food.ec.europa.eu/safety/novel-food/consultation-process-novel-food-status_en.

EU GMO Authorisation for Food and Feed n.d., 'GMO authorisations for food and feed – European commission', europa.eu.

EU GMO Register – GMO Register – European Commission, europa.eu.

EU Novel Food Status Catalogue n.d., *Food and Feed Information Portal Database | FIP*, europa.eu.

FDA 2023, 'Labeling of plant-based milk alternatives and voluntary nutrient statements; Draft guidance for industry', Docket No. FDA-2023-D-0451, https://public-inspection.federalregister.gov/2023-03513.pdf, Downloaded 8 March 2024.

Fischer, D 2023, 'Fischer reintroduces real MEAT act to end deceptive labeling of imitation meat products, stop smear campaign against real beef and pork, Press release 14 November 2023, accessed 10 January 2024, www.fischer.senate.gov/public/index.cfm/2023/11/fischer-reintroduces-real-meat-act-to-end-deceptive-labeling-of-imitation-meat-products-stop-smear-campaign-against-real-beef-and-pork.

FSANZ 2023a, *Advisory committee on novel foods*, www.foodstandards.gov.au/business/novel/novelcommittee.

FSANZ 2023b, *Exclusivity of use for novel foods and nutritive substances* | Food Standards Australia New Zealand, accessed 7 February 2024. https://www.foodstandards.gov.au/business/novel/exclusivity-of-use-for-novel-foods-and-nutritive-substances.

FSANZ 2023c, *Cell-based meat* | Food Standards Australia New Zealand, last updated 2023. https://www.foodstandards.gov.au/consumer/safety/Cell-based-meat.

Future of Edible Insects 2021, *Insects for food use is permitted by enforcement discretion in U.S.*, accessed 8 March 2024, https://thefutureofedibleinsects.com/tag/gras/.

Good Food Institute 2023, *Europe plant-based food retail market insights 2020–2022*, https://gfieurope.org/wp-content/uploads/2023/04/2020-2022-Europe-retail-market-insights_updated-1.pdf, Downloaded 8 March 2024.

Good Food Institute n.d., *The global health benefits of alternative proteins – the good food institute*, accessed 9 February 2024, gfi.org.

Lähteenmäki-Uutela, A, Rahikainen, M, Camarena-Gómez, MT, Piiparinen, J, Spilling, K & Yang, B 2021, 'European Union legislation on macroalgae products', *Aquaculture International*, *29*, pp.487–509, https://doi.org/10.1007/s10499-020-00633-x.

Maine Public 2022, accessed 4 February 2024, www.mainepublic.org/environment-and-outdoors/2022-06-01/seaweed-isnt-considered-enough-of-a-food-for-more-comprehensive-fda-safety-regulations.

National Milk Producers Federation 2021, *Bipartisan dairy pride act may further FDA enforcement progress*, accessed 10 January 2024, www.nmpf.org/bipartisan-dairy-pride-act-may-further-fda-enforcement-progress.

New South Wales Food Authority 2021, edible-insects.pdf (nsw.gov.au), Downloaded 7 February 2024.

Ohm Rørdam, M 2013, 'EU Law on food naming: The prohibition against misleading names in an internal market context', Copenhagen Business School. PhD Series 13–2013. EU Law on Food Naming: The prohibition against misleading names in an internal market context, econstor.eu, Downloaded 8 March 2024.

Plant-Based Foods Association 2019, *PBFA submits comments to FDA on labeling of plant-based milk*, accessed 10 January 2024, www.plantbasedfoods.org/pbfa-submits-comments-to-fda-on-labeling-of-plant-based-milk/.

Proveg.org 2021, *Great news for the plant-based sector: Europe rejects 'plant-based dairy censorship*, 6 May 2021, accessed 5 March 2024, https://proveg.org/news/great-news-for-the-plant-based-sector-europe-rejects-plant-based-dairy-censorship/.

Raciti, RL 2020, 'The terminology wars: The Dairy pride sct and its potential impingement on innovation', *Ohio State Business Law Journal*, *14*(2), pp.263–297, https://moritzlaw.osu.edu/sites/default/files/2021-07/11.-Raciti.pdf, Downloaded 8 March 2024.

Reuters 2023, Italy's parliament approves ban on lab-grown food amid tensions. Reuters, 16 November, Accessed 9 February 2024.

Ridler, G 2021, 'EU official rejects plant-based dairy ban', *Food Manufacture*, 26 May 2021, accessed 10 January 2024, www.foodmanufacture.co.uk/Article/2021/05/26/EU-officials-reject-plant-based-dairy-ban.

Rural and Regional Affairs and Transport Legislation Committee 2022, *Don't mince words: Definitions of meat and other animal products*, accessed 10 January 2024, www.aph.gov.au/Parliamentary_Business/Committees/Senate/Rural_and_Regional_Affairs_and_Transport/DefinitionsofMeat/Report.

Siddiqui, A, Mehany, T, Schulte, H, Pandiselvam, R, Nagdalian, AA, Golik, AB, Asif Shah, M, Muhammad Shahbaz, H & Maqsood, S 2023, 'Plant-based milk – Thoughts of researchers and industries on what should be called as "milk"', *Food Reviews International*, in press, https://doi.org/10.1080/87559129.2023.2228002.

Singapore Food Agency 2021, 'Singapore Food Statistics 2021', www.sfa.gov.sg/docs/default-source/publication/sg-food-statistics/singapore-food-statistics-2021.pdf, Downloaded 7 February 2024.

Singapore Food Agency 2023, 'Requirements for the safety assessment of novel foods and novel food ingredients', Updated 20 July 2023, www.sfa.gov.sg/docs/default-source/food-information/requirements-for-the-safety-assessment-of-novel-foods-and-novel-food-ingredients.pdf, Downloaded 8 March 2024.

Singapore Food Agency n.d.a, *Factsheet on alternative proteins*, accessed 9 February 2024, factsheet-on-alternative-proteins.pdf (sfa.gov.sg).

Singapore Food Agency n.d.b. *Factsheet on insect regulatory framework*, accessed 9 February 2024, sfa-insect-regulatory-framework-factsheet.pdf.

Stout, AJ, Zhang, X, Letcher, SM, Rittenberg, ML, Shub, M, Chai, KM, Kaul, M & Kaplan, DL 2024, 'Engineered autocrine signaling eliminates muscle cell FGF2 requirements for cultured meat production', *Cell Reports Sustainability*, *1*(1), p.100009, https://doi.org/10.1016/j.crsus.2023.100009.

Triton Algae Innovations, Ltd 2023, '*Chlamydomonas reinhardtii* dried biomass powder – Novel food application', Submitted to the European Commission.

U.S. FDA n.d.a, *Generally Recognized as Safe (GRAS)* https://www.fda.gov/food/food-ingredients-packaging/generally-recognized-safe-gras

U.S. FDA n.d.b, *GRAS notices and FDA letters*, www.fda.gov/food/gras-notice-inventory/recently-published-gras-notices-and-fda-letters.

van Huis, A, Van Itterbeeck, J, Klunder, H, Mertens, E, Halloran A, Muir, G & Vantomme, P 2013, 'Edible insects: Future prospects for food and feed security', *FAO Forestry Paper 171*, www.fao.org/3/i3253e/i3253e.pdf, Downloaded 8 March 2024.

Vegconomist.com 2023, France's vital meat submits premarket dossier to launch cultivated chicken in Singapore – Vegconomist – The vegan business magazine, accessed 10 March 2024.

Wassmann, B, Hartmann, C & Siegrist, M 2024, 'Novel microalgae-based foods: What influences Singaporean consumers' acceptance?', *Food Quality and Preference*, *113*, p.105068, https://doi.org/10.1016/j.foodqual.2023.105068.

Yeung, J n.d., 'Safety of alternative protein', *Singapore Food Agency*, accessed 10 January 2024, www.sfa.gov.sg/food-information/risk-at-a-glance/safety-of-alternative-protein.

7 Health Claims and Their Regulation

Comparing Australia and Europe

Siva Barathi (Sharl) Marimuthu and Anu Lähteenmäki-Uutela

7.1 Introduction

Nutritious foods are essential to a healthy lifestyle, because food consumed as part of a balanced diet promotes health and wellbeing, reduces illness and disease, and reduces healthcare costs. It is this desire for good health that drives the functional food market (Stanton 2016; Wang et al. 2002; Topolska et al. 2021; Diez-Gutiérrez et al. 2020). Functional foods are often perceived as providing physiological benefits in addition to basic taste and aroma (Nystrand & Olsen 2020). Breads fortified with iron and folic acid, breakfast cereals fortified with iron, margarine with plant sterols, yoghurt with certain bacterial strains, and iodised salt are just a few examples of functional foods. Such foods are often advertised to consumers for their health benefits.

Functional foods are deemed to play an important role in reducing the prevalence of heart disease, cancer, osteoporosis, diabetes, and hypertension (Victoria State Government n.d.; Alkhatib et al. 2017). Scientists have discovered physiologically active components in foods from plant and animal origins that can reduce the risk of chronic lifestyle diseases (Adefegha 2018; Das & Biswas 2016). Consumers, aware of the link between the nutritional benefits of functional foods and certain health conditions, are driving the demand for such foods. From a societal perspective, increased intake of such foods can be a useful strategy to improve public health. However, the term functional food varies as the literature in scientific and business studies shows many but overlapping definitions (Kwak and Jukes 2001; Bigliardi and Galati 2013; de Moraes Prata Gaspar et al. 2020).

Health-conscious consumers are often unclear of what functional foods are or what the term entails. From a consumer perspective, functional food implies processed foods fortified with specific nutrients (iron-fortified breakfast cereals), commonly known as superfoods (chia, goji), or any foods with health claims (Gupta and Mishra 2021; Zawistowski 2019). Functional food is not a legal term in Australia or in the European Union. Both jurisdictions regulate the marketing of functional foods through the assessment of health claims on food labels and during advertising. From a legal point of view, there is a

DOI: 10.4324/9781003392279-7

distinction between food and "food with medicalised claims" where regulators struggle to categorise all products (Lähteenmäki-Uutela 2010; Zawistowski 2019; Kim et al. 2019). However, not all consumers are aware of this distinction (de Boer and Bast 2015a).

In this chapter, we will examine the existing regulatory frameworks for health claims in Australia and the European Union. We will examine whether the existing controls are sufficient to protect consumers from misleading claims or medicalisation of food, and whether this is fair to the entrepreneurs developing innovative products. Both jurisdictions have their own strengths and weaknesses, yet both recognise that inadequate regulation will undermine consumer confidence and the potential public health impact of food health claims. Misleading claims appear to escape scrutiny in Australia when an industry-standard self-justification process is applied. The European Union, on the other hand, has a strict and bureaucratic approval process for health claims, which can hamper business innovation.

We will discuss how pitfalls could be mitigated by establishing additional measures in Australia. In the European Union, the fault of the system is its inflexibility to the point of hindering innovation. We recognise the competing demands created by regulatory controls, consumer wants and needs, and the pursuit of business success and macroeconomic growth to achieve the best outcomes for society. Regulatory reforms must not burden companies while addressing the mischief that companies can wreak. The reforms must strike a balance between preventing misleading claims and ensuring that consumers have an adequate flow of information, which would facilitate them in making an informed choice about their health.

We recognise that several articles have discussed and compared the regulation of health claims between jurisdictions. For example, in 2020 the regulatory review of health claims in functional foods was compared between Europe, the United States, and Japan (Díaz et al. 2020) followed by a comparison between Europe, the United States, Canada, Australia, and New Zealand in February 2021 (Kušar et al. 2021). Several international comparisons have been highlighted in the literature in the past (de Boer and Bast 2015b; Díaz et al. 2020; Greene et al. 2001). This chapter is an update of those articles, addressing the issue of health claim regulation and examining regulation from the perspective of competing demands at three (3) interfaces, namely government, consumers, and businesses. The chapter provides suggestions to address the pitfalls from these two perspectives.

In addition to these analyses, we provide an outlook and round off the paper by pointing out the role business plays in providing consumers with functional foods. It is recognised that these products do not only offer companies and businesses a great marketing opportunity for sales but also to do good in a societal sense. This puts the economy to the test, and we are aware of the challenges and the ethical balancing act that this entails. We recognise that there are many challenges for businesses, but there are also opportunities for the health of the citizens and to reduce the costs of a burgeoning healthcare system in the countries surveyed.

7.2 Medicalisation of Health Claims Escapes Regulation

In Australia, a functional food is regulated as a therapeutic good (i.e., a drug) if it is classified as a therapeutic good. In determining whether a product is a therapeutic good, consideration is given to the product's ingredients, the route of administration, as well as its intended use, that is, whether any therapeutic claims are made on the product's label or in other promotional materials relating to the product. The term "therapeutic good" in Australia or "medicine" in the European Union is broadly defined in legislation, so a wide range of products can fall under the classification.

Under the key terms in the Australian definition, therapeutic goods are products that present a therapeutic purpose, are suitable for a therapeutic purpose, or intended for a therapeutic purpose. In the European Union, medicines are products with a medicinal function or with medicinal claims. Therapeutic goods or medicine are different legal categories from foods with distinctive rules. All consumer regulations aim to protect consumers from exaggerated and misleading claims.

Both therapeutic/medical claims and health claims refer to the effects of food on health. While health claims in general refer to improving health or promoting health, therapeutic/medical claims refer to the prevention, cure, or treatment of disease. The difference is that therapeutic/medical claims suggest a more direct link to the prevention of acute diseases, while health claims are aimed at promoting health, maintaining health, or reducing the risk of disease. The regulatory implications of claims are so far-reaching that claims where foods are interpreted as therapeutic fall under the category of therapeutic goods (or food-medicine interface) in Australia and can be categorised as medicine in the European Union.

In both jurisdictions, functional foods that have a therapeutic claim in their advertising or labels are classified and regulated as medicinal products, meaning they are subject to regulatory drug safety controls to ensure continuous availability of safe and effective products. The control includes scientific testing at different stages, authorisation procedures, post-market surveillance, and reporting of adverse reactions. However, if they escape regulation as medicinal products, functional foods are not subject to medical safety control prior to distribution. Products that are legally categorised as foods are exempt from long and costly clinical trials used in drug regulation.

7.3 The Dilemma in Classifying Functional Foods as Medicinal

In practice, marketers often try to avoid categorising functional foods as medicines. In both Australia and the European Union, in the regulation of therapeutic products such as medicines, a risk management approach is applied to assess the safety and efficacy of the products. While ensuring they are safe and effective, the decision to place them on the market is based on an assessment of whether the benefits resulting from the consumption of the medicines outweigh the risks associated with the use of such products (Department of Health and Aged Care and Australian Government 2024).

In layman's terms, claims about functional foods that either suggest disease prevention or promote health benefits are deemed comparable and innocent. Consumers are in general unaware of the rules for each regulatory product category. If the real purpose of functional foods is to confer health benefits, but it does not prevent disease, the information placed on the labels or in advertising (both explicit and implicit) can blur their classification. Through clever wording (or art), it is possible to create food labels and advertisements that imply therapeutic use to consumers yet escape regulation as a therapeutic good in Australia or medicine in Europe.

We believe that consumers tend to misinterpret claims and advertisers use this to their advantage. Using their personal background knowledge to interpret health claims, customers' assessment of the health impact of a food product may not only be based on the actual words in the claim but also on their self-assessment. For consumers, words (both explicit and implicit) as well as cues such as images and health logos have a major impact on their decision-making (Hieke et al. 2016). Given behavioural biases and consumer vulnerability, the regulatory scrutiny of health claims made on functional foods requires careful thought.

It is a flaw in the system when exaggerated, misleading, and medical claims escape proper regulation. Global studies have shown that when claims are misleading, deceptive, or confusing and lack adequate regulatory control, consumers lose confidence, and claims lose their role in making healthier food choices (Hoffmann and Schwartz 2016; Federal Trade Commission n.d.). Another aspect to be considered is the need to strike a balance between information overload and information destruction. We do not deny that empowering consumers to make informed choices and guiding them to make healthier choices through valuable information is vital to all food claims and advertising. However, we must not lose sight of the fact that information overload can also lead to consumers missing out on valuable information (Roetzel 2019).

This requires a balance between ensuring valuable consumer information is provided and eliminating false, misleading claims. Consumers must be sufficiently and comprehensively informed to make a rational decision. Information can be distorted, omitted, or confused for various reasons (MacFarlane et al. 2020), particularly to increase sales. A company might be unable to provide information due to cost. Alternatively, a company may lack incentives if it sees no financial or other gains from investing in information dissemination. In some cases, however, a seller may have incentives to provide information in a competitive market to differentiate their products from those of others

(Craswell 1997). Failure to provide sufficient information is not considered misleading unless it is a false claim and it causes customers to believe that it is true (Richards 2021; Craswell 1985).

However, eliminating information can be costly to those who are not misled, as valuable information is lost to those who derive some benefit from the information (Holden et al. 2021). In other words, overemphasising the costs of misleading claims (or prohibiting health claims outright) and underemphasising the benefits of valuable information (elimination) can reduce deception but the benefits that could be gained from the information are lost. Information failure, like deception, can be addressed by regulation, for example by imposing mandatory disclosure, sanctions, or warnings to protect consumers from the consequences of insufficient information. Regardless of its form, any claim that is or may be misleading deserves strict regulation (Wu and Geylani 2020).

7.4 Codex Alimentarius 1997 Guidelines on Nutrition and Health Claims

We begin our in-depth discussion of the regulation of functional food health claims by examining the internationally recognised food standards, guidelines, and codes of conduct set out in the Codex Alimentarius. Developed by the Codex Alimentarius Commission (CAC), the code was created by the Food and Agriculture Organization (FAO) and the World Health Organization (WHO) to ensure consumer health through food safety and quality and to promote fair practices in the food trade.

7.4.1 Requirements in Codex Alimentarius

In many countries, the Codex Alimentarius serves as the basis for national legislation. Australia (since 1963) and the European Union (since 2003) are members of the Codex Alimentarius. The 1997 Codex Guidelines on Nutrition and Health Claims (the Guideline) describe a health claim as any statement that states, suggests, or implies that there is a relationship between a food, or a component of that food, and health (Codex Alimentarius 1997).

It states as follows:

- Nutrient function claims – A nutrition claim that describes the physiological role of the nutrient in growth, development, and normal functions of the body.
- Other function claims – These claims concern specific beneficial effects of the consumption of foods or their constituents, in the context of the total diet on normal functions or biological activities of the body. Such claims relate to a positive contribution to health or to the improvement of a function or to modifying or preserving health.
- Reduction of disease risk claims – Claims relating the consumption of a food or food constituent, in the context of the total diet, to the reduced risk

of developing a disease or health-related condition. Risk reduction means significantly altering a major risk factor(s) for a disease or health-related condition. Diseases have multiple risk factors and altering one of these risk factors may or may not have a beneficial effect. The presentation of risk reduction claims must ensure, for example, by use of appropriate language and reference to other risk factors, that consumers do not interpret them as prevention claims.

The requirements and terms of service are detailed and comprehensive to ensure high standards are met. We highlight in this chapter the aspects of (1) substantiation requirements, (2) a regulatory framework for qualifying and/or disqualifying conditions for eligibility to use certain information, (3) benefits claimed, and (4) labelling requirements. First, regarding the obligation to justify the standard, the Guidelines require that the health claim must be based on timely, relevant, and scientific substantiation, with sufficient level of evidence to demonstrate the nature of the claimed effect and the link to health. An essential prerequisite is also a recognised scientific assessment of the data, which is reviewed when new findings become available.

Second, the Guidelines suggest that what is important for an effective regulatory framework is, inter alia, a clear regulatory framework for qualifying and/or disqualifying conditions for eligibility to use the specific claim. This requirement implies the possibility for national competent authorities to prohibit claims made on foods containing nutrients or components in amounts that increase the risk of disease or an adverse health condition. This must also be accepted by the competent authorities of the country where the product is sold.

Third, regarding the claimed benefits, the Guidelines emphasise that the claimed benefits result from consuming an appropriate amount of the food or food component as part of a healthy diet and the claimed effect is attributed to a component of the food and a validated method for quantifying the food component, which supports the foundation is in place. In addition, claims that encourage or condone overconsumption of food or disparage good nutritional practices are prohibited (Codex Alimentarius 1997).

Finally, the labelling regulations require, among other things, that labels contain information such as:

- A statement of the quantity of any nutrient or other constituent of the food that is the subject of the claim.
- Target group, if appropriate.
- How to use the food to obtain the claimed benefit and other lifestyle factors or other dietary sources, where appropriate.
- If appropriate, advice to vulnerable groups on how to use the food and to groups, if any, who need to avoid the food.
- Maximum safe intake of the food or constituent where necessary.
- How the food or food constituent fits within the context of the total diet.

- A statement on the importance of maintaining a healthy diet (Codex Alimentarius 1997).

7.5 Regulation of Health Claims in Functional Food

Codex Alimentarius standards and regulations are implemented according to jurisdictions. In this section, we examine health claim regulations in the two jurisdictions, Australia and the European Union. The primary objective of this exploration is to provide a fundamental understanding that facilitates a rigorous assessment of the regulatory frameworks described in the following section. By examining the regulatory landscape of health claims in both jurisdictions, we aim to lay the groundwork for a critical and insightful analysis of the effectiveness and impact of these controls.

7.5.1 Australia's Regulation of Health Claims

Food marketers often face a multitude of requirements and regulations. In Australia, food law broadly encompasses rules on food safety, food labelling, and marketing claims. Food safety is governed by the Food Standard Australia New Zealand (FSANZ). Product labelling is also governed by the Australian Consumer Law (ACL) and industry-specific regulations, namely the Australian Competition and Consumer Act 2010 (Cth) Schedule 2. Food marketing is governed by several industry codes as well. The main code is the AANA Code of Ethics and others include;

- Children's Advertising Code
- Food and Beverages Advertising and Marketing Communications Code (FBAC)
- Environmental Claims Code
- Wagering Advertising Code
- Responsible Children's Marketing Initiative (RCMI)
- Quick Service Restaurant Initiative for Responsible and Marketing (QSRI).

Both Australia and New Zealand share a regulatory system for food composition and labelling that involves the government agencies of both countries (Curran 2002). The central regulatory bodies include a forum of ministers (the Forum), the Food Regulation Standing Committee (FRSC), and the Food Standards Australia New Zealand (Food Regulation Secretariat 2024). The guidelines are developed and set by the Australian and New Zealand Forum and supported by the FRSC, which is made up of government departments and agency heads.

Food standards are developed by the FSANZ (FSANZ 2023a). However, implementation and enforcement of policies, including food recall, is done at the state level by government agencies in the Australian states and territories and New Zealand through their respective food laws and other related legislations (FSANZ 2024a). Imports and exports and biosecurity issues are overseen by the Department of Agriculture, Water, and the Environment. In addition, the Implementation Committee for Food (ISFR) oversees the enforcement and enforcement processes (Food Regulation Secretariat 2024). Food labelling is regulated under the Australia New Zealand Food Standards Code, developed by FSANZ. In particular, Standard 1.2.7 of the Food Standards Code contains specific requirements for nutritional and related claims and allows three types of claims on food labels and related advertising.

In addition to the nutrient claims, over 200 pre-approved general health claims and 13 FSANZ pre-approved high-level health claims are allowed (FSANZ 2023b). Food businesses can also use the self-established food-health relationship, which is subject to a systematic review process in Appendix 6 of the Code; this process is explained later in this chapter (FSANZ 2023c). All health-related claims from abroad are also considered in Australia. In 2013, FSANZ incorporated 183 food health relationships previously authorised in the European Union in Schedule 4 of the Food Standards Code. In addition, 32 health claims authorised by the European Union have been reviewed, and of these, 29 claims are being followed up but are not currently included in the standards (FSANZ 2024b).

Indeed, a general health claim must be based on either FSANZ's 200 pre-approval in the Standards or the industry (food companies) self-justified process based on a systematic review according to Schedule 6 of Standard 1.2.7 before they can be allowed on labels and advertisements. To support the industry (food companies) in the self-substantiation process, FSANZ has developed guidelines that must be followed (FSANZ 2023d). To assess the self-substantiation process, the Getting Your Claims Right Guide (checklist) can be used to determine if a systematic literature review has been conducted in accordance with the requirements of the Food Standard Code.

Essentially, this process involves food companies maintaining cause-and-effect relationship records between foods (or food ingredients) and their health effects, and notifying the Chief Executive Officer of FSANZ (FSANZ 2023e). This notification is then included in the list of reported food relationships. Note that food companies must contact local law enforcement agencies before informing FSANZ about the self-established relationship between food and health. FSANZ does not approve or validate information added to the list nor does it enforce non-compliance. In fact, a clear disclaimer to this effect is placed on the website:

> FSANZ cannot guarantee and assumes no legal liability or responsibility for the accuracy, currency, completeness or interpretation of any information contained in the list of notified food-health relationships. FSANZ is not responsible for the enforcement of Standard 1.2.7 and does not assess compliance of the notified food-health relationships. Our role is only to administer the notification process. Publication by

> FSANZ does not indicate acceptance, approval or validation of the notified food-health relationship. Any concerns about the content of this list should be directed to an enforcement agency. Read the list of agencies and departments responsible for enforcement.
>
> Please note general level health claims based on notified food-health relationships may not be on food products in the marketplace.

Since FSANZ is not involved in the authentication process, no documents need to be submitted to FSANZ for systematic verification. Details on how and when to notify FSANZ, what details of food health relationships should be reported, what happens after notification, and how updates to the systematic review can be made are all set out on the website. There is also information about the delisting of the food relationship (FSANZ 2024c). Health claims are only permissible if, for example, they meet the prescribed requirements: (1) Nutrient content claims that have met the defined eligibility criteria for the specified nutrient, and (2) health claims at a general level that have met the nutrient profile assessment criteria and are supported by the quality evidence of the claim.

Whether pre-approved or self-substantiated by the industry, these health claims must be backed by scientific evidence with equal certainty. Nutrient content claims refer to the content of certain nutrients or substances in foods, such as good sources of calcium or low in fat. This claim may not be made unless the food contains the amount of calcium stated in the standard as a good source. Health claims at a general level suggest a nutrient or substance in a food that impairs health. An example is, "calcium is necessary for normal tooth and bone structure". Again, this claim is not permitted unless it contains at least the required amount specified in the Food Standards Code Schedule 4 and Standard 1.2.7, and must also meet certain other criteria set out in the Food Standards Code (FSANZ 2023f).

The high-level health claims relate to the effect of a particular food on a serious disease or a biomarker of a serious disease. Examples of serious diseases are coronary artery disease, osteoporosis, osteoporotic fractures, and neural tube defects. Examples of serious disease biomarkers include blood cholesterol and hypertension. An example of a high-level health claim might be that a diet rich in calcium and adequate levels of vitamin D may reduce the risk of osteoporosis in people aged 65 and over. An example of a biomarker health claim is that lower sodium or salt levels are a cause of the reduction in blood pressure. Some claims are not allowed in food labelling and related advertising. Therapeutic claims, whether expressed or implied, are prohibited on foods. Other prohibited claims include claims about kava, foods with more than 1.15% alcohol, and infant formula.

7.5.2 ***European Union Regulations on Health Claims***

In the European Union, the primary regulatory bodies that govern health claims are the European Food Safety Authority (EFSA) and the European

Commission, and the food labelling rules are found in Regulation EC/1924/2006. In the European Union, foods that contain health claims must be authorised at the European Union level. The authorisation process was created through Regulation EC/1924/2006. Authorisation is requested from the European Commission, and the EFSA assesses the scientific evidence behind the claims.

All authorised and non-authorised health claims can be found in the European Union Register. The European Union regulation distinguishes the types of health claims. The Function Health Claims (Article 13 claims) relate to the growth, development, and functions of the body; psychological and behavioural functions; or weight loss or weight control. There are hundreds of allowed claims under Article 13. Examples of authorised claims include "α-Linolenic acid contributes to the maintenance of normal blood cholesterol levels", "Magnesium contributes to normal psychological function", or "Glucomannan in the context of an energy-restricted diet contributes to weight loss".

The exact terms of use are specified for each claim. The first list of claims was developed in cooperation with all Member States of the European Union according to Article 13(1) and published by Commission Regulation EU/432/2012. The list of claims in the Register of the European Union is regularly updated as new claims are admitted subject to individual applications under Article 13(5). The risk reduction claims (or Article 14(1)(a) claims) are related to reducing a risk factor in the growth of a disease. Dozens of claims have been authorised and appear in the European Union Register, for example.

> Plant stanol esters have been demonstrated to reduce blood cholesterol. Blood cholesterol is a risk factor in the development of coronary heart disease.
>
> Supplemental folic acid intake increases maternal folate status. Low maternal folate status is a risk factor for the development of neural tube defects in the developing foetus.

Article 14(1)(b) claims refer to children's development. Dozens of claims have been authorised for example "Vitamin D is needed for the normal growth and development of bone in children" and "Essential fatty acids are needed for normal growth and development of children". The regulation provides for a five-year data protection period for applicants' proprietary data if the approval of health claims are based on this data. Several companies have requested and received privacy protection over the years.

An interesting feature of the European Union system is that the list of non-authorised claims is the longest of the European Union's health claim lists: it has thousands of claims. Significant efforts have been made by scientists and companies to evaluate these unsuccessful applications. For example, all claims about probiotic bacteria have been rejected, for example, "*Lactobacillus casei* helps balance the intestinal flora" or "*Bifidobacterium longum* strengthens the immune system". The reason for the rejection is insufficient scientific evidence of the health effects and/or insufficient characterisation of the food in question. Several studies are needed on a given food to demonstrate the cause-and-effect relationship between food consumption and the claim. The regulatory situation for health claims on botanicals has been unclear for many years.

Few applications have been approved, while hundreds have been denied and more than 1,500 applications have been suspended since 2012 (Merten-Lentz 2020). Being "on hold" at the European Union level means that national rules on botanical claims apply. National regulations vary widely and, as a result, a large body of health claims remains in disharmony. Medicinal claims are prohibited on foods such as any references to prevention, treatment, or cure of disease. The categorisation depends on product functions and on claims, and the categorisation between food and medicine is an obligation of the member states. Countries differ in the interpretation of what a medicinal function is, with food companies typically preferring countries where their product is categorised as food. Presenting medical claims always makes the product a drug that may require solid evidence to prove its apparent usefulness.

7.6 Critical Appraisal of the Australian System and the European Union

In fact, both Australia and the European Union have an intricate web of laws, rules, and regulations that meticulously monitor food labelling, marketing, and advertising. These regulations are also complemented by industry-specific codes that add an additional layer of governance. Table 7.1 serves as a concise compilation outlining the institutional framework of these two legal systems.

Together, these create comprehensive regulations that address almost all marketing and labelling aspects of functional foods. At first glance, regulations appear sufficient and even flawless, yet in reality they are far from perfect. The implementation and enforcement of these regulations may require some attention. In the following section, we examine the regulatory systems for health claim control in the two (2) jurisdictions and highlight some critical pitfalls in each. We then provide recommendations for practical improvements with tailor-made proposals for each country. In summary, a health claim is any statement about a relationship between food and health. This relationship is communicated to consumers who rely on it to improve their health.

7.7 Towards Better Regulatory Control in Australia

Australia has a wealth of food regulations to develop and implement workable strategies to ensure adequate and effective controls through existing food laws, codes, and regulations. The health and related claims are numerous,

Table 7.1 Institutional Framework for Health Claims on Functional Foods

	UN FAO/WHO: Codex Alimentarius	*Australia*	*European Union*
Regulatory Bodies	Codex Alimentarius Commission (CAC)	Forum of Ministers Food Regulation Standing Committee (FRSC) Food Standards Australia New Zealand (FSANZ)	European Commission European Food Safety Authority (EFSA)
Regulations	Codex Alimentarius	Australia New Zealand Food Standard Code (ANZSC)	Regulation EC/1924/2006
Types of Nutrition Claims	Nutrition claims (nutrient content claims and nutrient comparative claims)	Nutrient content claims	Nutrition claims
Types of Health Claims	Nutrient function claims Other function claims Reduction of disease risk claims	General-level health claims: over 200 approved High-level claims: 13 pre-approved	Function claims Disease risk reduction claims Claims referring to children's development

comprehensive, and a useful guide to the relationship between food and health. Enforcement of the Food Standard Code and its non-compliance (if any) occurs at the state level, where each state has its own law implementing the Food Code. However, one area that requires attention is the effectiveness of regulatory controls over health claims made on functional foods. Our analysis revealed several critical deficiencies in the justification of the health claim requirement.

The self-substantiation process is a requirement stipulated within Schedule 6 of the Food Standards Code. Typically, within this framework, industries or food companies have the option to use a pre-approved list of over 200 generic claims. However, should the proposed claims deviate from these established pre-approvals, there exists an avenue to create food health claims based on a systematic literature review (Lutz et al. 2019). At first glance, this might seem like a clear indication of safeguarding consumers while encouraging innovation. Nonetheless, the process of obtaining a permit through systematic literature review in Australia has been the subject of much debate, with several authors pointing out the shortcomings and limited development of the process.

The quality or adequacy of industry-provided review dossiers is not independently verified and remains unaudited unless a formal complaint is lodged. Even then, the following investigation is not timely (Neo 2019). Second, industry-funded research in general tends to favour results aligned with industry interests when claims may be exaggerated, misleading, unsubstantiated, or fall into the food medicine category (Fabbri et al. 2018). Third, the high workload and lack of sufficient labour in Australia is a significant problem. State and local officials lack the time and resources to assess the quality of evidence files, let alone prioritise investigative questions (Condon-Paoloni et al. 2015).

However, since 2019, the COVID-19 pandemic has exacerbated many of the existing challenges for governments around the world (Green and Loualiche 2021). Centrally, it concerns the resources required to assess the quality or investigate complaints. This resulted in continued substandard food health relations, delays in regulatory control processes, and delays in government agencies removing unsubstantiated claims from the FSANZ website and providing updates to complainants. A lack of skilled manpower, organisational capacity, and political commitment are often some of the most common barriers to effective food safety enforcement. So how can we ensure accuracy and timeliness of health claims and increase consumer confidence in food claims?

A functional regulatory approach to food safety is to independently review, consistently monitor adherence to food labelling laws, and promptly implement penalties to bring non-compliant parties towards regulatory conformity. Monitoring could be entrusted to a centralised authority that inspects and surveys industrial practices periodically, thereby expediting the alignment of industrial operations with food standards. Agency staff and personnel could undergo specialised training and receive adequate resources to develop necessary skills, knowledge to assess the calibre of evidence dossiers generated by industry, and prioritise investigations. Where appropriate, monitoring functions could also be outsourced to independent consultative industries or educational institutions.

7.8 Way Forward for the European Union

The European Union system is transparent and clear wherever health claims are permitted. The European Union register is easily accessible and searchable, and the register contains rejected applications, allowing operators to see how not to apply. EFSA's scientific opinion, on which the Commission's decision is based, is public. Sometimes the European Commission does not follow EFSA's opinion, which can raise questions about other decision-making bases besides science. EFSA is an impartial scientific body, and the Commission is the risk manager and policy maker. The Commission's decision must be supported by at least a majority of member states (Bucchini 2019). For example, the Commission decided against the EFSA report on omega-3 fatty acids. The challenge with the European Union Health Claims Act from a food science perspective is that fascinating scientific discoveries may not be communicated to consumers any time soon.

Claims can only be made after sufficient evidence has been collected and the multi-year regulatory process has been completed. Likewise, EFSA could issue its own opinions on selected connections between food and health without companies having to submit applications. As part of the regulatory fitness and performance programme (REFIT), the Nutrition and Health Claim Regulation EC/1924/2006 was recently evaluated and in May 2020, the Commission published the report on the evaluation (European Commission 2020). The report focused on two (2) unregulated topics: nutrient profiles and plant-based ingredients. Under the Regulation, the legality of food claims was conditional upon the product conforming with a nutrient profile, in which no claims could be allowed for unhealthy foods (foods with high fat, sugar, or salt content). However, due to political controversy and opposition from some member states, the Commission was unable to establish any nutrient profiles. The 2020 report noted that the goal pursued with nutrient profiles is relevant and should be considered. Some companies have reformulated their products, while others keep making claims about unhealthy foods.

The definition of unhealthy food shall be central to food law in the future. Nutrition and health claims should not be allowed on unhealthy foods where a practice that misleads consumers may have macro-level costs to the public health system. Plant-based products with health effects are deemed problematic by legal view in the European Union. Member states are responsible for classifying products as food or medicinal products. The distinction between plant-based foods with health claims and herbal medicinal products is fluid.

Around 2,000 health claims on plant-based foods are waiting for an assessment by EFSA or a decision by the Commission. This hold situation has lasted over a decade. In the absence of decisions by the European Union, member state regulations will apply, and consumers will continue to face waiting-list claims. The Commission has considered whether traditional practices can be used as a basis for claims and whether human intervention studies are not required (European Commission 2020). A possible solution is to market traditional foods as traditional herbal medicinal products. The European Union could look at the possibility of allowing claims based on preliminary evidence, like the United States and Japan models, for qualified claims. This means there would be food products on the markets where some evidence on the health impacts exists while a full understanding with high certainty and clear mechanisms are still lacking.

7.9 Commentary

Many health claims are without proper scientific substantiation; and marketers take advantage of consumers' vulnerability, knowing that they are influenced by traditional beliefs. Therefore, although the regulations appear detailed and comprehensive on paper, various loopholes prevent adequate regulation of health claims. Multinational food companies can use sophisticated tools to appear they care about people's health and circumvent strict government regulations. These companies invest in aggressive food product marketing campaigns and develop solutions to evade consumer protection laws and regulations (Reeve and Gostin 2019). As well as being a legal issue, misleading the consumer is also unethical. The marketer must recognise that the wording and images used in advertising and labels affect consumers' decision-making and health.

In marketing law and marketing ethics, consumers are traditionally assumed to be optimisers. The law focuses on guaranteeing buyers the information needed to make rational decisions. This focus on rational decisions is referred to as the information paradigm under the European consumer law (Gidlöf et al. 2013). Traditional marketing ethics are based on the notion of the average trader who is reasonably well-informed and smart. A person who has sufficient information is likely to make decisions that will maximise his or her welfare. Research in behavioural economics, consumer behaviour, and neuroscience has provided insights into how consumers make decisions in real-world situations (Kahneman and Patrick 2011). In practice, consumers have some notable limitations in making rational decisions.

The rationale for regulating information is not only to prevent harm to consumers and/or to address market failures, in particular information asymmetry between advertisers and consumers, but also to protect genuine advertisers' businesses from unfair advertisers (Klass 2020). Harm to consumers can be in the form of wasted money if the products do not perform as advertised. In addition, consumers are physically harmed when the products advertised are not safe, but falsely claim otherwise (Topol 2004). Misleading claims can also disappoint consumers (Heather and David 2019). In addition, some may be disappointed when products do not work as advertised and some may also suffer from dissatisfaction. Regulated information protects honest competitors from losing business due to misleading claims made by dishonest advertisers.

Because such advertising negatively impacts consumer perception, it may lead consumers to view any claims or advertisements or advertisements for certain products as potentially misleading. An honest seller who provides consumers with accurate and reliable information may fail to convince consumers of their credibility if consumers are unable to distinguish between honest and dishonest sellers (Klass 2020). Consumer confidence provides the foundation for the growth of a robust functional food market. When consumers lose confidence in health claims and health benefits, the whole system suffers (de Boer 2021). The public health benefits of functional foods may remain unrecognised. It is, therefore, of paramount importance that food claims are accurate, up-to-date, based on scientific evidence, and understandable for consumers. The system may also need to be adapted to meet the changing needs of consumers who are demanding more information from their food industry, including improved information visibility.

The food world is changing, where new foods are formulated, new production and delivery methods are introduced, and the system is increasingly digital. When applying the precautionary principle, it would be better to play it safe and do not introduce health claims or implicit therapeutic claims. Australia needs to overhaul regulatory measures and introduce rigorous and independent review of the self-justification process, coupled with increased oversight and inspection. This will give Australian consumers reasonable confidence in health claims on functional foods and their regulation.

The age-old problem of marketers pushing the envelope with product development and upselling, balanced against consumer ignorance and slow government response times to fill gaps, reveals a dire situation that benefits neither the consumer nor the business. That is not to say Australia's processes are lacking, but the machinery in place to achieve an outcome for society is subpar. In Europe, there is a strictly regulated procedure to approve health claims on foods and an EU list of permitted health claims. The same rules apply to the 27 countries of EU. The European regulatory system has been criticised, especially by nutritionists, food scientists, and food companies. The process of approving health claims is demanding and time-consuming, and impossible for small food businesses. The requirements for scientific evidence are extremely strict. For example, European consumers cannot read about the health benefits of probiotics in food labels. The roles of EFSA and the European Commission are unclear. Political concerns can sometimes override scientific evidence.

7.10 Conclusion

A comparative analysis of the regulation of health claims on functional foods showed, among other things, that effective controls appear necessary in developed countries such as Australia and the European Union. Although similar principles influence regulation, businesses face different rules and challenges and are constrained by differing regulatory procedures in the two areas. The analysis shed light on how Australia and the EU might deal with the challenges posed by the regulation. It offered a perspective on how to deal with some of the constraints and limitations found in regulation. However, limitations were identified that hampered a comprehensive analysis, in which we faced challenges usually found in a comparative study.

Comparing different approaches to solve a similar problem shows how problems can be approached in more than one way, but it has proven impossible to identify exactly comparable measures or benchmarks. Even if it were possible, it would not be possible to get an accurate scale. For example, the terminology used in one country might not exactly match the terminology used in another country. The terms can cover either a broader or a narrower range of categories. In addition, factors that have a significant impact on regulation in one country would not necessarily result in a similar impact in another. For example, some countries have more advanced technologies than others, and this has contributed to the wider dissemination of information.

In other countries, strong public interest groups challenge the freedom of information. These components influence the mechanics of health claims regulation, and determining a comparable point is not without its challenges. We acknowledge that each nation has a unique combination of regulatory strategies that were developed gradually and through various influences such as politics, culture, and social and economic structures. These combinations made it difficult to claim that a given factor would lead to a similar outcome in another country. Another challenge is also to achieve a balance between factors. The total ban on health claims made on food can undoubtedly simplify the administrative burden of regulatory control and enforcement but at the expense of several factors.

The form of reform must strike a balance between factors reform that does not unduly burden corporations but at the same time addresses the malevolence that corporations can bring. In addition, it must strike a balance between preventing the spread of unsubstantiated or medical claims and ensuring a flow of information for consumers that can facilitate informed decisions about their health. Finding the balance between these two extremes is not an easy task. To overcome these limitations and challenges, we analysed how the existing regulation of health claims on functional foods can be improved. This is possible because the key aspects of regulation compared, provided a framework for understanding the fundamentals of health claim regulation that policymakers can use to help shape the regulatory system.

Essentially, each country and its systems and processes highlight well-intentioned common goals aimed at protecting consumers while encouraging business innovation. The need to give the industry sufficient scope for much-needed development, freedom, and transparency is measured against government controls, which must be effective and, above all, fast. This is not an easy compromise to reach, but we believe that the foregoing (albeit initial) examination of each system in the nominated developed countries, such as Australia and the European Union, and selecting the best processes from those countries, offer us the best opportunity. We also recognise that much more investigative work needs to be done to achieve this.

In addition, the role of companies is crucial. Not only, as suggested in the previous paragraph, by creating a fertile and innovative environment for business, but business should be doing good for society and its broader stakeholders. While there must be an obvious structural element for this in the company's individual strategic and operational plans, there is also an essential ethical and social responsibility context that the company must serve. The greater good does not have to cost the company the bottom line, it can, in fact, be a sound and profitable business decision.

It is also important that a company can positively influence government policy for the benefit of all. After all, regulations on food health claims are just one of the possible regulatory ways to shape the food environment and influence consumer diets that have been lost. Creating healthy food environments, especially for children, and creating tax incentives for consumers also require nutrient profiling. Focusing government efforts on claims must not distract attention from the big picture of regulating food products, outlets, pricing, and advertising in general, which benefits food consumers and businesses. This then brings us to the next chapter which deals with corporate social responsibility of the food business in more detail.

References

Adefegha, SA 2018, 'Functional foods and nutraceuticals as dietary intervention in chronic diseases; novel perspectives for health promotion and disease prevention', *Journal of Dietary Supplements*, *15*(6), pp.977–1009.

Alkhatib, A, Tsang, C, Tiss, A, Bahorun, T, Arefanian, H, Barake, R, Khadir, A & Tuomilehto, J 2017, 'Functional foods and lifestyle approaches for diabetes prevention and management', *Nutrients*, *9*(12), p.1310.

Bigliardi, B & Galati, F 2013, 'Innovation trends in the food industry: The case of functional foods', *trends Food Science & Technology*, 31, pp.118–129.

Bucchini, L 2019, 'Nutrition and health claims in Europe: Oils & fats related claims, regulatory and labeling challenges', *OCL*, *26*, p.48.

Codex Alimentarius 1997, 'Guidelines for use of nutrition and health claims (CAC/GL 23-1997)', World Health Organization and the Food and Agriculture Organization of the United Nations, Rome, Italy.

Condon-Paoloni, D, Yeatman, HR & Grigonis-Deane, E 2015, 'Health-related claims on food labels in Australia: Understanding environmental health officers' roles and implications for policy', *Public Health Nutrition*, *18*(1), pp.81–88.

Craswell, R 1985, 'Interpreting deceptive advertising', *Boston University Law Review*, *65*(4), p.658.

Craswell, R 1997, '"Compared to what?" The use of control ads in deceptive advertising litigation', *Antitrust Law Journal*, *65*(3), pp.757–791.

Curran, MA 2002, 'Nutrition labelling: Perspectives of a bi-national agency for Australia and New Zealand', *Asia Pacific Journal of Clinical Nutrition*, *11*(2), pp.S72–S76.

Das, R & Biswas, S 2016, 'Nutraceutical-prophylactic and therapeutic role of functional food in health', *Journal of Nutrition & Food Sciences*, *6*(4), accessed 17 June 2021, www.omicsonline.org/open-access/nutraceuticalprophylactic-and-therapeutic-role-of-functional-food-inhealth-2155-9600-1000527.php?aid=76424.

de Boer, A 2021, 'Fifteen years of regulating nutrition and health claims in Europe: The past, the present and the future', *Nutrients*, *13*(5).

de Boer, A & Bast, A 2015a, 'Stakeholders' perception of the nutrition and health claim regulation', *International Journal of Food Sciences and Nutrition*, *66*(3), pp.321–328.

de Boer, A & Bast, A 2015b, 'International legislation on nutrition and health claims', *Food Policy*, *55*, pp.61–70.

de Moraes Prata Gaspar, MC, Garcia, AM & Larrea-Killinger, C 2020, 'How would you define healthy food? Social representations of Brazilian, French and Spanish Dietitians and Young Laywomen', *Appetite*, 153, p.104728.

Department of Health and Aged Care & Australian Government 2024, 'The TGA's risk management approach', www.tga.gov.au/resources/resource/guidance/tgas-risk-management-approach.

Díaz, LD, Fernández-Ruiz, V & Cámara, M 2020, 'An international regulatory review of food health-related claims in functional food products labeling', *Journal of Functional Foods*, *68*.

Diez-Gutiérrez, L, San Vicente, L, Barrón, LJR, del Carmen Villarán, M & Chávarri, M 2020, 'Gamma-aminobutyric acid and probiotics: Multiple health benefits and their future in the global functional food and nutraceuticals market', *Journal of Functional Foods*, *64*, p.103669.

European Commission 2020, 'Commission staff working document evaluation of the regulation (EC) No 1924/2006 on nutrition and health claims made on foods with regard to nutrient profiles and health claims made on plants and their preparations and of the general regulatory framework for their use in foods {SWD(2020) 96 final}', https://ec.europa.eu/food/system/files/2020-05/labelling_nutrition-claims_swd_2020-95_part-1.pdf.

Fabbri, A, Holland, TJ & Bero, LA 2018, 'Food industry sponsorship of academic research: Investigating commercial bias in the research agenda', *Public Health Nutrition*, *21*(18), pp.3422–3430.

Federal Trade Commission 'Health claims and fitness claim', *Health and Fitness Claim*, www.ftc.gov/news-events/media-resources/truth-advertising/health-claims.

Food Regulation Secretariat 2024, last updated 10 January 2024, www.foodregulation.gov.au/activities-committees/secretariat.

FSANZ n.d., *Safe food for life*, accessed 1 March 2024, www.foodstandards.gov.au/.

FSANZ 2023a, *About FSANZ*, last updated 21 December 2023, accessed 1 April 2024, www.foodstandards.gov.au/about-us.

FSANZ 2023b, *Food standard code*, last updated 6 December 2023, accessed 1 April 2024, www.foodstandards.gov.au/code/Pages/default.aspx.

FSANZ 2023c, *Nutrition, health and related claims*, last updated 21 December 2023, accessed 1 April 2024, www.foodstandards.gov.au/business/labelling/nutrition-health-and-related-claims.

FSANZ 2023d, *Information on establishing food-health relationships for general level health claims*, last updated 6 December 2023, accessed 1 April 2024, www.foodstandards.gov.au/publications/Guidance-on-establishing-food-health-relationships-for-general-level-health-claims.

FSANZ 2023e, *Notified food-health relationships to make a health claim*, last updated September 2023, accessed 1 April 2024, https://fhr.foodstandards.gov.au/.

FSANZ 2023f, *Nutrition, health and related claims*, last updated 21 December 2023, accessed 1 April 2024, www.foodstandards.gov.au/business/labelling/nutrition-health-and-related-claims.

FSANZ 2024a, *Food enforcement contacts*, last updated 14 February 2024, accessed 1 April 2024, www.foodstandards.gov.au/about/foodenforcementcontacts/Pages/default.aspx.

FSANZ 2024b, *Consideration of European union-authorised health claims*, last updated 5 January 2024, accessed 1 April 2024, www.foodstandards.gov.au/business/labelling/Consideration-of-European-Union-authorised-health-claim.

FSANZ 2024c, *Notifying a self-substantiated food-health relationship*, last updated 22 February 2024, accessed 1 April 2024, www.foodstandards.gov.au/business/labelling/nutrition-health-and-related-claims/notifying-fhr.

Gidlöf, K, Wallin, A, Holmqvist, K & Møgelvang-Hansen, P 2013, 'Material distortion of economic behaviour and everyday decision quality', *Journal of Consumer Policy*, *36*(4), pp.389–402.

Green, D & Loualiche, E 2021, 'State and local government employment in the COVID-19 crisis', *Journal of Public Economics*, *193*, p.104321.

Greene, HL, Prior, T & Frier, HI 2001, 'Foods, health claims, and the law: Comparisons of the United States and Europe', *Obesity Research*, *9*(S11), pp.276S–283S.

Gupta, E & Mishra, P 2021, 'Functional food with some health benefits, so called superfood: A review', *Current Nutrition & Food Science*, *17*(2), pp.144–166.

Heather, H & David, B 2019, Who are the experts? Examining the online promotion of misleading and harmful nutrition information, 1st edn, Routledge.

Hieke, S, Cascanette, T, Pravst, I, Kaur, A, Van Trijp, H, Verbeke, W & Grunert, KG 2016, 'The role of health-related claims and symbols in consumer behaviour: The CLYMBOL project', *Agro Food Industry Hi-Tech*, *27*(3), pp.26–29.

Hoffmann, D & Schwartz, J 2016, 'Stopping deceptive health claims: The need for a private right of action under federal law', *American Journal of Law & Medicine*, *42*(1), pp.53–84.

Holden, A, Nanayakkara, S, Skinner, J, Spallek, H & Sohn, W 2021, 'What do Australian health consumers believe about commercial advertisements and testimonials? A survey on health service advertising', *BMC Public Health*, *21*(1), p.74.

Kahneman, D & Patrick, E 2011, *Thinking, fast and slow*, Allen Lane.

Kim, JY, Kim, SJ & Jeong, S 2019, 'Chapter 31 – regulations on health/functional foods in Korea', in D Bagchi (ed.), *Nutraceutical and functional food regulations in the United States and around the world*, 3rd edn, Academic Press, pp.497–507, www.sciencedirect.com/science/article/pii/B9780128164679000319.

Klass, G 2020, 'False advertising law and new private law', in A Gold et al. (eds.), *False Advertising Law, in Oxford Handbook of New Private Law*, Oxford University Press (forthcoming).

Kušar, A, Žmitek, K, Lähteenmäki, L, Raats, MM & Pravst, I 2021, 'Comparison of requirements for using health claims on foods in the European Union, the USA, Canada, and Australia/New Zealand', *Comprehensive Reviews in Food Science and Food Safety*, *20*(2), pp.1307–1332.

Kwak, N-S & Jukes, DJ 2001, 'Functional foods. Part 2: The impact on current regulatory terminology', *Food Control*, *12*, pp 109–117.

Lähteenmäki-Uutela, A 2010, Foodstuffs and medicines as legal categories in the EU and China: Functional foods as a borderline case, LAP LAMBERT Academic Publishing.

Lutz, M, Arancibia, M & Stojanova, J 2019, 'Using systematic reviews in the scientific substantiation of health properties of foods and food constituents', *Medwave*, *19*(6), p.7664.

MacFarlane, D, Hurlstone, MJ & Ecker, UKH 2020, 'Protecting consumers from fraudulent health claims: A taxonomy of psychological drivers, interventions, barriers, and treatments', *Social Science & Medicine*, *259*, p.112790.

Merten-Lentz, K 2020, 'EU health claims and botanicals: Back in the spotlight amid Covid-19 crisis', *Food Navigator*, www.foodnavigator.com/Article/2020/05/08/EU-health-claims-and-botanicals-Back-in-the-spotlight-amid-COVID-19-crisis.

Neo, P 2019, 'Lack of evidence – researchers demands stricter FSANZ governance over food health relationships', www.foodnavigator-asia.com/Article/2019/04/10/Lack-of-evidence-Researchers-demand-stricter-FSANZ-governance-of-food-health-relationship-claims#.

Nystrand, BT & Olsen, SO 2020, 'Consumers' attitudes and intentions toward consuming functional foods in Norway', *Food Quality and Preference*, *80*, p.103827.

Reeve, B & Gostin, LO 2019, '"Big" food, tobacco, and alcohol: Reducing industry influence on noncommunicable disease prevention laws and policies comment on "addressing NCDs: Challenges from industry market promotion and interferences"', *International Journal of Health Policy and Management*, *8*(7), pp.450–454.

Richards, JI 2021, 'Key concepts in advertising: Deceptiveness', *Advertising & Society Quarterly*, *22*(3).

Roetzel, PG 2019, 'Information overload in the information age: A review of the literature from business administration, business psychology, and related disciplines with a bibliometric approach and framework development', *Business Research*, *12*(2), pp.479–522.

Stanton, R 2016, 'Changing eating patterns versus adding nutrients to processed foods', *Medical Journal of Australia*, *204*(11), pp.398–398.

Topol, EJ 2004, 'Failing the public health: Rofecoxib, Merch, and the FDA', *New England Journal of Medicine*, *351*(17), p.1707.
Topolska, K, Florkiewicz, A & Filipiak-Florkiewicz, A 2021, 'Functional food – consumer motivations and expectations', *International Journal of Environmental Research and Public Health*, *18*(10).
Victoria State Government, Better Health Channel 'Diet and heart risks', www.betterhealth.vic.gov.au/health/conditionsandtreatments/heart-disease-and-food.
Wang, M-Y, West, BJ, Jensen, CJ, Nowicki, D, Su, C, Palu, AK & Anderson, G 2002, 'Morinda citrifolia (Noni): A literature review and recent advances in Noni research', *Acta Pharmacologica Sinica*, *23*(12), pp.1127–1141.
Wu, Y & Geylani, T 2020, 'Regulating deceptive advertising: False claims and skeptical consumers', *Marketing Science*, *39*(4), pp.788–806.
Zawistowski, J 2019, 'Chapter 33 – regulation of functional foods in selected Asian countries in the Pacific Rim*', in D Bagchi (ed.), *Nutraceutical and functional food regulations in the United States and around the world*, 3rd edn, Academic Press, pp.523–560, www.sciencedirect.com/science/article/pii/B9780128164679000332.

8 Enriching Environmental Law and Improving Food Security Through an Innovative Interpretation of Human and Natural Rights

Alessandra Telch, Siva Barathi (Sharl) Marimuthu, and Anu Lähteenmäki-Uutela

8.1 Introduction

Can acknowledging human rights, in particular, the right to food and the right to a healthy environment alongside granting legal personality and rights to natural entities like landscape and ecosystem, bring about a viable solution to food insecurity and its related concerns?

It is essential to explore the notion of human and of nature via an innovative interpretation of human and natural rights; this will enhance the legal system with a fresh understanding of human and natural rights. Our initial inquiry is about the basis of human identity. By examining this question, we can begin to unravel the unique attributes that define us as a species. Our second inquiry is about assessing the extent to which we differ from all other forms of life. In this regard, exploring a new perspective to the interpretation of human and natural rights is important. To integrate this new approach into the legal systems that acknowledge both the extrinsic and intrinsic value of nature, a review of the bases of anthropology is necessary.

Human nature is a concept that denotes the fundamental dispositions and characteristics that humans are said to have naturally. The term is often used to denote the essence of humankind, or what it truly means to be human; this concept has been the subject of discussion and debate for centuries and it continues to be a topic of deep contemplation. Biologists search for human nature in our genes (Von Bertalanffy 1956), and social constructivists in our practices and institutions (Armstrong 2002). Clearly, humans are parts of natural ecosystems, and our food consumption practices, food cultures, and food security rely on ecosystem services.

8.2 What Does Granting Rights to Nature Mean?

An often overlooked yet deep-seated question is what granting rights to nature means and/or entails. As eloquently explained by Borrás, granting rights to nature is to "recognise our interconnectedness with the natural world",

DOI: 10.4324/9781003392279-8

acknowledging its legal "right to exist, persist and maintain its vital circle" (Borrás 2016). This mindset could significantly contribute to the evolution of legal systems and to the restructuring of economies to adjust to the planetary boundaries (O'Neill et al. 2018). It entails moving away from considering nature as a passive object or property to an "actor", an entity that shapes the world through its various expressions – animals, plants, landscapes, and ecosystems.

The difference between humans and non-human living objects is in the non-physical element: humans can comprehend and communicate verbally. The ability to converse in languages is intricately related to the mental sphere, with language serving as the most prominent expression. Language has been recognised as the primary means through which humans express their understanding. Consequently, non-human entities lack linguistic capacities and therefore find themselves in a passive role as subjects of human perception and innovation.

Humans, on the other hand, establish a justification for this privileged position and thereby hinder any effort to liberate anthropology from its inherent anthropocentrism. Yet non-human entities representing nature aspire to take on active roles, they can overcome the passivity imposed by limitations of symbolic expressions. Even if humans still have a limited understanding on this at present, nature is deemed as capable of thinking and communicating through various means. This involves recognising the capacity for emotions, cognitive processes, memory, the creation of unique global views, and the ability to communicate these perspectives to their own species and across species (Eduardo 2013).

The shift from the traditional narrative to recognising nature as a legal entity possessing significant capabilities facilitates forging a much more diverse and deeper connection between human and nature. It goes beyond the common belief that humans are exploiting or merely preserving nature for their own benefit. It emphasises the connection between human and nature and highlights that humans can only exist and truly understand themselves in this complex web of ecosystems and the natural environment. Put differently, humans should focus their efforts on preserving and improving the ecosystem, which broadly includes the relationship between animals and plants and their surroundings – water, soil, nutrients along with all living organisms. Like humans, these animals and plants deserve the fundamental right to survive, flourish, and reproduce.

In practice, however, contemporary human activities are the cause of disruption to entire ecosystems, with food production being the primary factor. Food represents a vital aspect of ecosystem services; addressing not only basic survival needs but also encompassing cultural and social dimensions (Choruma and Odume 2019). Regrettably, the downgrading of food status to merely another commodity has proven to have adverse impact, leading to the breach of basic human rights and the rights of nature. Reorienting food production towards sustainable agricultural practices can bring about a balance that allows for food production whilst also protecting the ecosystem services including water purification, climate control, and biodiversity of, for example, soil microbes and pollinators (Lamm et al. 2023).

Conversely, large-scale industrial agriculture is attributed to driving deforestation and other conversion of native habitats into cultivated lands. This results in loss of biodiversity, extensive water consumption for agriculture and livestock, and the transformation of recreational spaces into cropland (do Carmo Pônzio et al. 2023). Furthermore, this approach undermines cultural and landscape heritage and violates the rights of indigenous peoples of their lands, traditional livelihoods, and lifeways (Scheidel et al. 2023).

8.3 Human Rights-Based Approach and Legal Rights to Nature

What is the significance of being a holder of legal rights? In general terms, legal rights provide individuals with entitlement protection in various areas including land ownership, property, intellectual property, trademarks, and more. Proof of ownership in the form of certificates is often needed to show the ownership (Kumalasari 2021). Rights-holders are individuals or social groups that have specific entitlements in relation to specific duty-bearers. In the context of human rights, all human beings are rights-holders under the Universal Declaration of Human Rights (UDHR) (United Nations General Assembly 1948). This Declaration, ratified in 1948 by representatives from diverse regions each with its different legal and cultural background, underscores the universal nature of these rights, as can be noted in Article 1:

> **All** human beings are born free and equal in dignity and rights.

A human rights-based approach goes beyond acknowledging that the entitlement of rights-holders should be upheld, respected, safeguarded, and acknowledged. It also regards rights-holders as proactive individuals or entities whether acting individually or collectively through organisations and groups that represent their interests (Chalabi 2023). Despite this fundamental principle intended to embrace all of humanity, it is evident that in the ratifying states of the UN International Covenant on Civil and Political Rights or the UN International Covenant on Economic, Social and Cultural Rights, all individuals and groups do not have their human rights fully respected, protected, and fulfilled. Often, rights are incompletely realised for women and girls, members of racial and ethnic minorities, indigenous peoples, refugees, and young, old, or disabled people (United Nations Office for the High Commissioner of Human Rights 2010).

The challenge in achieving universal human rights stems from several factors. One primary factor is the multifaceted nature of a human rights approach where interests of one category of right holders may not align with the interests of others because of the underlying cultural, political, and social contexts. For example, landowners and non-landowners often have different interests and different rights (Lähteenmäki-Uutela et al. 2021). These differences lead to conflicts and hinder the simultaneous realisation of all rights. These obstacles and conflicts of interest can, however, be overcome in time. In fact, the concept of human rights is fluid; it is adaptable and evolves in response to the development and affirmation of new social, political, and cultural paradigms. This evolution results in the recognition of further rights such as environmental rights or the expansion of the categories of actors that can benefit from them, thereby creating new rights-holders such as nature itself. Traditionally, nature does not possess the features of a rights holder, it in fact has no independent legal status, the damages it eventually sustains do not factor in the determination of the repairing action, and it is not the recipient of compensation. In fact, natural objects have been historically treated by the law, and to a greater extent, by people, "as objects for man to conquer and master and use (. . .). The dominant motive has been to conserve them for us – for the greatest good of the greatest number of human beings" (Stone 1972).

As we explore further into the human rights-oriented approach to nature protection, we will see that the scope of protecting nature expands proportionally with our ability to establish connections between human wellbeing and the health of an ecosystem. The significant relationship between the continued existence and prosperity of humans on the one hand and the protection of ecosystems and landscapes on the other has gained prominence through the recognition of "ecosystem services" as the foundation for human life and development. The term was introduced by the Millennium Ecosystem Assessment in the 2003 and 2005 reports (Millennium Ecosystem Assessment 2003, 2005). It encompasses the benefits that people derive from ecosystems in terms of provisioning services, regulating services, cultural services, and supporting services. However, ecosystems are today susceptible to human pressure and drivers, albeit direct and indirect, leading to biodiversity loss and their capacity to provide those services (Lü et al. 2020). Consequently, these drivers have a detrimental impact on various aspects of human wellbeing, including water, food, health, livelihood and income, social relations and culture, security, and more (Sena and Ebi 2020). Destroying an ecosystem ruins the basis for the realisation of a good life and human rights for all (UN General Assembly 2019, 2021, 2022).

8.4 The Birth of Rights to Nature

The first specific instances of "formally" recognised rights to nature were established without the current consciousness about the complex relationship between man and nature. Therefore, they are inadequate to safeguard the interests of nature, especially when challenged by commercial and business interests. The development of national parks and protected areas to protect ecosystems, wildlife, and biodiversity is an example of such initiative. Initially, national governments created these natural parks with conservation in mind, shielding specific areas from human interference to ensure that future generations can continue to appreciate them. However, these initiatives are constrained by their geographical boundaries, objectives, and the fundamental principles upon which they were founded.

In this sense, the Act establishing the Yellowstone National Park recites:

> the **tract of land** in the Territories of Montana and Wyoming, lying near the head-waters of the Yellowstone River, and described as follows, . . . is hereby reserved and withdrawn from settlement, occupancy or sale under the laws of the United States, and dedicated and set apart as a public park or pleasuring-ground **for the benefit and enjoyment of the people**.
>
> (Miller 2010)

A famous essay by the explorer Adolf Erik Nordenskiöld on the establishment of the first European national parks through Sweden's Conservation Act of 1909 highlighted the adverse effect of the spreading human inventions across the countryside. He viewed this expansion as a harm to future generations, who might not even be able to imagine the landscape that their forefathers once knew (Niemi 2012). Around the world, we are now witnessing courts, lawyers, and policymakers engaging in exploring ways to contribute to the protection of ecosystems. Conferring rights to ecosystems is deemed a way to protect species from extinction. Courts have now begun to acknowledge environmental rights to establish responsibilities towards ecosystems.

Individuals have taken legal actions against States and other entities, citing commitments made by the international community and which were formalised in international environmental agreements. Indeed, the Paris Agreement on the climate and the Rio Declaration on biodiversity (Paris Agreement 2015; Rio Declaration 2003). They filed lawsuits when they believe that a particular action or lack of action is harming the environment, which in turn violates their rights to life, health, and healthy environment. On 9 April 2024, public hearings were held at the European Court of Human Rights on three climate change and human rights rulings (*KlimaSeniorinnen v. Switzerland*; *Carême v. France*; *Duarte Agostinho and Others v. Portugal and 32 Other States*), establishing a legal precedent informing how human rights law is interpreted to protect citizens from the climate crisis across all member states of the Council of Europe.

In this context, the recent judgment of the European Court of Human Rights in the case of *KlimaSeniorinnen v. Switzerland* is of particular interest. The Court went as far as to determine when and how states must take action to mitigate the effects of climate change to adequately protect their citizens – not without raising concerns of those who find it has gone too far beyond its role. With this judgment, the European Court of Human Rights condemned Switzerland for violating the European Convention on Human Rights. The case was originally brought by 2,500 women who complained of the "failure of the Swiss authorities to mitigate the effects of climate change", which they claimed was having a negative impact on their living conditions and health. Initial interpretations on the judgment have already been issued by experts in the field.

Analysing scientific evidence, severity of consequences, irreversibility of impacts, and the global nature of phenomenon, the Court found that climate protection shall carry considerable weight in weighing up any competing considerations. In its reasoning, the Court provided two requirements. First, the setting of overall ambition in relation to which the scientific and political consensus limits the discretion of individual states. Second, the selection of individual measures to meet such targets, for which states have a wider margin of appreciation. Transposing these to the context of climate risks requires states to set in place effective measures aiming at "net neutrality" within the next decades. States are required to act timely, and in an appropriate and consistent manner. Short-term action is necessary to avoid shifting the burden to the future generations.

The Court then laid out a test to assess whether the State's climate policies comply with obligations under the ECHR. In brief, states must:

- specify a target timeline for achieving carbon neutrality,
- set out intermediate greenhouse gas emissions reduction targets and pathways,
- Provide evidence showing whether they have duly complied,
- Keep the relevant greenhouse gas reduction targets updated with due diligence, and
- Act in good time and in an appropriate and consistent manner.

The Court noted several deficiencies in relation to compliance by Switzerland with these obligations, namely, absence of regulatory framework post-2024, absence of quantified national greenhouse gas budget, and past failure to meet greenhouse gas targets, and concluded for a violation of the right to privacy and family life (which the Court interpreted as freedom from environmental threats to one's personal life). The Court also gave its opinion on the right of access to a court, which is deemed to have been violated by the Swiss tribunals, since all three levels of judicial bodies in Switzerland rejected the case. Through the recognition of new rights of the European citizens, the Court demonstrates its innovative approach and pivotal role in shaping European law, while being a potential vehicle for the acknowledgement of rights in nature itself.

Other relevant actions are under the scrutiny of the Court (*Duarte Agostinho and Others vs. Portugal and 32 Other States*). Climate cases are justified by the idea that the rights of humans are harmed by states by not acting effectively for mitigating climate change. Human rights such as indigenous rights, rights of the child, and rights to a healthy environment now feature prominently in these legal actions. This perspective represents an innovative but not entirely revolutionary interpretation on human-nature relations. In terms of litigation, most cases in recent times still revolve around issues such as environmental impact assessment of projects and environmental permitting. These include projects such as erecting power plants, extracting natural resource extraction, developing renewable energy, and enabling climate adaptation.

The determinations made today on whether to grant permits for fossil fuel projects or to require renewable and circular projects can have an impact on the wellbeing of children and future generations. Environmental laws and environmental permitting do not entirely address climate change concerns. While there may be some regulations in place that govern environmental impacts, such as soil, air, and water, this may not address greenhouse gas emissions. Furthermore, mechanisms such as carbon trading or carbon quotas are viewed separately to these environmental impacts (Silvo 2021). Courts must now grapple with issues such as whether individuals can legally demand the gradual elimination of fossil fuels under the framework of international and national laws and acts.

One legal issue is whether forest fires occurring in a specific ecosystem and rainforest constitute a violation of the human rights of traditional and indigenous communities living in the rainforest (ADPF 746 Brazil). In this regard, the case of *Future Generations v. Ministry of the Environment and Others* (2018) is an interesting one, where the Supreme Court of Justice of Colombia has recognised the Colombian Amazon as a subject of rights that is entitled to protection, conservation, maintenance, and restoration led by the State and the Colombian territories. The Court referred to its previous decision where it declared the Atrato River as a subject of rights in 2016. An example in Europe is the granting of rights to nature is in the case of Vjosa River in Albania. It is the only wild river in Europe left, flowing freely from its origin in the Greek mountains down to the Adriatic almost without any deviation or infrastructure imposed by humans.

The river represents a complex ecosystem housing thousands of animal species, among them endangered ones. After several actions undertaken by local and international organisations advocating for its protection, the Albanian government agreed to the creation of the first Wild River National Park, and the establishment of a new legal category of Protected Areas. This legal innovation has a particularly important meaning in the local historical and political context, characterised by the Communist past and the challenge of ongoing democratisation process, of which the declaration of the National Park created the favourable conditions to change perspective and gradually establish the river as a legal personhood, addressing environmental concerns that were not considered before (Acevedo 2023).

Two other countries that granted rights to nature are New Zealand and India. In 2017, the Whanganui River in New Zealand and the Ganges and Yamuna Rivers in India were granted legal status. In Australia, in the State of Victoria, a law protecting the Yarra River and its First Nation custodianship was passed (O'Donnell and Talbot 2018). The Murray-Darling River System (Rights of Nature) Bill 2021 in New South Wales and the Rights of Nature and Future Generations Bill 2019 in Western Australia came close to passing but are yet to progress further (Alexandra et al. 2023). Globally, lawsuits to protect ecosystems and the climate are made against governments, corporations, and individuals. These lawsuits serve as a driving force for courts to take on an active role in ensuring implementation of international agreements, local constitutions, and local environmental laws. Indeed, these rulings can inspire legislators with new interpretations and legal solutions.

8.5 Legal and Cultural Prerequisites

There are challenges and obstacles involved in enforcing the concept of rights of nature and in the role of law addressing these challenges. This raises important questions that are discussed in this section. These obstacles can be categorised into two main types: general and specific obstacles. General obstacles can be traced back to human cultural heritage while specific ones relate to the specific obstacle pertaining to the intricate legal premises required for a comprehensive grasp and application of the rights of nature.

Within the realm of general obstacles, the most significant challenge is the ability to confer legal personality to entities that have traditionally been without one. Today, conferring legal rights directly to nature itself poses difficulties since it is not commonly perceived as an entity capable of possessing such rights. However, the same mechanism that permitted in the past to recognise the existence of corporations and nations, could also be applied to ecosystems. Christopher Stone's perception in *Should Trees Have Standing* predicted the question we are currently attempting to reconstruct. He examined legislative developments and legal precedents to facilitate the ideas we are exploring today.

> Each time that there is a movement to confer rights onto some new entity, the proposal is bound to sound odd or frightening or laughable.

There are illustrations in terms of fictional reality: those born from the creation of fictitious elements and their relatively widespread acceptance, for example, money, nations, as well as rights, laws, and corporations. This concept is appropriately described in the *Legend of Peugeot* by Harari (2014). It clarifies how the rise of the renowned automotive company marks the establishment of a fresh collective narration or myth; one that thrives solely within the collective imagination and endures while this collective imagination persists. Over time, the influence of fictional reality has gradually increased, to the extent that today, as pointed out by Harari (2014), "the survival of trees and rivers . . . depends on the imaginary stories that *Homo sapiens* has invented".

Just as modern societies, gods, law, and judicial systems require a foundation in a shared belief and narrative to exist, the effective enforcement of the rights of nature relies on a strong foundation accepted by a sufficiently large community. Another significant obstacle revolves around defining the identity of "nature" as a rights holder. How do we define nature? In our inclination to protect and engage with the natural world, humans tend to prioritise the animal world at the expense of the plant kingdom.

Renowned botanist Stefano Mancuso addressed this seemingly straightforward yet critical issue. He pointed out that our understanding of reality is closely tied to mechanisms and concepts inherent to the animal kingdom, despite plants constituting 85% of the living beings, while animals make up 0.3% (Mancuso 2017). In the scientific community, it is often the case that findings in the plant world are not considered legitimate until they are aligned in the animal world. Likewise, movements advocating for recognition and protection of animal rights have been more prevalent, compared to movements for the recognition of rights to plants and marine or terrestrial ecosystems.

This topic remains highly discussed and unresolved, and the transition from advocating for the protection of animal rights to recognising nature's rights in its entirety may seem illogical to those individuals currently engaged in efforts to implement effective instruments for the protection of animals. Even if we can identify the entity to which rights are granted, there are still questions about what kind of rights nature should have. Should it have the same kind of rights as humans? Additionally, when there is an entity with rights, there is also someone responsible for ensuring those rights are upheld, namely the duty-bearer. Does this mean that there should be a government authority tasked with monitoring and holding individuals accountable if they violate the rights of nature?

While these questions remain unanswered, legislative initiatives have emerged globally, transcending factors such as the form of government, economic system, and the legal framework. What distinguishes these efforts is the approach and method they employ. In developing countries, there is a growing trend to recognise the rights to a healthy environment and the rights of nature in newly drafted constitutional charters. For instance, the recently rejected draft of the new Chilean Constitution included provisions that recognised individuals' right to access water and granted nature itself the right to protection and respect. This raised concerns among businesses and investors.

In contrast, developed countries that established constitutional charters are in the process of integrating and revising these aspects in the original text. For example, in February 2022, the Italian Parliament approved the amendment to Articles 9 and 41 of the Constitution, extending the Constitutional protection to the environment and ecosystems. These changes clarified the terms of applicability of environmental crimes introduced in 2015.

The modified articles are as follows (changes indicated in capital letters).

> Articolo 9: La Repubblica promuove lo sviluppo della cultura e la ricerca scientifica e tecnica. Tutela il paesaggio e il patrimonio storico e artistico della Nazione. TUTELA L'AMBIENTE, LA BIODIVERSITÀ E GLI ECOSISTEMI, ANCHE NELL'INTERESSE DELLE FUTURE

GENERAZIONI. LA LEGGE DELLO STATO DISCIPLINA I MODI E LE FORME DI TUTELA DEGLI ANIMALI.

Article 9: The Republic promotes the development of culture and scientific and technical research. It protects the landscape and the historical and artistic heritage of the Nation. IT PROTECTS THE ENVIRONMENT, BIODIVERSITY AND ECOSYSTEMS, ALSO IN THE INTEREST OF FUTURE GENERATIONS. THE LAW OF THE STATE REGULATES THE WAYS AND FORMS OF PROTECTION OF ANIMALS.

Articolo 41: L'iniziativa economica privata è libera. Non può svolgersi in contrasto con l'utilità sociale o in modo da recare danno alla sicurezza, alla libertà, alla dignità umana, ALLA SALUTE, ALL'AMBIENTE. La legge determina i programmi e i controlli opportuni perché l'attività economica pubblica e privata possa essere indirizzata e coordinata a fini sociali E AMBIENTALI.

Article 41: Private economic initiative is free. It may not be carried out in conflict with social utility or in such a way as to harm security, freedom, human dignity, HEALTH, ENVIRONMENT. The law determines the programmes and appropriate controls so that public and private economic activity may be directed and coordinated for social AND ENVIRONMENTAL purposes.

Before these amendments were approved, the Italian constitutional text did not contain any references to the environment, except for a constitutional amendment in 2001, which introduced the subject of "environmental protection" among the exclusive state legislative powers. In the past, both the legal doctrine and the Italian Constitutional Court attempted to establish a constitutional basis for the environmental policies by relying on other provisions. First, through a broad interpretation of the concept of "landscape" as described in Article 9. Initially, this concept was primarily associated with aesthetics, but as environmental concerns gained importance, it evolved to encompass the protection of land and the ecosystem.

However, this interpretation failed to apply to situations where the environmental impact did not affect the physical "form" of the country such as the use of fertilisers in agriculture or air pollution. The judicial system subsequently interpreted the "right to health" (Article 32) as encompassing the right to a healthy environment. The second approach involved emphasising environmental protection as part of the "duties of solidarity" outlined in Article 2 of the Constitution. This interpretation is grounded on the assumption that the environment, rather than just an expression of a right, is fundamentally linked to the responsibilities of political, economic, and social solidarity – a principle explicitly stated in other European constitutional texts (Grasso 2006).

What does it entail to implement these new principles? It fundamentally involves integrating these valuables such as the environment, biodiversity, and ecosystem, into the critical decision-making process that the government, whether on a national or local level, undertakes when formulating policies and allocating resources. Take the construction of new works, for example, evaluating the suitability (and legitimacy) of a new project will no longer be driven solely based on preserving the "landscape" but also considering these other assets. The aim is to assess, on a case-by-case basis, whether the project will bring greater benefit to the environment, biodiversity, and ecosystems considering the interest of the future generations, than the potential harm it may cause to the landscape.

There are uncertainties regarding the introduction of this intergenerational responsibility, and it is unclear how it relates to the concept of sustainable development. The use of the term "also" raises questions about whether it refers to an existing interest of current generations or of the environment itself. Furthermore, it raises the question of *who* has the authority to protect the environment following the reform of the constitutional text.

8.6 Transitioning from Food as Commodity to Food as Common Good: Legal Instruments and Policies

Recognition of the importance of granting rights to nature for climate change mitigation, adaptation, and better living conditions is not something imposed top-down by the State and/or legislators to citizens. Instead, it is a process driven by individuals, groups, organisations, and entities in various forms, reflecting as a statement of the international community. States, along with non-state actors, are the uncommon stakeholders working to formalise the awareness that the social and ecological fragmentation seen in the current global framework can only be addressed through the recognition of the rights of nature.

All these actors share a common premise: that "everything in the world is connected" (Francis, Encyclical letter "Laudato Si: On Care for our Common Home"). They believe the key to ensuring the wellbeing of all beings (human and non-human) lies in shifting from an anthropocentric approach towards a holistic one. Among the ones most likely to appreciate this interconnectedness are those intimately connected to the natural world. This includes the indigenous communities living in harmony with their environment and, on a more practical level, farmers, and cattle breeders. Various agricultural paradigms advocate for the respect of nature and its expressions as the only way to ensure food safety and, more generally, the subsistence of humankind.

This revolutionary approach is embodied in the words and acts of R. Zierock, an agrarian philosopher and pioneer of the biodynamic wine scene. He believed that the ultimate goal of farmers shall be to create harmony between man and nature:

> Die Seele des Pflegers der Erde kann nur zufrieden und glücklich sein, wenn die Erde immerwährend lebt und die Herrlichkeit ihrer Schöpfung bewahrt wird.
>
> (Zierock 1995)

[The soul of the caretaker of the Earth can only be content and happy if the earth lives perpetually and the glory of its creation is preserved.]

To fully embrace this vision, we must undergo an intellectual and cultural transformation.

Nature should no longer be seen as mere property under the law but as a recognised legal entity with the right to exist and regenerate in all its forms. In essence, it calls for a profound reimagining of our relationship with the natural world. The disruption of the cultural and physical connection between people and nature has led to disastrous impacts on the environment and humans' health and livelihood. Food systems count today as the main threat to biodiversity, driven by an ongoing process of commodification of food, dilution of the supply chain, and agricultural and food policies diverging from sustainable development goals. If we are to meet the needs of the global population with respect to food safety and security, the shift from food as a commodity to a common good shall be prioritised.

As food security is one of the most relevant problems in the modern world economy, there has been a growing body of Food Laws and Regulations issued at a global level governing the production and trade of food, such as the Codex Alimentarius (the international food code established under the United Nations), and the various agreements related to food trade agreed under the WTO. With the deepening of the international division of labour, the development of world trade in agriculture and food, and the acceleration of globalisation, food has been depicted as a commodity: a private, economic good valued as a fungible resource, which is sold at a price determined by the (global) market and regulated by international agreements and subsidies.

However, in recent food discussions on food security, two trends can be noted. First, the importance of the role of government regulation. This stems from the idea that decisions or approaches to food security need to consider not only the technical aspects of the problem, but also the social, economic, environmental, and political aspects. This can be achieved only by the system of state economic regulation, and in this case, the private sector of the economy is given a secondary role. The state is recognised as having a dual function: it forms the country's food complex and regulates its activities in the market; it provides favourable legal, political, and organisational conditions for sustainable development, ensures food security from internal and external risks, and protects from threats.

The latest situation makes the state's regulatory role as a guarantor of food independence and security especially relevant. Second, the interdependence of the different concerns mentioned previously (social, economic, environmental, and political) favours the emergence of the idea of food as a common good: it is held in community, independently from its private or public ownership; it represents a non-fungible resource for peoples' livelihood, depending on its provenience and nutritional values. It is valued beyond pricing, considering all cultural, social, and environmental aspects connected to its production and consumption.

8.7 Conclusion

The chapter explored potential solutions for addressing concerns about food security and issues related to food security whilst also acknowledging basic human rights, in particular, rights to food and healthy environment. Alongside this, the chapter explores the notion of providing rights to nature as a viable solution for addressing food insecurity. It requires an in-depth analysis of legal and cultural framework for acknowledging, implementing, and enforcing these rights. We found the evolution towards this new awareness of the concept of right to nature to be complex. We learned that it would be ineffective to understand this concept solely through the lens of juridical-normative nature. When seeking progress, we need to consider a range of factors and not merely the laws. First, progress requires development and maturation of multiple cultural, social, and political premises; and second, focusing solely on law as expression of legislative power while neglecting other theories and interpretation will be superficial.

In real life, the legal dimension is not segregated from society, its people, and their land. In a globalised world, this means extending beyond geographical boundaries of states' territories (Natalino 2002). In other words, the complexity and interconnectedness that characterise the natural environments on which mankind depends cannot be adequately protected by focusing on regulatory development, in the absence of a profound understanding of the connection between human wellbeing and nature. There is a need to make humanity aware of the dependence of our species on the health of the Earth's ecosystems. This concept is well represented by the lengthy battle involving a wealthy Chilean industrialist and a group of local environmentalists, the outcome of which was cited by the New York Times as a "landmark transaction" and the case itself an example of "modern-day conservation" (David 2024).

The entrepreneur Robert Hagermann acquired over years the ownership of the Cochamó Valley, an ecologically sensitive area that was fragmented into more than 200 small properties, with the intention of developing a business through the construction of a hydroelectric facility. The Valley is surrounded by national parks and is habitat to animal and botanical species that would be irremediably harmed by any human intervention, which would inevitably determine a disruption of the ecosystem. This plan encountered resistance from Rodrigo Condeza, a local wilderness guide and leader of the nonprofit organisation Puelo Patagonia: after a period of intense discussions, the organisation proposed to buy the property, financing the purchase through fundraising. Finally, the businessman agreed: the land was sold to the conservationists, guaranteeing that this ecological corridor of inestimable value is preserved.

This outcome is achievable solely due to the exceptional alignment of legal, financial, and political resources. There shall be no legal instrument capable of protecting these lands as effectively as the activism of an increasing number of local and non-local environmentalists, the creation and management of a funding campaign, and the legal and administrative support of various non-profit organisations. This multisectoral mindset and approach, blending of components and parties, is indispensable to foster the safeguarding of nature by acknowledging its own rights. The premises are there for the judiciary to be recognised as an adequate medium to investigate the link between human subsistence and rights and the subsistence of animal and plant species and their own rights, understanding the need to do it in light of the overriding interest in the protection of nature.

References

Acevedo GT 2023, 'The Vjosa Wild River National Park as a legal innovation: Creating transformative change in Albanian river governance', https://studenttheses.uu.nl/handle/20.500.12932/45297.

ADPF 746 Brazil, Federal Supreme Court. (Fires in the Pantanal and the Amazon Forest).

Alexander E, Michael H & Rolf, 'Rights of nature are being recognised overseas: In Australia, local leadership gives cause for optimism', *The Conversation*, 27 December, https://theconversation.com/rights-of-nature-are-being-recognised-overseas-in-australia-local-leadership-gives-cause-for-optimism-212851.

Armstrong, SJ 2002, 'Being human: Ethics, environment, and our place in the world, by Anna L. Peterson. Berkeley, *University of California Press* (2001). Reviewed by Susan J. Armstrong', *Journal of Political Ecology*, *9*(1), pp.9–11, accessed 7 December 2023, https://doi.org/10.1525/california/9780520226548.003.0005.

Borrás, S 2016, 'New transitions from human rights to the environment to the rights of nature', *Transnational Environmental Law*, *5*(1), pp.113–143, https://doi.org/10.1017/s204710251500028x.

Chalabi, A 2023, 'A new theoretical model of the right to environment and its practical advantages', *Human Rights Law Review*, *23*(4), https://doi.org/10.1093/hrlr/ngad023.

Choruma, DJ & Odume, ON 2019, 'Exploring farmers' management practices and values of ecosystem services in an agroecosystem context – a case study from the Eastern Cape, South Africa', *Sustainability*, *11*(23), p.6567, https://doi.org/10.3390/su11236567.

David, G 2024, 'How locals saved "the Yosemite of South America"', *New York Times*.

do Carmo Pônzio, M, Pasqualotto, N, Zanin, M, Chiarello, AG & Pardini, R 2023, 'Landscape heterogeneity can partially offset negative effects of habitat loss on mammalian biodiversity in agroecosystems', *Journal of Applied Ecology*, *61*(1), pp.120–133, https://doi.org/10.1111/1365-2664.14543.

Duerte Agonstinho and Others vs. Portugal and 32 Others. European Court of Justice. Application no. 39371/20; Neubauer et al vs. Germany. Federal Constitutional Court. Case No. BvR 2656/18/1, BvR 78/20/1, BvR 96/20/1, BvR 288/20. Fliegenschnee et al. v. Federal Ministry for Digitalisation and Business Location. Administrative Court of Vienna.

Eduardo, K 2013, *How forests think: Towards anthropology beyond the human*, The Regents of the University of California.

Francis, Encyclical letter Laudato Si: On Care for our Common Home.

Grasso, G 2006, 'L'ambiente come dovere pubblico "globale": Qualche conferma nella giurisprudenza del giudice delle leggi?', in *Convegno annuale del Gruppo di Pisa, "I doveri costituzionali: la prospettiva del giudice delle leggi"*, Acqui Terme e Alessandria, 9–10 June.

Harari, YN 2014, *Sapiens: A brief history of humankind*, Random House.
Kumalasari, RB 2021, 'Legal protection for village communities against land rights in the construction of a national strategy project through a complete systematic land registration system (study of pasuruan district land registration)', *International Journal of Multicultural and Multireligious Understanding*, *8*(7), p.48, https://doi.org/10.18415/ijmmu.v8i7.2879.
Lähteenmäki-Uutela, A, Lonkila, A, Huttunen, S & Grmelová, N 2021, 'Legal rights of private property owners vs. sustainability transitions?', *Journal of Cleaner Production*, *323*, p.129179, https://doi.org/10.1016/j.jclepro.2021.129179.
Lamm, AJ, Lamm, K, Trojan, S, Sanders, CE & Byrd, AR 2023, 'A needs assessment to inform research and outreach efforts for sustainable agricultural practices and food production in the western United States', *Foods*, *12*(8), p.1630, https://doi.org/10.3390/foods12081630.
Lü, Y, Yang, Y, Sun, B, Yuan, J, Yu, M, Stenseth, NC & Obersteiner, M 2020, 'Spatial variation in biodiversity loss across China under multiple environmental stressors', *Science Advances*, *6*(47), https://doi.org/10.1126/sciadv.abd0952.
Mancuso, S 2017, *Plant revolution-le piante hanno già scritto il nostro futuro*, Giunti.
Millennium Ecosystem Assessment 2003, *Ecosystems and human well-being: A framework for assessment*, Millennium Ecosystem Assessment and Island Press, www.millenniumassessment.org/en/Framework.html.
Millennium Ecosystem Assessment 2005, *Ecosystems and human well-being: Biodiversity synthesis*. World Resources Institute, Washington, DC.
Miller, C 2010, *The evolution of the conservation movement, 1850–1920*, Created and maintained by the Library of Congress, accessed May–June 2009, http://lcweb2.loc.gov/ammem/amrvhtml/conshome.html.
Natalino, I 2002, *Norma e luogo. Problemi di geo-diritto*, Laterza, Roma-Bari.
Niemi, SA 2012, *Nordenskiöld, an early pioneer of Nordic conservation*, Environment and Society Portal, Arcadia.
O'Donnell, E & Talbot-Jones, J 2018, 'Creating legal rights for rivers: Lessons from Australia, New Zealand, and India', *Ecology and Society*, *23*(1), https://doi.org/10.5751/es-09854-230107.
O'Neill, DW, Fanning, AL & Lamb, WF 2018, 'A good life for all within planetary boundaries', *Nature Sustainability*, *1*(2), pp.88–95.
Paris Agreement 2015, 'Paris agreement to the United Nations framework convention on climate change', accessed 12 December 2015, T.I.A.S. No. 16-1104.
Rio Declaration 2003, 'Rio declaration on environment and development', (A/CONF.151/26, vol.I).
Scheidel, A, Fernández-Llamazares, Á, Bara, AH, Bene, DD, Davíd-Chavez, DM, Fanari, E & Whyte, KP 2023, 'Global impacts of extractive and industrial development projects on indigenous peoples' lifeways, lands, and rights', *Science Advances*, *9*(23), https://doi.org/10.1126/sciadv.ade9557.
Sena, A & Ebi, K 2020, 'When land is under pressure health is under stress', *International Journal of Environmental Research and Public Health*, *18*(1), 27 December, p.136, https://doi.org/10.3390/ijerph18010136. PMID: 33375481; PMCID: PMC7796245.
Silvo, K 2021, 'Climate impacts and environmental permit procedure', Publications of the Government's Analysis, Assessment and Research Activities 2021:43, Finland.
Stone, CD 1972, 'Should trees have standing? – towards legal rights for natural objects', *Southern California Law Review*, *45*, pp.450–501.
UN General Assembly 2019, A/74/161. Report of the Special Rapporteur on the issue of human rights obligations relating to the enjoyment of a safe, clean, healthy and sustainable environment.
UN General Assembly 2021, A/76/179. Healthy and sustainable food: Reducing the environmental impacts of food systems on human rights.

UN General Assembly 2022, Resolution A/76/L.75. The human right to a clean, healthy and sustainable environment.
United Nations General Assembly 1948, *The Universal Declaration of Human Rights (UDHR)*, United Nations General Assembly, New York.
United Nations Office for the High Commissioner of Human Rights 2010, 'Minority rights: International standards and guidance for implementation', UN New York and Geneva, 1045585_HR_PUB10_10_3_SIGNA.pdf (ohchr.org).
Von Bertalanffy, L 1956, 'A biologist looks at human nature', *The Scientific Monthly*, *82*(1), pp.33–41, www.jstor.org/stable/21839.
Zierock, R 1995, *Das Pentagon*, Azienda Agricola Foradori.

9 Intellectual Property Supporting a Green Framework for Sustainability

Elham Ghaffarian, Mark Perry, and Siva Barathi (Sharl) Marimuthu

9.1 Introduction

It is concerning that 795 million people are undernourished and more than 333 million people faced severe food insecurity in 2023 (World Food Program 2023). They are predominantly situated in developing countries. This lamentably high rate of malnourishment and hunger continues even in the current era of modern technology, which offers the ability to increase productivity in the agriculture sector. For instance, today, biotechnology gives rise to genetically modified crops that are resistant to climate change, salinity, and drought. Other information-based technologies offer smart systems, such as the Internet of Things and Robotics, to give accurate and comprehensive data about crop needs, soil behaviour, meteorological predictions, and automation on farm (Chhachhar et al. 2014).

Real-time data help farmers predict the accurate need for water, fertiliser, and pesticide (Grigera et al. 2007). Decision support systems for irrigation can reduce the risk of over- or under-irrigation which both have dire consequences on crop growth and yield. These technologies will increase food security and make food more nutritious (Pan et al. 2018; Smith 2013). Harnessing the potential benefits of modern technology and innovation for food security requires investments in research and development (R&D). Universities have had a long history of conducting R&D in the agricultural sector.

Research and scientific findings may contribute to food security when universities are able to translate their findings into industrial applications. This process has been called the "Third Mission" of universities (Trencher et al. 2014). Creating a safe environment and clear pathway for transferring agricultural R&D from universities into industry relies on a transparent intellectual property system, particularly patent rights. Engaging in R&D is both time-consuming and costly, and most universities get funds from government, industry, or donations. This makes intellectual property rights, particularly patent mechanisms, a framework that can build an environment with less risk for investment (Zhao 2006).

Despite the existence of intellectual property international regulators such as the World Intellectual Property Organization and its Trade-Related Aspects

DOI: 10.4324/9781003392279-9

of Intellectual Property Rights (TRIPS) agreement, IPRs are laws governed by national jurisdictions with specific characteristics based on the national social, cultural, and financial norms of each society (Abbott and Cottier 1999). Uncertainty about the realm of patent laws can deter cooperation between universities and industrial bodies, particularly those based in another nation, that aim to invest in agricultural R&D (Gans et al. 2008). Green patents aim to accelerate the development of green technologies by improving the clarity of patent policies, requirements, and examination processes (Dechezleprêtre 2013).

Embedding green IP in the national IP framework should encourage investment in that area of R&D and increase cooperation with universities and other research institutes. In this chapter, we provide a background of the current state of food security and discuss the important role of agricultural sustainability in food security. It follows by examining how agricultural sustainability can be enhanced by research and development. The subsequent sections delve into innovation and development breakthroughs by universities. Through this exploration, we hope to shed light on the importance of green patents in stimulating and promoting the diffusion of green technologies between nations and different sectors that can shape a more sustainable future and ensure food security.

9.2 Food Security

Providing sufficient, safe, and nutritious food for all people is one of the major global concerns historically and in the 21st century. Food security is defined by the Food and Agricultural Organisation (FAO) of the United Nations as:

> Food security exists when all people, at all times, have physical and economic access to sufficient, safe and nutritious food that meets their dietary needs and food preferences for an active and healthy life.
>
> (FAO 1996)

Food security is simple in definition yet a complex task in practice and may even be impossible for a single country to accomplish alone. That is why food security has been recognised as one of the Sustainable Development Goals (SDGs) specifically as the second goal, “Zero Hunger” (Brooks 2016). Food security is a complex and multidimensional concept encompassing four key pillars: availability, access, utilisation, and stability (Clapp et al. 2022). However, these pillars are affected by complex externalities, including climate change (Hertel 2015), population growth, the availability of arable land and other natural resources (Premanandh 2011), food prices (Mc Carthy et al. 2018), various civil inequalities (Banik 2019), political violence, insufficient purchasing power, and geopolitical, historical, cultural, and economic aspects (Alonso et al. 2018).

As mentioned by the FAO (2022) report, approximately 828 million people in 2021 did not have access to food (FAO 2022). This represents a rise of approximately 46 million since 2020 and 150 million since the outbreak of the COVID-19 pandemic (FAO 2022). The report presents compelling evidence that the world is failing in efforts to eliminate hunger and malnutrition, and this is a perturbing development (FAO 2022). The reality of food security depends on the activities and efficiencies of agriculture. This sector has always played a vital role in food security by increasing local domestic production and increasing its national economic status, particularly in developing countries with agricultural-based and rural-based economies.

Any food security policy must consider agriculture and any small changes in the sector may improve or jeopardise food security. This has been highlighted in international forums, as mentioned in the jointly published report by the FAO, the International Fund for Agricultural Development (IFAD), the United Nations Children's Fund (UNICEF), the UN World Food Programme (WFP), and the World Health Organisation (WHO): Repurposing agricultural policy, through increasing healthy and nutritious products whilst giving respect to the environment, is necessary for food security.

9.2.1 The Role of the Sustainable Agriculture Sector on Food Security

From a broad perspective, food security is linked to agriculture sustainability. Achieving sustainability in these sectors requires meeting the needs of present and future generations while being mindful of the environmental, social, and economic dimensions. The FAO defines sustainable agricultural development as "the management and conservation of the natural resource base, and the orientation of technological change in such a manner as to ensure the attainment of continued satisfaction of human needs for present and future generations" (FAO 1996).

In terms of food security, everyone at any given time should have access to enough nutritious and healthy food to have an active life. However, when accounting for population growth, there is high pressure on agriculture sectors to provide the food and fibre needs of people in sustainable manners that not only are safe for the environment but also improve social and economic development.

9.2.2 Agricultural Sustainability Challenges

There are various challenges to reaching long-term sustainable agriculture production and food security of which the most important challenges are population growth, climate change, and food waste. Population growth: Feeding the ever-growing population is one of the main challenges of the agriculture sector which pushes it to produce more and more. The global population is estimated to reach 9.7 billion by 2050 which means at least 70% more food will be required (FAO 2022). Climate change: There is a complex relationship between agriculture and climate change. On the one hand, climate change has direct impacts on crops, livestock, and fisheries production (Campbell et al. 2016).

Furthermore, rising temperatures, depletion of water resources, loss of soil fertility, extreme weather events, salinity, and acidification have led to a huge decline in the quality and quantity of agricultural productivity. Climate change's dire consequences are extreme in tropical regions where most people suffer from malnutrition and food insecurity (Wheeler and Von Braun 2013). However, as reported by the Intergovernmental Panel on Climate Change (IPCC), the negative impacts of climate change on food security can be overcome by innovation and technology. On the other hand, the agriculture sector emits 25% of global greenhouse gases (IPCC 2006). Earlier studies show that the current technological advancement in carbon absorption applied in the agriculture sector can considerably reduce greenhouse gas emissions (Lal 2004). However, the contribution of agricultural activities to climate change is more than just greenhouse gas emissions. Unsustainable agriculture impacts biodiversity loss and natural resource depletion by excessive use of water resources for irrigation, and uncontrolled application of pesticides and fertilisers on arable land – without land reclamation, agriculture causes climate change.

Food waste: Despite the strong literature on increasing productivity, including increasing agricultural products, introducing new food supply, and improving the quality of agricultural production including organic crops, lab corps, and genetically modified crops, food waste management is barely discussed in the research agenda (Alexander et al. 2013). Food waste in the supply chain occurs in two phases: Pre- and post-consumer phases (Pham et al. 2015). Pre-consumer waste is generated during agriculture, processing, and distribution, while post-consumer waste arises during the preparation of meals and consumption. Reducing food waste is necessary for future food security. About 1.3 billion tonnes or one-third of the food produced in the world for human consumption annually are lost or wasted throughout the supply chain, from production to consumption (Gustavsson et al. 2011). The current technological advancements can address waste management, though it should be noted that food waste management requires more than technological advancement. Different technologies including biotechnology, thermal, and thermochemical technology can be applied to the food supply chain – particularly in agriculture – to reduce food waste (Pham et al. 2015).

However, there is an urgent need for social innovations such as education programmes that focus on consumer behaviour towards a healthy lifestyle and sustainable consumption for innovation and technology adaptation (Al-Obadi 2022). The current situation regarding agricultural and food sustainability is not ideal. To feed the world population without compromising the needs of future generations, a combination of scientific and technological advancements, innovative business investments, and green approaches are necessary for the agricultural sector. Agricultural R&D plays a role in promoting cooperation between academic and business communities, stimulating the adaptation of green innovation and technology in agriculture.

9.2.3 Role of R&D in the Agriculture Sector

Over the past five decades, agricultural productivity around the world has been greatly enhanced by the application of agricultural R&D, which has helped to improve the livelihoods of millions of the world's poorest people. Sustainable growth in agricultural productivity is necessary to address the demand for more food, which continuously grows because of the increase in population and income (Heisey 2001). Meeting the demand for food for the ever-increasing world population will have to be met by increasing agricultural production (Heisey 2001).

Traditionally, increasing agricultural productivity has relied on allocating more land for agricultural activities, eventuated with deforestation, desertification, and biodiversity loss over the years (Godfray et al. 2010). The Green Revolution opened a new door for combating famine and starvation globally. The Green Revolution is a term used to describe a set of agricultural advancements that were initiated during the 1940s and 1950s. It is based on improved seeds and more fertilisers and pesticides driven by agricultural R&D (Heisey 2001). These innovations resulted in notable increases in global food production. The Green Revolution was founded on developing new, high-yielding strains of crops, such as wheat and rice, alongside using fertilisers, pesticides, and irrigation technologies, all aimed at enhancing crop yields (Pingali 2012).

In other words, the Green Revolution was not that *green* (in the modern sense of the term). Empirical studies have demonstrated how the Green Revolution contributed to food security over the years (Hazell and Ramasamy 1991; Ahmad et al. 2004; Schmalzer 2019). The Green Revolution addressed food security not through increasing the demand on more arable land but through applying more pesticides and fertilisers. It addressed food security but not in a sustainable manner. The uncontrolled use of chemical-based pesticides and fertilisers results in an unhealthy environment with soil and water pollution (Pimentel 1996).

As evidenced by many countries, agricultural R&D has been a major contributor to the world's ability to produce more food from limited agricultural land over the past 40 years (Heisey 2001) – avoiding the Malthusian nightmare that was anticipated by many in the 1960s – through the investment in agricultural science and technology programmes (Alston and Pardey 2013). To reap the benefits of R&D in agricultural productivity, yet avoid the irreversible environmental effects of the Green Revolution, redirecting the R&D to produce more actual *green* and environmentally friendly technologies to increase agricultural productivity with zero or minimal environmental effects, is the significant approach for the future.

Green R&D can help to achieve agricultural sustainability by developing new farming practices, improving soil health, reducing greenhouse gas emissions, and increasing the efficiency of water use or organic farming (Willer and Zerger 1999). Green R&D can also help to develop new crop varieties (Ndjeunga et al. 2015) that are resistant to pests and diseases. Japanese scholars have illustrated how green R&D can reduce the need for chemical pesticides (Takagi and Ueji 1997). In addition, green R&D can help to develop new technologies and tools that can increase the efficiency of farming operations, such as precision agriculture and digital farming (Paunov and Planes-Satorra 2019).

These technologies can help to reduce the environmental impact of agriculture while also increasing productivity and profitability for farmers. Policymakers require scientific assessments and knowledge for the decision-making process in this knowledge-based era (Rivera-Ferre 2012). Particularly in agrifood chains, any decision can affect the whole economy. Hence, there is a need for more targeted knowledge that is specifically focused on problem-solving (Berbegal-Mirabent et al. 2015), and further innovation is necessary to tackle the food problem. In the context where R&D is necessary for green innovation technology and knowledge diffusion for food security, universities have acquired an increasingly significant role as institutions to facilitate the creation and transfer of knowledge (Pinto and Fernandes 2021).

9.3 The University – R&D in Innovation and Technology Accessibility

Traditionally, research, education, and training have been the core mission of universities; however, there has been pressure on universities to contribute more to society, known as the "Third Mission" (Laredo 2007). Universities in the 21st century started to play a crucial role in social progress besides training academics by increasing accessibility to knowledge worldwide, providing basic data and information for the different research areas, (Altbach 2009), and creating innovative technologies.

R&D is also a valuable mechanism for technology and know-how gap reduction for indigenous peoples (Fu et al. 2011). The university's contribution to technology transfer through R&D is important in developing countries to tackle the financial obstacles for technology transfer such as licensing fees. R&D cooperation can remove existing obstacles to technology transfer (Laredo 2007). Moreover, developing countries would be able to create a high volume of data and information as a cornerstone for future research via R&D cooperation. It forms the link and bridge for local talent to be in contact with international scholars (Altbach 2009). It is important for many reasons, and one of them is to reduce any brain drain. Intelligent local individuals and scholars, through universities, can bring knowledge and science to their society.

According to the literature on the benefits of universities contributing to R&D in both developed and developing countries, the question is "Why do research and development activities mostly concentrate in industrial-developed countries" (Pimentel 1996)? Indeed, why are developing countries still looking to import imitation products or use older technology and innovation? Or why do developing countries lag behind developed countries in benefiting from R&D by universities at an international level? Among the factors that may bring universities with other industrial partnerships together in R&D cooperation is the existing protective mechanism to protect intellectual assets. This mechanism is an intellectual property framework, particularly patent rights.

9.4 Intellectual Property Rights as a Mechanism for Knowledge Flow

The 21st century is the century of knowledge. Knowledge is the fuel for future innovation and new creations (Mashelkar 2001). The ability of nations to fulfil the application of knowledge assets would improve both social wealth and development status (Mashelkar 2001). In this scenario, the agricultural sector is an important income source for nations, particularly in developing countries, and must access the knowledge-based sector to provide food security as well as national security (Falcon and Naylor 2005).

Patent protection can increase the flow of knowledge by giving inventors and researchers exclusive rights to their innovations, at the same time encouraging them to disclose their inventions in exchange for legal protection. This disclosure of how the invention is made, which is required for all patent applications, ensures that new knowledge is made available to the public and accelerates the diffusion of technological advances. Ensuring patent protection also attracts investment and enables pendency inventors to develop their ideas in the market because it reduces the risk of piracy or imitation.

Conveying knowledge as innovation and technology into the market needs a supportive environment, and IPRs play a key role in creating such an environment. A better understanding of IPR is essential for agricultural R&D cooperation. Effective IP strategies at the national and international levels help accelerate the translation of agricultural research into practice. In this context, to increase knowledge growth in the agriculture sector demand for a viable and transparent intellectual property framework is going to become essential across the globe.

9.4.1 Diverse Perspective on Intellectual Property Rights' Effect

Everyone is entitled to protect intangible products such as creative writing, music, and inventions under the specific conditions and requirements of intellectual property rights as mentioned by Article 27 of the Universal Declaration of Human Rights.

Article 27, Universal Declaration of Human Rights

1. Everyone has the right freely to participate in the cultural life of the community, to enjoy the arts, and to share in scientific advancement and its benefits.
2. Everyone has the right to the protection of the moral and material interests resulting from any scientific, literary, or artistic production of which he is the author.

Furthermore, the World Intellectual Property Organization and TRIPS set standards and principles to harmonise the basic IP framework for member nations for IP protection. The TRIPS Agreement provides a transparent IP framework, which enables R&D innovations to be protected by various regimes including copyright, trademark, geographical indications, industrial design, patents, layout designs of integrated circuits, and protection of undisclosed information.

> **Article 7, TRIPS Agreement**
>
> The protection and enforcement of intellectual property rights should contribute to the promotion of technological innovation and to the transfer and dissemination of technology, to the mutual advantage of producers and users of technological knowledge and in a manner conducive to social and economic welfare, and to a balance of rights and obligations.

Meanwhile, IP diversity at the national level is completely clear, so that developing countries may believe that less extreme IP protection can increase their access to national innovation and economic growth (Conversely, developed countries have strong IP frameworks (Kanwar and Evenson 2009)). There is no consensus on whether strong IP protection can be good or bad for developing countries (Dutfield and Suthersanen 2005). However, studies from 64 developing countries illustrate the positive impacts of IPR protection of innovation on economic development (Chen and Puttitanun 2005). Regardless of the strength of the IP framework, transparent and clear rules are vital to promote innovation and R&D, in which the agriculture sector needs to reduce food insecurity.

Uncertainty in the national IP framework protection reduces collaboration and hinders knowledge diffusion (Czarnitzki et al. 2015). Cooperation in R&D, especially in complicated projects, is essential. Various inputs, such as skills, knowledge, and considerable budgets allocated to achieve more valuable outputs, have uncertain outcomes where IPRs cannot guarantee a reliable platform for this cooperation. For instance, patents may hinder R&D collaborations. Only relying on a solid and transparent patent basis gives a propensity for R&D players to cooperate (Manap et al. 2016).

9.4.2 Weak Intellectual Property Protection System

There are two special features of weak intellectual property protection that make it challenging to fully understand the concept. First, there is uncertainty and ambiguity in its definition which is why some authors (Helfer 2004; Watal 1998) consider international IP protection standards, particularly the TRIPS Agreement, as a benchmark for evaluating the weakness or strengths of the IP system. Being a signatory of the TRIPS Agreement does not make national IP protection more or less effective or efficient if the national legislation does not underpin and support the implementation of these standards.

Furthermore, the existence of historical and current evidence on the efficiency of weak IP protection, predominantly in Asian Nations, and Japan,

Taiwan, and South Korea (Kumar 2003), increases the doubt around strong IP protection, which is deemed as a Western profit mechanism to protect their technology or transfer them under the unfair condition to developing countries (Kumar 2003). Between 1960 and 1993, when the United States saw strong IP protection as an indispensable strategy to increase innovation and investment in R&D, Japan had taken diverse engineering methods to accelerate the national innovation development process (Kumar 2003).

More recently, China has been an instance of a country with lax IP protection but leading in economic development and R&D. There are different justifications for the success of so-called weak IP protection over time as mentioned by IP utilitarians and the different national variations that influence the productivity and efficiency of the IP system.

Also, China has specific human resources, low labour costs, and a high capability for imitation that fuels its economy (Cao 2014). Therefore, reaching an exact conclusion as a solution to whether a strong or weak IP system is a better mechanism for increasing investment in R&D needs wide information about the specific conditions of each country such as economic status. However, the rare progressive outcomes of weak IP protection shall not underestimate the evidence from most of the countries in which strong IP protection makes a secure environment for more R&D.

9.5 Green IP Boost R&D in Different Intellectual Property Systems

As highlighted in the previous section, existing international harmonisation standards are not enough for every country to have the same IP system. Every nation, as mentioned by TRIPS, must have its own choice to design a national IP system that results in a different typology in IP systems across the world. Meanwhile, agricultural sustainability and food security are global concerns that cannot be tackled if all nations do not have access to green innovation and technologies that are able to increase agricultural products with zero or less harm to the environment. Each country must be able to use its own IP system, particularly the patent system in order to increase innovation and investment in R&D.

Innovation needs investment in R&D, and it is arguable that a weak IP system reduces investment because inadequate support increases the risk of infringement counterfeiting. Investors in this environment are reluctant to invest in R&D and cooperate with universities. A green patent framework is a strategy that can incentivise investments in green innovation and technology, regardless of the weakness or strength of the whole IP framework, including patent, copyright, trademark, trade secrets, or geographical indications (Nitta 2005).

The *green* patent is a relatively new concept; it was introduced in 2009 and is part of the legal system of some countries (Dechezleprêtre 2013). The United Kingdom, the United States, Australia, Canada, Japan, South Korea, Brazil, and China are countries where the patent system, particularly in terms of filing and review, has been amended to accelerate the diffusion of green technologies (Lu

2013). An important issue for the IP system of these countries that have a green patent strategy is that China and Brazil have weak domestic IP protection (Lu 2013). China is one of the countries that feature an imitation-based market.

However, by embedding green patents within the current IP framework, these countries are going to be leaders in renewable energy, particularly biofuel, hydropower, and solar energy (Gould and William 1996). The green patent framework is not harmonised at the international level yet, which we believe, is a privilege, especially for developing countries that have weak IP protection. To optimise the use of patent rights, every nation shall have specific initiatives that are suited to its income level, infrastructure, and culture. When a unique green patent framework is legislated, it consequentially boosts R&D in green technology or agricultural technology.

9.6 Conclusion

It is undeniable that agricultural sustainability will bring food security if agriculture performs sustainably by applying green technologies and innovation. Universities can foster R&D, which has a prominent role in providing green technology that needs to be transferred into the market to address sustainability. Each country can consider its own version and have a patent system to incentivise and foster more investment in R&D. Implementing a green patent scheme which can happen in developing countries or in so-called weak patent systems indicates the flexibility of such a scheme.

References

Abbott, F & Cottier, T 1999, *The international intellectual property system: commentary and materials*, Kluwer Law International, pp. 1999–2122, ISBN: 9789041181930.
http://digital.casalini.it/9789041181930.

Ahmad, I, Shah, SAH & Zahid, MS 2004, 'Why the Green Revolution was short run phenomena in the development process of Pakistan: A lesson for future', *Research*, *4*(1), pp.281–288.

Alexander, C, Gregson, N & Gille, Z 2013, 'Food waste', *The Handbook of Food Research*, *1*, pp.471–483.

Al-Obadi, M, Ayad, H, Pokharel, S & Ayari, MA 2022, 'Perspectives on food waste management: Prevention and social innovations', *Sustainable Production and Consumption*, *31*, pp.190–208.

Alonso, EB, Cockx, L & Swinnen, J 2018, 'Culture and food security', *Global Food Security*, *17*, pp.113–127.

Alston, JM & Pardey, PG 2013, 'Agricultural R&D and food security of the poor', *Economic Papers: A Journal of Applied Economics and Policy*, *32*(3), pp.289–297.

Altbach, PG 2009, 'Peripheries and centers: Research universities in developing countries', *Asia Pacific Education Review*, *10*, pp.15–27.

Banik, D 2019, 'Achieving food security in a sustainable development era', *Food Ethics*, *4*, pp.117–121.

Berbegal-Mirabent, J, García, JLS & Ribeiro-Soriano, DE 2015, 'University–industry partnerships for the provision of R&D services', *Journal of Business Research*, *68*(7), pp.1407–1413.

Brooks, J 2016, 'Food security and the Sustainable Development Goals' in Patrick Love (ed.), *Debate the Issues: New Approaches to Economic Challenges, OECD Publishing*, Paris. DOI: https://doi.org/10.1787/9789264264687-27-en
Campbell, BM, Vermeulen, SJ, Aggarwal, PK, Corner-Dolloff, C, Girvetz, E, Loboguerrero, AM, Ramirez-Villegas, J, Rosenstock, T, Sebastian, L, Thornton, PK & Wollenberg, E 2016, 'Reducing risks to food security from climate change', *Global Food Security*, *11*, pp.34–43.
Cao, Q 2014, 'Insight into weak enforcement of intellectual property rights in China', *Technology in Society*, *38*, pp.40–47.
Chen, Y & Puttitanun, T 2005, 'Intellectual property rights and innovation in developing countries', *Journal of Development Economics*, *78*(2), pp.474–493.
Chhachhar, AR, Qureshi, B, Khushk, GM & Ahmed, S 2014, 'Impact of information and communication technologies in agriculture development', *Journal of Basic and Applied Scientific*, *4*(1), 281–288.
Clapp, J, Moseley, WG, Burlingame, B & Termine, P 2022, 'The case for a six-dimensional food security framework', *Food Policy*, *106*, p.102164.
Czarnitzki, D, Hussinger, K & Schneider, C 2015, 'R&D collaboration with uncertain intellectual property rights', *Review of Industrial Organization*, *46*, pp.183–204.
Dechezleprêtre, A 2013, 'Fast-tracking green patent applications: An empirical analysis', ICTSD Programme on Innovation, Technology and Intellectual Property, no. 37.
Dutfield, G & Suthersanen, U 2005, 'Harmonisation or differentiation in intellectual property protection? The lessons of history', *Prometheus*, *23*(2), pp.131–147.
Falcon, WP & Naylor, RL 2005, 'Rethinking food security for the twenty-first century', *American Journal of Agricultural Economics*, *87*(5), pp.1113–1127.
FAO 1996, 'Rome declaration on World food sand World food summit plan of action', World Food Summit 13–17 November 1996, Rome.
FAO 2022, 'UN report: Global hunger numbers rose to as many as 828 million in 2021', www.fao.org/newsroom/detail/un-report-global-hunger-SOFI-2022-FAO/en.
Fu, X, Pietrobelli, C & Soete, L 2011, 'The role of foreign technology and indigenous innovation in the emerging economies: Technological change and catching-up', *World Development*, *39*(7), pp.1204–1212.
Gans, JS, Hsu, DH & Stern, S 2008, 'The impact of uncertain intellectual property rights on the market for ideas: Evidence from patent grant delays', *Management Science*, *54*(5), pp.982–997.
Godfray, HCJ, Beddington, JR, Crute, IR, Haddad, L, Lawrence, D, Muir, JF, Pretty, J, Robinson, S, Thomas, SM & Toulmin, C 2010, 'Food security: The challenge of feeding 9 billion people', *Science*, *327*(5967), pp.812–818.
Gould, DM & William, CB 1996, 'The role of intellectual property rights in economic growth', *Development Economics*, *48*(2), pp.323–350.
Grigera, G, Oesterheld, M & Pacín, F 2007, 'Monitoring forage production for farmers' decision making', *Agricultural Systems*, *94*(3), pp.637–648.
Gustavsson, J, Cederberg, C, Sonesson, U, Van Otterdijk, R & Meybeck, A 2011, Global Food Losses and Food Waste- Extent, Causes and Prevention.
Hazell PB and Ramasamy C (Editors) 1991, *The green revolution reconsidered: The impact of high-yielding rice varieties in South India*, International Food Policy Research Institute by Johns Hopkins University Press, Baltimore, MD.
Heisey, PW, 2001, 'Agricultural Research and Development, Agricultural Productivity, and Food Security,' 33685, United States Department of Agriculture, Economic Research Service.
Helfer, LR 2004, 'Regime shifting: the TRIPs agreement and new dynamics of international intellectual property lawmaking', Yale Journal of International Law, 29, p.1.
Hertel, TW 2015, 'The challenges of sustainably feeding a growing planet', *Food Security*, *7*(2), pp.185–198.

IPCC 2006, 'Generic methodologies applicable to multiple land-use categories', *Agriculture, Forestry and Other Land Use*, *4*, pp.2–6.

Kanwar, S & Evenson, R 2009, 'On the strength of intellectual property protection that nations provide', *Journal of Development Economics*, *90*(1), pp.50–56.

Kumar, N 2003, 'Intellectual property rights, technology and economic development: Experiences of Asian countries', *Economic and Political Weekly*, *38*, pp.209–226.

Lal, R 2004, 'Soil carbon sequestration impacts on global climate change and food security', *Science*, *304*(5677), pp.1623–1627.

Laredo, P 2007, 'Revisiting the third mission of universities: Toward a renewed categorization of university activities?', *Higher Education Policy*, *20*, pp.441–456.

Lu, B 2013, 'Expedited patent examination for green inventions: Developing countries' policy choices', *Energy Policy*, *61*, pp.1529–1538.

Manap, NA, Shapiee, RB, Tehrani, P & Shariff, AABM 2016, 'Protecting R&D inventions through intellectual property rights', *Journal of Intellectual Property Rights*, *21*, pp.110–116.

Mashelkar, RA 2001, 'Intellectual property rights and the Third World', *Current Science*, *81*, pp.955–965.

Mc Carthy, U, Uysal, I, Badia-Melis, R, Mercier, S, O'Donnell, C & Ktenioudaki, A 2018, 'Global food security–Issues, challenges and technological solutions', *Trends in Food Science & Technology*, *77*, pp.11–20.

Ndjeunga, J, Mausch, K & Simtowe, F 2015, 'Assessing the effectiveness of agricultural R&D for groundnut, pearl millet, pigeonpea and sorghum in West and Central Africa and East and Southern Africa', in *Crop improvement, adoption, and impact of improved varieties in food crops in Sub-Saharan Africa*, CABI, Wallingford, UK, pp.123–147.

Nitta, I 2005, 'Proposal for a green patent system: Implications for sustainable development and climate change', *Sustainable Develoment Law & Policy*, *5*, p.61.

Pan, Y, Smith, SC & Sulaiman, M 2018, 'Agricultural extension and technology adoption for food security: Evidence from Uganda', *American Journal of Agricultural Economics*, *100*(4), pp.1012–1031.

Paunov, C & Planes-Satorra, S 2019, 'How are digital technologies changing innovation?: Evidence from agriculture, the automotive industry and retail', OECD Science, Technology and Industry Policy Papers, No. 74, OECD Publishing, Paris, https://doi.org/10.1787/67bbcafe-en.

Pham, TPT, Kaushik, R, Parshetti, GK, Mahmood, R & Balasubramanian, R 2015, 'Food waste-to-energy conversion technologies: Current status and future directions', *Waste Management*, *38*, pp.399–408.

Pimentel, D 1996, 'Green revolution agriculture and chemical hazards', *Science of the Total Environment*, *188*, pp.S86–S98.

Pingali, PL 2012, 'Green revolution: Impacts, limits, and the path ahead', *National Academy of Sciences*, *109*(31), pp.12302–12308.

Pinto, EB & Fernandes, G 2021, 'Collaborative R&D the key cooperation domain for university-industry partnerships sustainability–position paper', *Procedia Computer Science*, *181*, pp.102–109.

Premanandh, J 2011, 'Factors affecting food security and contribution of modern technologies in food sustainability', *Journal of the Science of Food and Agriculture*, *91*(15), pp.2707–2714.

Rivera-Ferre, MG 2012, 'Framing of agri-food research affects the analysis of food security: The critical role of the social sciences', *The International Journal of Sociology of Agriculture and Food*, *19*(2), pp.162–175.

Schmalzer, S 2019, *Red revolution, green revolution: Scientific farming in socialist China*, University of Chicago Press.

Smith, P 2013, 'Delivering food security without increasing pressure on land', *Global Food Securitly*, *2*(1), pp.18–23.

Takagi, K & Ueji, M 1997, 'Use, research and development of pesticides in relation to sustainable agriculture in Japan', *Japan Agricultural Research Quarterly*, *31*, pp.13–20.

Trencher, G, Yarime, M, McCormick, KB, Doll, CN & Kraines, SB 2014, 'Beyond the third mission: Exploring the emerging university function of co-creation for sustainability', *Science and Public Policy*, *41*(2), pp.151–179.

Watal, J 1998, 'The TRIPS agreement and developing countries: Strong, weak or balanced protection?', *World Intellectual Property*, *1*(2), pp.281–307.

Wheeler, T & Von Braun, J 2013, 'Climate change impacts on global food security', *Science*, *341*(6145), pp.508–513, https://doi.org/10.1126/science.1239402.

Willer, H & Zerger, U 1999, 'Demand of Research and Development in Organic Farming in Europe. Paper prepared for the FAO-Workshop "Research Methodologies in Organic Farming" at the Forschungsinstitut für biologischen Landbau (FiBL), October 1998', Proceedings-First SREN Workshop "Research Methodologies in Organic Farming" at the Research Institute of Organic Agriculture (FiBL), Food and Agriculture Organisation (FAO), pp.57–92.

Zhao, M 2006, 'Conducting R&D in countries with weak intellectual property rights protection', *Management Science*, *52*(8), pp.1185–1199.

10 Corporate Social Responsibility and Embedded Sustainable Business Practices

Peter Dawson and Siva Barathi (Sharl) Marimuthu

10.1 Introduction

Corporate Social Responsibility (CSR) is a long-held view that a business should be socially accountable to all its stakeholders, including the general public. Stemming from that view it is incumbent on businesses to act sustainably in terms of its economic, social, and environmental impacts. Intuitively, it is in the long-term interests of a business to act in a socially responsible way. Specifically, in a way that delivers not only wealth and economic growth but delivers a balanced social good that loops back and reinforces an overall benefit to society.

Central to this theme is the need to balance and protect the environment, including the promotion of sustainable industry practices that give priority to positive societal outcomes, and, notable in this respect, the pressing need for addressing food security in an uncertain global context. Regarding food security and the production of nutritious food, which form a common thread in this book, it is emphasized that while CSR has direct relevance to food as a product of business activity, it is also important to note that CSR has a broader focus as part of the machinery of business which produces many economy-wide goods and services for the benefit of a broad range of stakeholders. However, some examples of food as a product of business are used.

Importantly, a business setting that is geared toward sustainable practices, including a profitable bottom line and the promotion of societal good is becoming expected. These aspects are also noted as priorities by the UN in its Sustainable Development Goal (SDG) proclamation which are explained in a subsequent section of this chapter within a business context.

While CSR has historically been more of an aspirational objective, countries are now moving towards providing a regulatory reporting framework for CSR and the lead in this regard is the EU which has now embedded specific reporting requirements as part of a business's annual reporting obligations. Australia is now taking limited steps to incorporate aspects of CSR in its annual accounts and the professional accounting bodies are currently pursuing this important change. Thus, a legal imperative now exists which adds a mandate to drive change.

DOI: 10.4324/9781003392279-10

10.2 Corporate Social Responsibility in Perspective

In terms of Corporate Social Responsibility, no discussion would be complete without briefly examining the important role of business in society, notwithstanding the criticism often directed at businesses for marketing marginal claims about the essential benefits of their products and services. Business is, indeed, the 'engine room' of our large economies of scale and society relies on the wealth creation at play. This complex interconnectedness should not be understated, and it would be somewhat disingenuous to imply otherwise.

Depending on the jurisdiction, business has to cope with a myriad of governance rules and legislation, wrestle with the requirement for scientific evidence, search for a marketing position based both in fact and the need to obtain sales and be seen as a good corporate citizen which is vital for the shareholders and, ultimately, the board. It is not in the best interests of businesses to do damage and businesses must not only add wealth but support a healthy lifestyle and dietary habits for their customers. Reputation is fragile and, once lost, cannot be regained easily. How then do we view the drivers of business and its philosophy when it comes to selling the benefits of a particular product or service?

Whether large or small, businesses have a corporate social responsibility that extends to all stakeholders. Business operates within a particular code of conduct framework, strategic and operational plan framework, audit and legislative framework, sales target framework, and importantly, cultural framework.

Societal and consumer benefits cannot be one-dimensional and assessed solely through the lens of prescriptive governmental controls, self-regulation, and consumer awareness (or lack thereof). Ultimately, businesses are the drivers of wealth and employment, and they support positive consumer behaviour because one would expect that it is in their interest to do so. Bonsu S (2020) notes that 'Corporate social responsibility implies not only trust by consumers but also a strategic embedding within the organization.'

In terms of relevance, Stakeholder Theory is well known, and it is not the objective here to promote this theory. That said, there is an element of truth in the stakeholder theory proposition noted by Freeman E et al. (2010), that interconnected relationships (customers, business, government, shareholders, and the broader community) are not only vital but also critical to a healthy business environment, a healthy and sustainable health system, and a healthy and sustainable economy. This interconnectedness requires not only governance rules, it requires trust and trust is essential in 'organization-stakeholder relationships' and, on this basis, if a firm is to be considered successful then a societal benefit must ensue. To suggest that this type of goal congruence can be achieved is an ideal worthy of pursuit.

In an overly prescriptive business environment, and for context we can use the example of the regulation of food products, it is noteworthy to remember that the support and encouragement of business to promote corporate social responsibility is necessary if the balanced achievement of consumer good is to be attained. In support of this 'ideal,' it is worth mentioning that modern business practice should not only work towards having a formalized 'corporate social responsibility' position, the value proposition should also be reworked towards the adoption of a 'triple bottom line' position whereby an all-inclusive goal of financial sustainability, positive social impact, and positive environmental impact are goals. It is submitted that this value proposition is the way forward and this goal is supported. Of course, this only highlights the tensions that can exist between business, government as an intermediary, and consumers. When we add the complexities of international trade, cultural differences, and wealth distribution, then those tensions are exacerbated.

10.3 Corporate Social Responsibility Globally

The current global geopolitical environment is changing rapidly and while it is expedient to focus on developed countries such as Australia, Europe, the United States, and many Asian countries, we cannot ignore the dynamics of our broader international markets. Business is increasingly global, and change is rapid. One only has to examine and reflect on the changes being wrought across the Middle East, the increasing geopolitical influence of Russia, China, and Iran, the upheaval in Ukraine, the emergence militarily of China, and the assertive promotion of its trade links and economic goals, and the massive growth in market potential of India and the broader Asian countries.

The dynamics of such rapid geopolitical change and its impact on mature, emerging, and potential markets are profound. The norms of business and goal setting to maximize profit, social benefit, and protect the environment can be subverted and lost when attempting to wrestle with such change. Indeed, it may be unwise for businesses to attempt to enter markets that are clearly unstable, thus skewing the social good component to safer markets.

Once again for context and by way of example, if we are to rationalize and achieve the greater community good in terms of sound nutrition, the promotion of attractive food products within varied and complex economies globally, then it must start with engagement and communication at government and community level to enable a strategic picture to be painted of what constitutes sound nutrition having regard to local circumstances. This will obviously vary depending on the receptiveness of governments to investment, the often sensitivity of religious constraints, the instability of some militarized societies, and the overall sophistication of the economy under investment consideration.

We have, thus, broadened our focus to recognize that most examinations of corporate social responsibility at play have focused on theoretical constructs targeting developed stable economies and societies. Of course, this is not the reality of real-world global business and if we are to engage globally and improve nutrition for citizens of all countries and circumstances, then we cannot assume that one size fits all in terms of business investment and communication strategy.

Businesses must accept compromise when dealing with governments, societies, and economies that have vastly different priorities to traditional Westernized structures. This is not to say that, for example, the overall goal of improved nutrition should be subjugated, but rather all investment and communication strategies should always be framed with the goal of an ethical and sustainable future for whatever target market is being pursued.

Businesses will need to become engaged equally with governments, consumers, and the nuances of the particular target market having regard to what 'sound nutrition' may look like. This, in turn, will determine what corporate social responsibility will look like as well. This position will obviously involve compromise, but it will also require business to be adaptable if the true intent of corporate social responsibility is to be achieved, and benefit is to accrue to a particular society through its target market. Thus, a target market in this context must not be simply a dumping ground and a potential source of cheap labour but rather a fertile ground for improving education, technology, and economic and environmental outcomes. The challenge for global business is to bring all these complexities and variabilities together, to frame a workable idea of corporate social responsibility, as it applies to the many challenging contexts globally.

It is beyond the scope of this chapter to individualize an examination of all the variables that exist globally that may act to support or inhibit the goal of sound corporate social responsibility. It is, however, well established that it is good for business, consumers, government, the economy, and the environment if businesses can work within the broader social context of a target market wherever that target market is located. While there may be much at play to work against this ideal, it is, nevertheless, an unarguable starting point that businesses must embrace if an overall good is to be attained and to be in a position to work within and, perhaps, influence regulatory change as needed.

When a business is faced with the prospect of arguing a position in a difficult and sometimes unstable market, the risk is that it will lack a way forward and the variabilities and uncertainties of international business will cause it to lose perspective of what is important in terms of gaining positive outcomes for societies. The position to be argued must be one that headlines the pursuit of improved conditions for consumers and delivers clear benefits for the particular government in terms of long-term growth. That position must be one of sustainability and there can be no more prominent or influential focus than sustainability in our modern and global marketplace. As noted, it captures and forms the bedrock of all we do and allows as consumers, regulators, businesses, and within society more broadly, wherever the target marketplace is located and whatever geopolitical or local tensions exist.

Keeble B (1998) noted that during the 1980s, the World Commission on Environment and Development published a report titled the 'Brundland Report' which offered a baseline description of sustainability which stated that 'humanity has the ability to make development sustainable to ensure that it meets the needs of the present without compromising the ability of future generations to meet their own needs.' This is what is now referred to as 'intergenerational equity.' This also translates to the 'triple bottom line' and takes account of the linkages between the environment, the economy, and society.

The economy and society can be seen as operating alongside the environment, but the economy and society cannot operate without due consideration to the impacts on the environment. Sustainable development and the production of foods offering sound nutrition can be seen as a core responsibility of both businesses and governments worldwide. Indeed, business has an ideal opportunity to drive the agenda in this space given their capacity to influence innovation, production, and consumer behaviour.

As an example of business taking the lead in this area, the global Sustainability Accounting Standards Board (SASB) has taken a prominent role by looking to embed five sustainability concepts for business in the future. Cavicchia M (2021: 10–11) notes that these concepts or dimensions are:

1. Environment – environmental impacts of the resource needs of the particular business;
2. Human capital – the rights of the workforce of the particular business;
3. Social capital – this concept relates to the reputation of the particular business as it operates within the target market or the target country, that is, does it have a social license to operate;
4. Business model – again, this concept identifies the need for the particular business to combine environmental, human and social considerations as it attempts to create value; and
5. Leadership and governance – the willingness of the particular business to comply with the laws and regulations of the industry and country. Once again, this is for a global business operating within complex markets, cultures and often volatile geopolitical situations.

Further, in 2015 the United Nations adopted several Sustainable Development Goals (SDGs) as a means of building a template to address poverty, protect the environment, and work towards enhancing peace and prosperity by 2030. Of course, one could argue that this is just another meaningless timeline, but it is nonetheless an important principle that we should embrace, and it is worth repeating those SDGs here in support of what is clearly a common good for societies, consumers, and governments of all persuasions worldwide.

The United Nations is of the view that each of its 17 SDGs are interconnected and that 'action in one area will affect outcomes in others, and that development must balance social, economic and environmental sustainability.' The goals are as follows and it is suggested that these goals form the basis for business as it approaches its planning framework and embarks on new ventures in target markets and negotiation with governments. The proposition is that it makes good business sense to do so and will address the many difficulties when selling a 'value add' proposition in otherwise difficult settings and cultures. For pragmatic business reasons, the goals could be termed principles and could form an important linkage back to the business planning process:

1. *No poverty.* This is a vital principle for business to adopt and fits nicely with the objective of targeting the most vulnerable and supporting communities.
2. *Zero hunger.* Functional food, dietary, and nutrition considerations are an essential selling point, particularly for children. The business could, thus, target sustainable agriculture and improved technology which will also send a direct signal to investors.
3. *Good health and wellbeing.* Improving life expectancy and targeting repeat business through reduced mortality and overall health standards embeds the business as a good corporate citizen.
4. *Quality education.* This is the bedrock of all immature and potential markets, and it is seen as a priority for business to encourage and support education as it strives for an informed market population to drive sustainable growth.
5. *Gender equality.* A significant gap in some world markets exists partly because there is an underutilization of human capital. Nowhere is this more pronounced than in some Middle Eastern and African countries and no longer can business accept such a disparity if it is to prosper in emerging and immature markets.
6. *Clean water and sanitation.* Direct investment in this area is essential if standards of living are to rise in line with market potential.
7. *Affordable and clean energy.* This is directly linked to market modernization and growth and goes 'hand in hand' with improved living standards and long-term sustainability.
8. *Decent work and economic growth.* Full productive work generates long-term economic and market growth, and it is in the interests of business to secure talent and employment security which, in turn, generates income.
9. *Sustainable industrialization.* Investment in modern industrial technologies and communications drives value-added products and supports sustainable growth.
10. *Reduce inequality.* Income inequality, discrimination, the lack of equal opportunities, and the lack of a modern financial system place a handbrake on growth and impede target market development.
11. *Sustainable cities and communities.* Making cities safe and sustainable through proper planning can be directly influenced by business through investment, representation, and negotiation with the government.
12. *Responsible consumption and production.* The effective management of food consumption, food waste, and losses through the supply chain, including effective recycling, is a responsibility of business as it establishes a long-term presence in a target market.

13. *Climate action.* If true sustainability is to be established then business needs to minimize its footprint and take a long-term view of business return, including working with government and agencies to build climate change policies and procedures into its strategic and operational plans.
14. *Life below water.* Minimizing damage and ensuring effluent is managed effectively also needs to be built into the planning process. Out of sight is not out of mind and oceans, streams and ecosystems need to be protected at all costs if markets are to be secured.
15. *Life on land.* Similarly, forests and habitat, including biodiversity considerations are critical to long-term market growth and success and need to be factored into the planning process.
16. *Peace, justice, and strong institutions.* Strong law and order and governance frameworks support business growth and also support consumer growth in target markets. Wealth creation cannot exist without these crucial elements.
17. *Global partnerships.* Globally, growth is impeded if international partnerships at the government level, government agency level, NGO level, and business level are not pursued. Business is uniquely positioned to exert influence for the benefit of consumers and enhance wealth creation within target markets.

Of course, there are many risks for businesses adopting the approach suggested, not the least of which are, high upfront costs and a less-than-attractive bottom line, initially. However, the alternative is equally less attractive through underdevelopment, underutilization, and the loss of long-term market potential. A narrow short-term profit focus is counterproductive, and a global entrepreneurial approach is required to support a long-term sustainable outcome for both businesses and consumers.

10.4 Does Corporate Social Responsibility Matter

Intuitively, businesses understand that to operate successfully, then due consideration must be given to customers, staff and employees, the community, and the strategic and sustainable direction of the enterprise. Factors such as staff and employee empowerment lead to improved morale and retention, the building of a positive brand image, improving productivity and customer retention and loyalty, creating competitive advantage through sustainable practices such as caring for the environment, giving back to the community through educational programs and alleviating poverty where possible are all practices and strategies designed to not only improve the 'look' of the business but also designed to improve the bottom line. It also carries the added advantage of attracting positive investor sentiment.

As noted by Murphy C (2024: 3–6)

> research shows that 87% of American consumers are more likely to buy a product from a company that advocates for an issue they care about, and

76% would refuse to purchase a product if they found out a company supported an issue contrary to their beliefs.

As also indicated by Murphy C (2024), Corporate Social Responsibility can be projected via the smallest of changes to practices. Examples include targeting charity donations, establishing a social mindset within the business, and partnering with the community and like-minded businesses. Specific examples include a 2010 Coca-Cola initiative to empower women employees across their businesses by targeting upskilling programs and access to support services. Additionally, Visa has introduced access to cash services in markets where customers face financial barriers.

In support of this theme Fernando J (2024: 1–4), indicates that Corporate Social Responsibility is a conscious business model choice. Thus, ethical and financial embedding occurs through a planning process that focuses on product research and development to promote sustainability, social responsibility and accountability, and customer good.

Fernando J (2024) expands on this proposition by providing recent examples. In 2022, Starbucks (the 'coffee king') indicated that care for its workforce and the environment were priorities. Practical initiatives such as medical and educational support for employees and staff, and setting targets for 50% reductions in business emissions, water consumption, and waste by 2030 were given as priorities. Home Depot and General Motors were also notable for their commitment to the adoption of Corporate Social Responsibility targets – Home Depot to the use of 100% renewable energy by 2030 and General Motors won a sustainability leadership award by the allocation of $60M for Corporate Social Responsibility initiatives. Business periodicals and magazines continue to publish rankings for good corporate citizenship.

Corporate Social Responsibility does matter, and it matters not only in terms of the foregoing but it matters in terms of its adoption as a particular philosophy. In other words, it encapsulates the fact that business not only operates within the confines and constraints of the market, but also society more broadly, both locally and internationally.

Kenton W (2024: 1–4) cites Conscious Capitalism as a 'socially responsible economic and political philosophy' which, in effect, means that business is responsible for pursuing profits but not at the expense of operating ethically. Conscious Capitalism imposes a mindset that harmonizes the interests of all stakeholders, not just one or two interest groups. In terms of that mindset, it is worthwhile to relay the four guiding principles:

1. A business has a higher purpose than simply making profits; it engages and inspires;
2. A business connects with all stakeholders and concentrates on the whole 'business ecosystem;'
3. A business projects 'conscious leadership' and emphasizes inclusiveness;
4. A business displays a 'conscious culture' that is embedded as one of 'trust and cooperation among all stakeholders.'

Kenton W (2024) notes that large companies such as Starbucks and Costco have adopted the concept of Conscious Capitalism.

Of course, detractors could say that investors may wish the focus to be on high returns and that the private sector should not be responsible for the delivery of outcomes that should be the purview of policymakers. In response, I think the reality suggests otherwise, and business currently continues to factor in a socially responsible approach that produces a sustainable outcome, which is good for businesses remaining profitable.

10.5 Evidence Suggesting the Adoption of a Corporate Social Responsibility Approach is Gaining Momentum

Stobierski T (2021: 1–4) provides some details that indicate the increasing adoption of a socially responsible business approach. In particular, it is noted that 'an estimated 90% of companies on the S&P 500 index published a CSR report in 2019, compared to just 20% in 2011.' Thus, the figures seem to support the movement towards the adoption of business practices that incorporate corporate social responsibility. In effect, this is a movement away from simply goal setting to more of a standardization which is built into strategic thinking. This is driven by customers taking into account the CSR policy before making a purchase, investors before they invest, prospective employees before they agree to work for a particular organization, and management before they undertake business planning.

As noted, Stobierski T (2021) provides 15 interesting statistics that are worthy of summary below categorized according to customer and investor, employee, and executive beliefs:

1. 70% of Americans believe companies have a responsibility to make the world a better place;
2. 70% of consumers prefer to deal with companies wanting to make the world a better place and 73% of investors preference companies that are environmentally socially responsible;
3. 41% of millennial investors investigate a company's CSR credentials, compared to lower figures for Gen X and Baby boomers;
4. 25% of consumers and 22% of investors avoid companies that have questionable CSR policies;
5. 55% of American consumers believe companies should have a firm positive position on social, environmental, and political issues;
6. 93% of employees support companies that show purpose;
7. 95% of employees believe businesses should benefit all stakeholders, not just some;
8. 70% of employees preference companies that display purpose;
9. 92% of employees will recommend a company as a preferred employer providing the company has a strong purpose;

10. 90% of employees working at companies with a strong sense of purpose believe they are more motivated and loyal;
11. 90% of executives believe that a strong sense of company purpose provides employee satisfaction;
12. 46% of executives believe that their company has a strong sense of purpose;
13. 58% of businesses that have a strong sense of purpose experienced 10% or more growth over the last three years;
14. Executives overall believe that value adding for customers, impacting society in a positive way, inspiring innovation, and positive change are three top reasons driving an organization's purpose;
15. 99% of executives believe disruptions similar to COVID impact the move towards CSR.

These statistics are strong indicators of a broad social consciousness that not only exists but is growing. They also strongly suggest that consumers, investors, staff, and management are coming to regard Corporate Social Responsibility as a key driver of future-proofing businesses.

10.6 Is There a Need for the Adoption of Mandatory Reporting of Aspects of Corporate Social Responsibility, including the Australian position

As the embedding of corporate social responsibility reporting frameworks appears to be on the uptake, they are still mostly unregulated arrangements. One exception is the European Union where EU Directive 2022/2464 introduces mandatory sustainability reporting for all targeted EU businesses as well as third-country linked businesses. Pantazi T (2024) covers in some detail aspects of this initiative. These aspects are worthy of a brief summary here and they provide an example of the first moves towards formalizing a legal framework for Corporate Social Responsibility in a global setting, from which other countries and jurisdictions can mirror in the future (the EU Corporate Sustainability Reporting Directive or CSRD).

As noted by Pantazi T (2024), the relationship between Corporate Social Responsibility and the law has been an arguable one. Because CSR never carried a clear definition its position has been more aspirational rather than one of 'hard law' and has previously been managed under the provisions of the EU's Non-Financial Reporting Directive or NFRD. CSR tended to follow the indirect legislative requirements outlined in areas such as 'human rights, environmental protection and anti-bribery.' Further, it tended to follow the recommendations of various international bodies and also the intent of various corporate law provisions. Of course, one should not discount the ever-increasing pressure applied by market forces, consumer and investor sentiment, and the overall increase in awareness of the need for businesses to act sustainably as outlined in the foregoing sections of this chapter.

The legal requirement for non-financial reporting is based on the need to ensure that risks to both the economy and environment are minimized and, insofar as the European Union is concerned, it brings together earlier regulations that were designed to achieve an outcome based on sustainability, although the previous focus was piecemeal rather than comprehensive. Importantly, Pantazi T (2024) notes that entities 'are expected to publish their first reports under the new regime starting from financial year 2024 (large entities). Other categories of undertakings will have to comply as of the financial year 2025.' Note that more entities will fall under the new requirements progressively from 2026 and separate standards will be developed for small to medium enterprises. Critical to the success of these mandatory requirements is that they will capture third-country undertakings which have a connection to the EU entity.

In terms of materiality as a binding legal rule, Pantazi T (2024) notes that under the Directive 'undertakings should report information necessary to understand the undertaking's impacts on sustainability matters as well as information necessary to understand how sustainability matters affect the undertaking's development, performance and position.' This is referred to as the 'double materiality principle' and all sustainability reporting disclosures will be published under a separate section of the annual financial statements. In addition, auditable assurances will be a progressive requirement in terms of the need for stakeholders to be able to make assessments.

The type of information reported will be both quantitative and qualitative and will include sustainability policies, goals and performance, greenhouse gas emissions and targets, employee satisfaction, governance outcomes, employee and staff diversity, and human rights impacts. Short to medium and long-term goals will be reported as well.

Of course, having a legally imposed reporting base is one thing, but how will the effectiveness of any sanctions for incorrect or misleading reporting play out in reality? Unfortunately, as noted by Pantazi T (2024), 'the CSRD makes no particular reference to public enforcement issues and sanctions.' Thus, deferral to the normal regulatory provisions relating to annual financial statements will be required as necessary and this can involve variability between EU member states. That said, resorting to civil measures such as shareholder enforcement or even company law provisions may be required. Failing that, consumers may take an action relating to incorrect reporting and misleading information, and in EU law the legal instrument for undertaking such an action is the Unfair Commercial Practices Directive (UCPD). However, it seems that this may be limited in scope.

As indicated by Pantazi T (2024), 'the potential of private enforcement is substantially limited and the aim of the directive is firmly focused on the needs of investors and financial participants, for which the clarity and comparability of information will certainly be beneficial.' Clearly, this is in line with the normal provisions of the information provided under the annual financial reports and their purpose. Regrettably, this probably falls short of fulfilling the objective of the need for full stakeholder engagement under sound Corporate Social Responsibility principles. That said, operationally, companies will be required to report both previous and future sustainability data and will be required to have their CSR information audited by third-party auditors to improve the chances of completeness and accuracy.

In terms of the Australian position, and as mentioned earlier, with the exception of the European Union, most Corporate Social Responsibility reporting frameworks are still unregulated. That still applies to Australia but reporting standards will soon be changing.

As noted by Sheedy C (2024)

> larger businesses are increasingly shaping their engagement and sustainability strategies around reporting standards that will soon come into force. Small and medium-sized businesses in Australia should be developing their carbon emissions reporting capability to better engage with their clients and customers that are grappling with impending mandatory rules.

Specifically, 'for big businesses, such reporting will soon be mandatory, but for small businesses it is often expected too.'

Whether it's a large or small to medium-size business, sustainability reporting will impact all businesses due to the interconnectedness of enterprises through the value chain due to 'scope 1, 2 and 3' emissions reporting requirements (Sheedy 2024). In essence, scope 1 refers to direct controllable emissions, scope 2 refers to purchased emissions (electricity for eg), while scope 3 refers to emissions from the other interconnected businesses within the primary business's value chain.

While the impending Australian-mandated position is not as comprehensive and far-reaching as the European Union, it is nonetheless changing the way Australian businesses will be required to formally report their sustainability impacts in relation to emissions and emission targets. Indicative timelines for the introduction of this mandatory reporting in Australia range from 12 months for large enterprises and up to ten years for other smaller to medium-sized enterprises. Of course, indicative timelines are not important in terms of when the implementation will take effect, rather the materiality of this change lies in the importance of the implementation itself.

10.7 Conclusion

Corporate Social Responsibility has grown from simply a business model designed to improve social outcomes and garner stakeholder support with the aim of improving the bottom line, to a progression towards mandatory annual reporting as part of the entity's annual reports. In the European Union, mandatory CSR reporting is in place in line with the legal requirements of the EU's Corporate Sustainability Reporting Directive (CSRD). No doubt, similar initiatives will occur more broadly, and in Australia changes are afoot.

No change happens in isolation and stakeholder pressure, whatever the motive, will continue to drive change in this space. This is indicative of the growing view that we must act in a more sustainable way when it comes to producing consumer goods, and how we treat our finite environmental resources.

In essence, all stakeholders, whether consumers, investors, management, society more broadly, regulators, and governments are becoming more in tune with the need for transparency and accountability in the pursuit of sustainable development and sustainable business practices. Corporate Social Responsibility does matter, and it is clearly in the best interests of business, its stakeholders, and the environment to embrace an honest implementation of its principles and practices.

References

Bonsu, S 2020, 'Deceptive advertising: A corporate social responsibility perspective', *International Journal of Health and Economic Development*, *6*(2), pp.1–15.

Cavicchia, M 2021, 'So, what do we mean when we talk about sustainability', Special Edition, 'Green new world, accounting for an ethical and sustainable future', *Public Accountant,* September, pp.10–11.

Fernando, J 2024 'What is CSR? corporate social responsibility explained', *Investopedia*, Investopedia.com.

Freeman E, Harrison, JS, Wicks, AC, Parmar, BL & de Colle, S 2010, 'Stakeholder theory', in *The state of the art*, University of Richmond School of Business, Management Faculty Publications.

Keeble, B 1988, 'The Brundtland report: "Our common future"', *Medicine & War*, *4*, pp.17–25.

Kenton, W 2024 'Conscious capitalism: Definition, 4 principles, and company examples', *Investopedia*, Investopedia.com.

Murphy, C 2024, 'Why social responsibility matters to business', *Investopedia*, Investopedia.com.

Pantazi T 2024, 'The introduction of mandatory corporate sustainability reporting in the EU and the question of enforcement', *European Business Organization Law Review*, https://doi.org/1001007/s40804-024-00320-x.

Sheedy, C 2024, 'How to get started with sustainability and emissions reporting', *Public Accountant*, Institute of Public Accountants, publicaccountant.com.au/features/sustainability-emissions-reporting.

Stobierski, T 2021, '15 eye opening corporate social responsibility statistics', *Business Insights Harvard Business School online business insights*, online.hbs.edu.

United Nation, *Sustainable development goals: 17 goals*, https://sdgs.un.org/goals.

11 Eradicating Malnutrition

Capacity to Access Nutritious Food

Mia Mahmudur Rahim and Abhay Vir Singh Kanwar

11.1 Introduction

The right to food is not limited to just having enough to eat. It also encompasses the ability to access and enjoy a diet that is both nutritionally appropriate and culturally relevant. The capabilities approach, developed by economist Amartya Sen and philosopher Martha Nussbaum, emphasizes the importance of focusing on people's abilities to do and be what they value, rather than just meeting their basic needs. The capability approach is a framework for evaluating wellbeing and development that goes beyond traditional economic models by focusing on the real freedoms individuals have to achieve their potential in terms of both 'doings' and 'beings'. This approach acknowledges that every individual has their own unique values and objectives, and, therefore, the right to food should not be limited to a one-size-fits-all solution.

Palasuberniam (2018) delves deeper into how the capabilities approach can be applied to the right to food by identifying the abilities necessary to enjoy this rightfully. These abilities include access to food, the ability to choose a culturally and nutritionally appropriate diet, freedom from hunger and malnutrition, participation in decision-making related to food policies, and engagement in cultural food practices. However, implementing the capabilities approach presents challenges, particularly in addressing issues of poverty and inequality. A comprehensive approach is necessary. This includes better access to education, healthcare, and basic necessities. It also involves empowering marginalized communities to participate in decision-making processes.

This chapter stresses the importance of viewing the right to food as a complex concept that demands a comprehensive approach to addressing food security and nutrition issues. It highlights the significance of the capabilities approach in guiding policies and practices that promote food security and nutrition for everyone.

11.2 Nutritious Food, Malnutrition, and Capability Approach

11.2.1 Nutritious Food

Nutritious food is defined as food that contains essential nutrients like vitamins and minerals. It provides the body with energy and the necessary

DOI: 10.4324/9781003392279-11

building blocks for optimal functioning. A balanced diet consisting of various fruits, vegetables, whole grains, lean proteins, and healthy fats is considered nutritious. Eating nutritious food is crucial for maintaining good health and preventing diseases. It helps improve energy levels, supports a robust immune system, aids in weight management, reduces the risk of chronic diseases, and promotes better mood and mental health. Consuming nutritious food is essential for overall wellbeing and should be incorporated into one's daily diet (Drewnowski and Evans 2001; Rozin 2005).

Obtaining specific data on the distribution of individuals receiving nutritious food in various countries can be challenging and, in some cases, unavailable. Nevertheless, it has been reported that approximately one out of every three people did not have access to sufficient food in the year 2020 (Food and Agriculture Organisation 2021). Additionally, in 2021, 29.3% of the global population, or 2.3 billion people, experienced moderate to severe food insecurity (World Health Organisation 2022). These numbers suggest that many global populations are not receiving nutritious food. It is important to note that access to healthy food is influenced by various factors such as economic conditions, availability of resources, and government policies (United Nations 2023).

11.2.2 Malnutrition

Malnutrition refers to deficiencies, excesses, or imbalances in a person's intake of energy and/or nutrients (World Health Organisation 2020). It can occur when the body does not receive enough nutrients or has an excess of certain nutrients (World Health Organisation 2020). There are four types of malnutrition: undernutrition, macronutrient undernutrition, micronutrient undernutrition, and overnutrition (Clinic 2023). Undernutrition is a deficiency of nutrients, while macronutrient undernutrition refers to a deficiency of proteins, carbohydrates, and fats. Micronutrient undernutrition is a deficiency of vitamins and minerals. Overnutrition, on the other hand, is excessive consumption of nutrients and can lead to obesity and various non-communicable diseases (Clinic 2023).

The number of people facing malnutrition continued to rise in 2020 to between 720 and 811 million people worldwide (World Health Organisation 2021). Africa, Asia, Latin America, and the Caribbean saw the most significant increases in the number of people suffering from malnutrition in 2020 (World Health Organisation 2021). Nearly one in three people in these regions did not have access to adequate food in 2020 (World Health Organisation 2021).

11.2.3 Capability Approach

The capability approach is a theoretical framework that prioritizes the wellbeing of individuals and recognizes the importance of their capabilities in achieving it. This approach has been adopted by several disciplines, including social justice and development ethics, and has influenced the human development approach. It has also gained recognition in moral and political philosophy. The roots of this approach can be traced back to Aristotle and Karl Marx, but Amartya Sen and Martha Nussbaum are credited with its development.

Aristotle's moral and political philosophy emphasizes virtue ethics and the common good. He believed that living well and flourishing (eudaimonia) was the goal of life, attainable through character development and virtues (McK eon 1941). Aristotle stressed the importance of a just and peaceful society that promotes the wellbeing of its citizens and enables them to pursue happiness in a well-ordered community. His 'politics of the mean' advocates for balanced and moderate governance to foster a harmonious society where people can cultivate virtue and achieve eudaimonia. Central to the capability approach is the idea of functioning and capabilities, which draws parallels to Aristotle's emphasis on the actualization of human potential and the ability to lead a life in accordance with one's values and goals (Nussbaum 1988). Karl Marx's moral and political philosophy is primarily characterized by his revolutionary communist views (Callinicos 2011). Marx believed that work could be creative and fulfilling, rejecting the notion of work as a necessary evil. His theory of historical materialism suggests that societies rise and fall based on their advancement or hindrance of human productive power (Cohen 1983). Marx's economic analysis centres on capitalism and the extraction of surplus value from the proletariat. He predicted the eventual breakdown of capitalism and the rise of communism. Marx's emphasis on freedom and empowerment is echoed in the capability approach's concern for individuals' capabilities to choose and act in ways that they value.

The capability approach can be seen as a fusion of utilitarianism and Rawlsian principles, drawing on the focus on wellbeing from utilitarianism and the emphasis on justice and fairness from Rawlsian principles (Sheng 2012). This blend results in a nuanced framework that places the expansion of individuals' capabilities at the heart of evaluating societal wellbeing and justice. As such, this approach is widely recognized for its capacity to address the limitations of previous egalitarian theories by offering a more holistic and person-centered framework that considers individuals' capabilities, freedom, and the diverse factors that shape their ability to lead lives they have reason to value. This nuanced approach provides a more comprehensive understanding of wellbeing and social justice, addressing the oversights of earlier egalitarian perspectives. It considers abstract concepts such as non-exploitation and non-discrimination and individual needs and abilities. Sen defines basic capabilities as the functions necessary for an individual to sustain their life and acknowledges the limitations of categorizing capabilities and basic capability as the sole guide for moral good.

The capability approach strives to achieve total utility equality and bridge the gaps between utilitarianism and Rawlsian justice. It focuses on the idea that an individual's wellbeing can be achieved by developing their capabilities. It differs from other theories focusing on equality by emphasizing an individual's wellbeing before distribution. The capability approach and the concept of cost-benefit analysis also represent different approaches to evaluating wellbeing and policy decisions, with the capability approach emphasizing human capabilities and freedoms, while cost-benefit analysis focuses on economic evaluation (Smith et al. 2012). While they are distinct, there are opportunities for these frameworks to complement each other, particularly by integrating non-monetary considerations into economic evaluations, thereby aligning more closely with the multifaceted concerns of the capability approach.

The capability approach, in the context of ensuring nutritious food, focuses on individual agency and the key capabilities necessary for healthy growth and development (Standford Encyclopedia of Philosophy 2023a). It recognizes that access to nutritious food is essential for overall wellbeing (Wells 2023). By addressing social structures and the unequal distribution of resources, the capability approach aims to break the cycle of unhealthy choices and empower individuals to access nutritious food. This approach emphasizes the importance of capabilities such as staying away from disease, eating well, staying happy and playful, staying healthy and nourished, practicing autonomy in childcare, and having earning opportunities (Chakraborty et al. 2020; Haisma et al. 2018). By enhancing these capabilities, programs and interventions can be developed to improve access to nutritious food, particularly in vulnerable regions like the poorest countries in Asia and sub-Saharan Africa (Chakraborty et al. 2020). By promoting emancipation and empowerment, the capability approach aims to break the cycle of unhealthy choices and provide individuals with the means to access nutritious food and improve their overall wellbeing (Gombert et al. 2017).

11.3 Capability Approach Towards Access to Nutritious Food

Ever since Amartya Sen propounded the capability approach in response to utilitarianism and Rawlsian idea of justice, it has been one of the most contested and accepted moves to furnish egalitarianism amongst various alternatives. Since this approach aims at an individual's wellbeing as an end product by emphasizing centrally located beings and doings, it has become one of its rallying points. The centrally located beings and doings facilitate individuals to access one of the most basic conditions for survival. It encompasses the ability to have access to adequate nutrition, shelter, healthcare, education, and social participation, free from stigma or illness (see Walker and Unterhalter 2007: 25). To Sen, poverty can be rated as one of the most acute forms of capability failure as it entails the absolute inability of individuals to choose something valuable intrinsic to human life. While explicating centrally located beings and doings, Sen tries to bring in the idea of a capability set. It is this set of capabilities that an individual should imbibe to avoid the conditions of acute forms of capability failure, which may entail malnutrition.

When Sen elaborates poverty as one of the most acute forms of capability failure, for it entails the absolute inability of individuals to choose something valuable which are intrinsic to human life, on the other hand, the problem of malnutrition seems to be far more entrenched and endemic to the extent that in millions of cases, children are not even exposed to minimal life chances so that they can even survive biologically. In 2020, approximately five million children under the age of five died globally, with India being one of the countries with the highest number of under-five deaths (Kaur 2023). This country ranked in the lowest quartile in the Child Development Index (CDI), along with countries like Congo and Ghana (Mathur et al. 2022). The CDI measures child wellbeing using education, health, and nutrition indicators. In terms of child malnutrition, India faces significant challenges. The Global Hunger Index reports that India has a child malnutrition rate of 37.4%, with 20.8% underweight and 37.9% experiencing stunting (Wiemers 2023). This has been the situation in many other developing countries like Nigeria. In 2019, the national under-five mortality rate in Nigeria was reported to be high (UNICEF 2023). Inadequate nutrition is a vital contributing factor to child mortality (Geza and Ndlovu 2023).

Having recapitulated the endemic nature of malnutrition, what is much more pressing is its biological spillovers on the infant when she or he is in its nascent and one of the most formative months of life. The concerns over the biological spillovers due to malnutrition have been raised by Coursin and others (Coursin 1972; Alderman et al. 2003; Hoddinott et al. 2012; Jha 2019). Coursin elaborates on how malnutrition is crucial in inter-generational socioeconomic mobility (Coursin 1972: 190). It also assumes special importance as it is seen as a disease aggravated and exacerbated by other diseases. It gets manifested in many forms like retardation in growth in the very early years of childhood, on a physical note, but in many acute cases, it may also entail into deficit in cognitive development. As severely malnourished children are quite often slow on cognitive functions and have poorer psychomotor development along with poorer fine motor skills, which entails their lower activity levels, comparatively less interaction with their environment, and decreased rate of acquiring skills. The previously mentioned are the immediate causes of malnutrition and its long-term consequences. They manifested in intergenerational transmission of poor nutrition, which further entails psychological and physiological malfunctioning across generations.

Given the endemic nature of malnutrition with its national, geographic, and especially gendered versions along with one of the severe biological spillovers, Choudhary and Parthasarathy (2009: 584–594) elaborate on socioeconomic spillovers that trigger as well as ensure malnutrition. According to them, migration contributes to a greater extent to malnutrition. When many people move from rural areas to urban areas, they are constantly subsumed by rampant violence, flimsy housing, filthy living conditions, and hunger and malnutrition (Winegarden et al. 2021; Jennings 2016). Circumstances of such sort have dire consequences on an individual's bodily health (Schanbacher 2019). When blended with the depreciated health of an individual, the urban squatter entails high rates of infant mortality. The reason behind such an abysmal form of condition is multi-layered. It ranges from a lack of access to employment opportunities and a dearth of education avenues; if employed, then there is a lack of tenure security (Choudhary and Parthasarathy 2009: 584–594). But most potent of all is one's vulnerability to health crises in general and malnutrition in particular. As access to food, accompanied by adequate care, is entirely missing, which are primarily some of the prerequisites in maintaining the two. The previously mentioned measures of vulnerability to health crises and malnutrition facilitate comprehending household access to food and an individual's nutritional status, respectively, in urban areas (Suarez-Orozco 2019). If an individual fares well on nutritional indicators, on the one hand, followed by access to health parameters, the blend of it facilitates augmenting the household income, on the one hand, and, on the other hand, helps in affirming sound household behavior, which also entails a congenial environment even in the urban squatter.

11.3.1 Poverty – An Absolute Capability Failure for Nutritious Food?

When the problem of malnutrition is widespread and it jeopardizes one of the most crucial capabilities required for an individual's biological survival, which further entails socio-economic spillovers, it is on this note that the theory of poverty, which by Sen is seen as 'absolute capability failure', needs revision. Merely rating poverty as one of the stages of 'absolute capability failure' may sidestep various other factors that may cause the conditions of deprivation. These factors, apart from economic deprivation, may be culturally induced and socially stirred. In many circumstances, poverty is percolated due to religious and political practices. Given the ambiguity of poverty as a condition of 'absolute capability failure' simply evades when it comes to capturing one of the most important conditions required for biological survival. Akin to the ambiguity reflected in the concept of poverty as a condition of absolute capability failure, similar uncertainty can be confronted in Amartya Sen's concept of capability set, which, if imbibed, can facilitate an individual to ebb the risk of running into absolute capability failure. According to Sen, the ability to have adequate nourishment and shelter, to avoid preventable illnesses and premature death, to receive education and healthcare, and to participate in society without feeling ashamed, are some of the essential capabilities that can be considered as part of the capability set. However, Sen acknowledges that there is no clear consensus on what basic capabilities should be included in the set, as the definition of 'basic' can vary depending on interpretation.

Based on the above explanation, it is difficult to determine whether poverty is a critical factor in addressing malnutrition. While some argue that poverty is one of the most basic capabilities required for an individual's biological survival, others, like Sen, have a broader view of basic capabilities. However, Alkire (2005) argues that basic capabilities can be delivered to individuals without their prior knowledge. It is important to draw attention to the fact that malnutrition levels in some areas are extremely high and pose a threat to individual survival. Given this situation, it is worth considering what capabilities can be provided without the informed consent of the individuals by the government machinery. In general parlance, we may conclude that the capability set proposed by Amartya Sen can be considered as one of the essential capabilities to which every individual must adhere. Still, even a cursory analysis of the capability set proposed by Sen would delineate that the capabilities proposed in the capability set are not about one or two kinds of capabilities. It is not just about having the basic necessities of life, such as food and shelter. It also involves having the ability to avoid sickness and death, access to education and good health, and engage in social interactions without experiencing shame. Therefore, it is not appropriate to compare the capability set proposed by Amartya Sen with other capabilities when defining the basic capabilities proposed by Sabina Alkire. Alkire's capability approach emphasizes functioning, capabilities, and agency. Functioning includes things people value, such as health, education, and social and political participation. But capabilities are the freedom to perform valuable functions. They show people's real options. She stresses that capabilities are valuable in themselves. They empower people to live meaningful lives and achieve their goals. She also recognizes that social, economic, and political conditions, as well as individual traits and abilities, affect capabilities. As such, she emphasizes agency along with functioning and capabilities. Agency is the ability to choose and act. People have different powers, resources, and opportunities, which can increase or limit their agency. Her work has advanced the capability approach in research and policymaking, improving human development understanding.

11.3.2 Education – A Basic Capability to Access Nutritious Foods?

In his discussion of fundamental capabilities required to prevent different types of capability failure, Sen outlines the following abilities: having access to sufficient food and shelter, avoiding preventable illnesses and premature death, having access to education and good health care, and being able to interact socially without feeling ashamed. Drawing from these basic capabilities proposed by Sen (2000) argue about basic capability by borrowing from Alkire (2005), which rates education as one of the most basic capabilities. Elaborating further, Terzi (2007) construes how the absence of education would ensue in the feeble-mindedness of the child, and on the other hand, its presence would enable her or him to equip several other complex capabilities. When malnutrition diminishes the life chances of infants and ceases the biological survival of an individual, education as a capability-building apparatus makes no sense, if we argue from the vantage point of an infant. However, elaborating further, education, as one of the most basic capabilities raises many concerns in grooming an individual through informal learning and formal schooling.

By considering the normal trajectory of a new born, it is not difficult to ascertain that informal learning, which includes orientation about the surrounding environment and knowing about oneself and one's body, takes place when an infant has crossed the postnatal stage. This phase comes when she or he is between one and two years. When it comes to formal schooling, which includes fine motor skills, comes much after the phase of informal learning. With respect to that, if an infant must be secured from malnutrition, which jeopardizes his life chances with the very idea of conception by a malnourished mother, education has no role to play. However, if education is to be considered one of the most basic capabilities according to the definition of Alkire (2005), then it must be delivered without the informed consent of the child. However, the very method by which education is delivered considers the acceptance level of the child. For this, by taking into consideration the growth trajectory of an infant, we need to delve into the capabilities that can be delivered when she or he is just born. If an infant has to be made capable as soon as she or he is born, it is indicative of the fact that education cannot be one of the basic capabilities required for biological survival.

11.3.3 Health as a Basic Capability – Need for Bifurcation?

While education is an important aspect of a child's growth and development, Ruger (2009) and Venkatapuram (2013) argue that it should be considered as a capability that ensures an individual's health and ability to be healthy once they have attained a certain level of psychosocial competence during the formative months. Venkatapuram, when arguing about the capability to be healthy, articulates a conception of health that enables a person to achieve or exercise a cluster of basic human activities and channel opportunities. These human activities primarily aim to live life with dignity and capture opportunities in which health as a capability is not merely seen as performing vital functions of life. Still, the capability to be healthy Venkatapuram should aspire for larger goals, which should have moral entitlements to avail cluster of abilities that no one can reject. Though the given scenario of malnutrition largely falls within the confines of the capability to be healthy, even Venkatapuram's version of the capability to be healthy reiterates ambiguity, as it aims at a cluster of capabilities that can make an individual healthy. If we peruse the delivery mechanisms of the public distribution system on an empirical plain, it would be self-evident that public health outlets do not even subscribe to minimal interventions that can facilitate an individual's survival as a biological being. On the other hand, the promise that Venkatapuram's version of the capability to be healthy adheres to is too big to be realized on a practical plane. Detailing it further, he aspires to adhere to such capability to be healthy in which everyone lives a life of dignity and not merely perform vital biological functions.

Considering the conditions in India in general and the villages in particular, small infants become so vulnerable due to several structural constraints that they cannot perform minimal biological functions. Though crucial, restoring them to their dignity seems too far-fetched a dream. By taking note of both theoretical and empirical strands, it is self-evident that neither education as a capability nor merely the capability to be healthy can address the acute fix of malnutrition. When the problem of malnutrition broadly falls within the confines of health, arguably, the capability to be healthy needs to be segregated. Ruger (2009) proposes the concept of central as well as non-central capabilities within the capability to be healthy. When central capabilities address the minimum life functions and non-central capabilities, take note of other complex functions. If an individual becomes vulnerable to inefficient health mechanisms, her central health capabilities cannot be channeled. Hence, an individual cannot sustain herself as a biological being. Most of the reports on malnutrition show that before getting any intervention, most infants do not even realize their whole biological beings as they are not restored to their central capabilities.

11.4 Access to Nutritious Food – A Basic Capability

From the above-mentioned discussion, we can discern the characteristics of the basic capabilities and conclude that neither education as a capability nor merely health as a capability can address the problem of malnutrition. One of the prominent attributes of the basic capabilities is that its absence may potentially harm an individual, and its presence prepares an individual to acquire several other complex capabilities. According to Alkire (2005), an essential capability can be one that can be delivered to an individual without their informed consent.

There are back-and-forth linkages between these three capabilities: the capability to access nutrition, the capability to be healthy, and the capability to be educated. Owing to their back-and-forth linkages, the exact trajectory in which they should be restored coincides with the development of the human body and needs further evaluation. By now, it is needless to explicate the sweeping scenario of malnutrition amongst most infants and the capability to access nutrition as one of the most basic capabilities. Arguing about the dilemmas that come to the forefront in restoring nutrition to one of the most vulnerable sections of society would bring in Sen's concept of agency.

Agency is the choice to which every individual is restored to realize her or his beings and doings. If palliative care is delivered to the target communities, who remain vulnerable to economic shocks, which entails their biological fragility, acting as an agency meets one of the most basal conditions of continued existence. Referring to the attributes of the basic capabilities, if the capability to access nutrition and ethical health is not timely delivered to the target communities, it would further push them to a much more dilapidated disposition regarding their diminished life chances. However, in the cases in which the interventions given show positive outcomes, those kids, after passing the postnatal stage, realize their further beings and doings with the help of an advanced complementary capability set. What we understand is that if an individual is biologically prepared to perform one of the basic functions, she or he is taken care of on health indicators first and educational parameters afterward. With respect to that, education and merely health cannot be rated as one of the most basic capabilities, given the malnutrition scenario. When the conditions of malnutrition take a toll on the biological survival of an individual, in such an acute fix, avoiding the capability to be educated and the capability to be healthy as a whole can be sidestepped. Rather than save an individual from the crises emerging from malnutrition, which endangers the very idea of life, she or he should mandatorily be restored to the capability to access nutrition. Moreover, this capability is a kind of capability to which every infant can be restored without informed consent, as it ensures the very basis of life. Comparing the capability to access nutrition to the capability to be educated and healthy, it is not difficult to argue that it is relatively homogenous. However, when a child crosses the postnatal stage and becomes enabling to equip themselves to access education, many other variables come into play, which determine and become predetermined due to the environmental orientation.

In a nutshell, capabilities must be realized in a timely fashion and in accordance with an individual's biological development. Acquiring varied capabilities necessitates a proportional level of biological and psychosocial competencies. Just as an infant in its prenatal stage cannot be made capable enough to acquire education, similarly, when an infant has crossed the postnatal stage, it would be too late to take note of her or his basic nutritional demands. This brings in another concept of capability approach: 'conversion factors'. In social science, conversion factors refer to the elements or factors that influence an individual's ability to transform personal and structural resources into actual achievements or agency (Bazzani 2023). These factors include social norms, public policies, and other societal influences that shape an individual's ability to achieve wellbeing and exercise their freedoms. They are significant in assessing how much a person can transform available resources into the doings and beings they value and have reason to pursue (Stanford Encyclopedia of Philosophy 2023b). Conversion factors are essential in understanding how societal contexts impact an individual's capabilities and functions (Nambiar 2013; Walker 2019).

Sen defines three conversion factors: personal conversion factors, social conversion factors, and environmental conversion factors (Sen 2000: 71–73). Suppose an infant remains malnourished due to the inaccessibility of nutrition. In that case, she or he will be unable to adapt biological beings to doings by using personal conversion factors. Inadequacy on the part of an individual to exist as a biological being indicates that she or he will not be able to realize social and environmental conversion factors. The previously mentioned explanation again reiterates the capability to access nutrition as one of the most basic capabilities, which should be followed by a capability to be healthy in broader terms, entailing biological preparedness to channel education as one of the capabilities from several other capabilities that can necessitate the overall welfare of an individual.

11.5 Conclusion

Within the broad capability approach, access to nutrition is a more fundamental capability than being healthy or educated. Dealing with the problem of malnutrition as a category provokes us to engage with the specific stakeholders concerned with the problem of malnutrition. Having concerned stakeholders involved in the delivery mechanisms helps ensure precision, reduces the problem of malnutrition, and guarantees overall welfare. However, the lack of such interventions makes it harder to evaluate the biological and financial repercussions on the target communities. When the availability of a crucial intervention determines biological survival and further facilitates the potential for assimilating various other complex capabilities, such as achieving overall health and education, it highlights the interconnection between different capabilities and underscores the importance of realizing them in accordance with an individual's biological potential. Since all the capabilities are interlinked and have cumulative effects with reference to one of the most basic capabilities to achieve the overall welfare of an individual, it calls for the idea of justice.

With respect to the capability to access nutrition, only nutritional justice can go a long way in accomplishing other capabilities like overall health and education. If we explicate the requirements to furnish justice on nutritional terms, it calls for such delivery mechanisms that are context-free in terms of culture, religious orientation, and socioeconomic inclination. It is so, as nutritional justice merely calls for mechanisms that can minimally provide nutritional access to an infant. When discussing nutritional justice and accessibility to nutrition, the capability to access nutrition is relatively uniform and straightforward compared to other capabilities such as higher education, skill development, and infrastructure development. As a result, it does not require a substantial financial budget or a massive infrastructural setup. Instead, delivering nutritional justice requires an ethical nutritional paradigm that focuses on precise managerial practices, resource mobilization, and community participation. NGOs working for citizens typically deliver this paradigm. Therefore, the importance of access to nutrition as a basic capability and its connection to other capabilities, such as health and education, does not need to be debated.

References

Alderman, H, Behrman, JR & Hoddinott, J 2003, 'Nutrition, malnutrition and economic growth', in G López-Casasnovas, B Rivera & L Currais (eds.), *Health and economic growth: Findings and policy implications*, MIT Press, Cambridge, pp.169–194.

Alkire, S 2005, *Valuing freedoms: Sen's capability approach and poverty reduction*, Oxford University Press, USA.

Bazzani, G 2023, 'Agency as conversion process', *Theory and Society*, *52*, pp.487–507.

Callinicos, A 2011, *The revolutionary ideas of Karl Marx*, Haymarket Books, New York.

Chakraborty, B, Yousefzadeh, S, Darak, S & Haisma, H 2020. '"We struggle with the earth every day": Parents' perspectives on the capabilities for healthy child growth in haor region of Bangladesh', *BMC Public Health*, *20*, pp.1–14.

Choudhary, N & Parthasarathy, D 2009, 'Is migration status a determinant of urban nutrition insecurity? Empirical evidence from Mumbai city, India', *Journal of Biosocial Science*, *41*(5), pp.583–605.

Clinic, C 2023, *Malnutrition* [Online], accessed 24 October 2023, https://my.clevelandclinic.org/health/diseases/22987-malnutrition.

Cohen, GA 1983. 'Reconsidering historical materialism', *NOMOS: American Society for Political and Legal Philosophy, 26*, p.227.
Coursin, DB 1972, 'Nutrition and brain development in infants', *Merrill-Palmer Quarterly of Behavior and Development, 18*, pp.177–202.
Drewnowski, A & Evans, WJ 2001, 'Nutrition, physical activity, and quality of life in older adults: Summary', *The Journals of Gerontology Series A: Biological Sciences and Medical Sciences, 56*, pp.89–94.
FAO 2021. *The world is at a critical juncture*, Food and Agriculture Organization, New York.
Geza, W & Ndlovu, M 2023, *2023 Global hunger index: The power of youth in shaping food systems* [Online], Concern Worldwide, accessed 25 October 2023, https://reliefweb.int/report/world/2023-global-hunger-index-power-youth-shaping-food-systems.
Gombert, K, Douglas, F, Carlisle, S & Mcardle, K 2017, 'A capabilities approach to food choices', *Food Ethics, 1*, pp.143–155.
Haisma, H, Yousefzadeh, S, Boele V & Hensbroek, P 2018, 'Towards a capability approach to child growth: A theoretical framework', *Maternal and Child Nutrition, 14.*
Hoddinott, J, Rosegrant, M & Torero, M 2012, *Hunger and malnutrition*, Copenhagen Consensus, Copenhagen.
Jennings, J 2016, *Killing civilization: A reassessment of early urbanism and its consequences*, UNM Press.
Jha, R 2019, 'Introduction: Hunger and malnutrition as major challenges in the 21st century', in *Hunger and malnutrition as major challenges of the 21st century*, World Scientific.
Kaur, B 2023, *India ranks 111 in global hunger index; report makers reject Indian government objections* [Online], accessed 13 October 2023, https://thewire.in/health/india-ranks-111th-among-125-countries-in-global-hunger-index-report.
Mathur, R, Jaitli, N & Amarnath, H 2022, *Child development index in India: Performance at district level*, National Institute of Public Finance and Policy, New Delhi.
McKeon, R 1941. 'Aristotle's conception of moral and political philosophy', *Ethics, 51*(3), pp.253–290.
Nambiar, S 2013, 'Capabilities, conversion factors and institutions', *Progress in Development Studies, 13*, pp.221–230.
Nations, U 2023, *Peace, dignity and equality on a healthy planet* [Online], United Nations Organisations, New York, accessed 24 October 2023, www.un.org/en/global-issues/food.
Nussbaum, M 1988, 'Nature, function, and capability: Aristotle on political distribution', in *Oxford studies in ancient philosophy: Supplementary volume*, Oxford University Press, Oxford.
Rozin, P 2005, 'The meaning of food in our lives: A cross-cultural perspective on eating and well-being', *Journal of Nutrition Education and Behavior, 37*, pp.107–112.
Ruger, JP 2009, 'Global health justice', *Public Health Ethics, 2*, pp.261–275.
Schanbacher, WD 2019, *Food as a human right: Combatting global hunger and forging a path to food sovereignty*, Bloomsbury Publishing, USA.
Sen, A 2000, 'Development as freedom', *Development in Practice, 10*, p.258.
Sheng, CL 2012. *A new approach to utilitarianism: A unified utilitarian theory and its application to distributive justice*, Springer Science & Business Media.
Smith, R, Lorgelly, P, Al-Janabi, H, Venkatapuram, S & Coast, J 2012, 'The capability approach: An alternative evaluation paradigm for health economics?', in A. Jones (ed.), *The Elgar companion to health economics*, 2nd edn, Edward Elgar Publishing.
Stanford Encyclopedia of Philosophy 2023a, *The capability approach* [Online], Stanford University, accessed 24 October 2023, https://plato.stanford.edu/entries/capability-approach/.
Stanford Encyclopedia of Philosophy 2023b, *The capability approach* [Online], accessed 15 October 2023, https://plato.stanford.edu/entries/capability-approach.

Suarez-Orozco, M. 2019, *Humanitarianism and mass migration: Confronting the world crisis*, University of California Press, CA.
Terzi, L 2007, 'The capability to be educated', in M Walker & E Unterhalter (eds.), *Amartya Sen's capability approach and social justice in education*, Palgrave Macmillan, New York.
UNICEF 2023, *Under-five mortality* [Online], accessed 14 October 2023, https://data.unicef.org/topic/child-survival/under-five-mortality/.
Venkatapuram, S 2013, *Health justice: An argument from the capabilities approach*, John Wiley and Sons, NJ.
Walker, M 2019, 'The achievement of university access: Conversion factors, capabilities and choices', *Social Inclusion*, *7*, pp.52–60.
Walker, M & Unterhalter, E 2007, *Amartya Sen's capability approach and social justice in education*, Palgrave Macmillan, New York.
Wells, T 2023, *Sen's capability approach* [Online], Internet Encyclopedia of Philosophy, accessed 23 October 2023, https://iep.utm.edu/sen-cap/.
WHO 2021, *The world is at a critical juncture* [Online], World Health Organisation, accessed 24 October 2023, www.fao.org/state-of-food-security-nutrition/2021/en/.
WHO 2022, *Global hunger numbers rose to as many as 828 million in 2021*, World Health Organisation, New York.
Wiemers, M 2023, *India* [Online], Global Hunger Index, accessed 25 October 2023, www. globalhungerindex. org/india.html.
Winegarden, W, Tartakovsky, J, Jackson, K & Rufo, CF 2021, *No way home: The crisis of homelessness and how to fix it with intelligence and humanity*, Encounter Books, New York.
World Health Organisation 2020, *Malnutrition* [Online], accessed 24 October 2023, www.who. int/news-room/questions-and-answers/item/malnutrition.

12 Future Food and Islam

A Perspective From Malaysia

Asril Amirul Zakariah, Mohd Lotpi bin Mohd Yusob, and Murshamshul Kamariah Musa

12.1 Introduction

Chapter 12 is divided into several sections, each addressing important aspects of how Islamic dietary laws intersect with new food technologies in Malaysia. The first section highlights the impressive growth of the halal food industry, driven by both the expanding global Muslim population and the rising interest from non-Muslim consumers who appreciate the ethical and hygienic standards of halal food. It also introduces the idea of future foods, like lab-grown meats and insect-based proteins, and questions how these new food sources fit with halal principles. In 'General Principles of Permissibility and Non-Permissibility under Shariah', the chapter explores the core Islamic dietary laws from the Quran and hadith and considers how these laws apply to modern food technologies. It discusses the different views within Islamic jurisprudence on whether new types of food can be considered halal, emphasizing the need for careful consideration by Islamic scholars. The above is followed by 'Specific Reasons of Permissibility and Non-Permissibility' which digs deeper into the reasons why certain foods are forbidden in Islam, such as those that are harmful, intoxicating, or impure. It explains how these rules might apply to new food sources, stressing the importance of ensuring that these foods are safe and ethically produced according to Islamic standards.

The section on 'Halal Certification Challenges in Malaysia' discusses the difficulties faced by the halal food industry, especially small- and medium-sized businesses, in meeting the strict requirements for halal certification. It outlines the comprehensive process, including sourcing ingredients, production methods, and ensuring proper handling and transportation; all regulated by the Department of Islamic Development Malaysia (JAKIM).

'The Regulatory Framework for Halal Certification' provides an overview of the guidelines and standards that ensure the integrity of halal certification in Malaysia. It explains the role of JAKIM and other regulatory bodies in maintaining consumer trust and industry credibility through rigorous certification processes.

DOI: 10.4324/9781003392279-12

Finally, the Conclusion brings together the insights from the previous sections, highlighting the need for ongoing research and collaboration among scholars, food scientists, and industry stakeholders. It emphasises the importance of integrating Islamic principles with new food technologies to tackle global challenges like food security and sustainability while maintaining the standards of halal and *ṭayyib* consumption. The chapter aims to contribute to the broader conversation about ethical consumption practices within the Muslim community and beyond, offering a thorough understanding of how the landscape of future foods is evolving in line with Islamic dietary laws.

12.2 The Intersection Between Future Food and Islam

The future of halal food is a topic of immense interest and importance. It refers to the anticipated growth and evolution of the halal food industry. According to industry forecasts, the global halal food market is expected to reach a staggering value of almost four trillion USD by 2028 (Zafar et al. 2023). This impressive growth is propelled by several factors. The primary driver is the growing Muslim population worldwide, which naturally leads to a higher demand for halal food (Mujar and Hassan 2014). However, the demand is not limited to the Muslim population. There is a rising trend among non-Muslim consumers who are choosing halal food due to its ethical and hygienic production methods (Nurrachmi 2018). This broadening consumer base significantly contributes to the expansion of the halal food industry.

The positive economic forecast suggests increasing supply and demand for halal food. By considering all forms of constraints to meet consumer demand, future food should be considered to bridge the supply gap. In this context, the concept of future food introduces a new perspective on halal food. The question of whether future food can be deemed or accepted as halal is important for consumers and industry alike. This perspective involves the need of consolidating Islamic principles with the non-conventional production and preparation methods of future food that emerge with advancements in food technology. These new methods include innovative technologies such as lab-grown meat or plant-based meat substitutes, and unconventional sources of food such as insects or algae, which are novel and uncharted in the context of halal food.

The development of lab-grown meats, also known as cultured or cell-based meats, presents a modern ethical and technological challenge to the traditional concept of permissible food and beverage in Islamic dietary laws (Ruling on Eating Synthetic Meat Produced by Using Stem Cells 2018). As advancements in biotechnology continue to revolutionise the food industry, questions arise about the permissibility of consuming lab-grown meats within the framework of Islamic jurisprudence. The views on these new methods and sources shall need to be thoroughly evaluated for their compliance with halal principles, presenting new challenges and opportunities for the halal food industry.

The primary sources of Islamic law – the Quran and hadith – that govern or at least influence Muslim beliefs, practices, and behaviours, amongst others, provide the principles for determining the permissibility of food consumption. Given the unprecedented growth and nature of future foods, Islamic jurists need to address the specific characteristics of this novel food product in relation to the established guidelines of ḥalal and *ṭayyib* consumption. Halal and *tayyib* are principles in Islamic dietary regulations that influence Muslims' food choices and consumption. *Halal* refers to foods and beverages that are permitted under Islamic law, as detailed in the Quran and Hadith.

According to the translation by Abdullah (2000) this includes following restrictions such as not consuming pork (The Holy Quran 2:173) or alcohol (The Holy Quran 2:219), ensuring that animals are slaughtered according to Islamic standards (The Holy Qur'an 5:5), and preventing contamination with prohibited substances. *Tayyib*, on the other hand, goes beyond basic permissibility and focuses on the wholesomeness, purity, and overall quality of food (The Holy Quran 2:168). It encourages Muslims to seek out food that is not only halal but also ethically sourced, nutritious, and good for both the body and the soul (Alzeer et al. 2018). When we delve into the subject of halal food and its future, we are navigating between two unique yet interconnected perspectives, the genuine halal status of the food and the halal certification of the food.

A full picture of the current situation of the halal food sector, as well as its prospective future trajectory, can be obtained by utilising these views. The true halal status of a specific food pertains to its adherence to Islamic dietary regulations. This implies that the food has satisfied all the criteria outlined in Islamic law, as observed by Muslims. While there are slight variations in serving halal cuisine among various sects of Islam, there exists a common understanding and interpretation of this concept. This mutual comprehension is apparent when the principle of necessity is implemented, permitting specific exemptions to the halal regulations in particular situations.

In contrast, the certification of halal foods is a distinct sector. Regardless of regulation, the certification bears the ubiquitous halal emblem that is identifiable by consumers. According to the Department of Islamic Development Malaysia (JAKIM), the halal logo in Malaysia is a certification that has been granted. The certification offers a dependable guarantee of the halal status of food, thereby fostering consumer trust in the acquisition and consumption of products that have obtained halal certification (Quoquab et al. 2020).

It is important to note that the halal certification process is comprehensive. It involves not just the food ingredients, but also the entire production and handling process. This includes the sourcing of ingredients, the manufacturing process, packaging, storage, and transportation. These suggest that halal certification covers both upstream and downstream food production. Therefore, as we consider what lies ahead for the future of halal food, it will be crucial to ensure that these new methods and flow of food production comply with halal principles. This will require ongoing research, dialogue, and collaboration among scholars, food scientists, and industry stakeholders, and the key points are highlighted in this chapter.

12.3 General Principles of Permissibility and Non-Permissibility Under Shariah

As Malaysia moves forward, the integration of food and Islamic principles has become increasingly important. With a predominantly Muslim population, Malaysia places great emphasis on the halal concept and its application in the food industry. This has shaped a unique perspective on upcoming food trends and technologies within the context of Islamic beliefs and practices. In this paper, we will explore how shariah and its emerging framework view future food development, considering changes in the food landscape, technological advancements, and halal principles.

By examining this viewpoint, our goal is to clarify how these factors could impact not only the future of halal food in Malaysia but also beyond its borders. Islam has provided rules, in general and specifically, for every aspect of life, including food. The purpose of the rule on food is no other than to ensure that Muslims, other than being obedient by faith, consume healthy and suitable substances. This is related to the ultimate purpose of rules in Islam: to protect the life and mind of the human being. Such protections are enshrined in jurisprudential discussion as *maqasid al-shariah* (the main purposes of shariah).

Therefore, this writing aims to elucidate those rules and frame them as a schematic parameter in determining the halal status of food. The writing will also address the *maqasid al-shariah* behind those rules. The intersection of future foods and the halal notion under Islam has sparked controversies and debates (Siaw and Rani 2012). On one hand, there is a growing concern among some Malaysian Muslims that future foods such as lab-grown meats and insect-based proteins may not align with the halal guidelines set by Islam (Rahim et al. 2023). They question the source and nature of these foods as well as the methods used in their production.

On the other hand, there are also Malaysian Muslims who believe that as long as these future foods meet the halal requirements and do not violate any Islamic principles, they can be considered permissible to consume (Hamdan et al. 2021). These contrasting viewpoints highlight the need for a thorough examination of future food developments from an Islamic perspective (Kashim et al. 2015). With better advancements in food technology and the emergence of alternative sources of protein, the halal concept faces new challenges and debates within the Malaysian Muslim community. It is evident that the traditional understanding of halal food needs to be reevaluated in the face of these innovative developments.

The controversies surrounding future foods have led to a deeper exploration of Islamic jurisprudence and the *maqasid al-shariah*, which serve as the guiding principles for halal food (Wahyudi et al. 2021). The intricate discussions within the Islamic legal literature shed light on the significance of ensuring the protection of human life and wellbeing through individual responsibility, including consumption choices that align with permissible and healthy substances. This highlights the evolving nature of the halal concept and its adaptability to contemporary food trends and technologies. Moreover, these discussions emphasise the importance of examining the entire process of food production, from the ingredient source to the processing methods (Kashim et al. 2015).

Furthermore, the debate over lab-grown meats and insect-based proteins has prompted Malaysian Muslims to delve into the source and production methods of these foods in relation to Islamic principles (Kashim et al. 2023). The need to establish comprehensive parameters for determining the halal status of these future foods has become more apparent, requiring a nuanced understanding of both traditional Islamic teachings and modern scientific advancements (Hossain 2019). The challenge lies in striking a balance between the preservation of Islamic dietary laws and embracing technological advancements that have the potential to address future food scarcity.

As Malaysian Muslims navigate the complexities of future food developments, it is important to engage in open dialogues that encompass diverse perspectives and interpretations of halal guidelines. The evolving landscape of food and technology calls for a holistic approach that considers the fundamental purposes of shariah and their application to contemporary challenges. By aligning with the *maqasid al-shariah*, Malaysian Muslims can frame a comprehensive framework for evaluating future foods through the lens of Islamic beliefs and practices. This inclusive approach will not only impact the future of food in Malaysia but also contribute to the global discourse on the intersection of food, technology, and religious principles.

Within the realm of Islamic legal literature, the term *tha'ām* or *ath'imah* is a word that can be used to refer to 'food'. The term refers to anything, apart from substances that are intoxicating, that is ingested in the form of food and drink without regard to whether or not it is typically consumed. A distinct and detailed chapter on the laws of food and beverage is typically allotted by the jurists in the book of Fiqh which is written in accordance with Islamic jurisprudence. The Quran and hadith are the primary sources utilised in the process of establishing whether a food item is halal.

When it comes to defining the parameters for halal food, both sources construct literal rules and provide technical legal guidance. When it comes to shariah, the general premise is that everything is regarded as permissible unless it is specifically stated otherwise by the rules (*shara'*). Islamic jurists, on the other hand, have a disagreement over the jurisprudential implications of this principle. To determine whether a material or subject matter can be considered permissible, there are three different points of view about the original rule.

Unless *shara'* makes a clear statement to the contrary, the first group is of the opinion that everything is subject to the prohibition. Ibnu Hamid, Qadhi Abu Ya'la of the Hanbalite, and Mu'tazilite sects have expressed their opinion in this manner. 'He has already explained to you what He has forbidden to you, except when compelled by necessity (The Holy Quran 6:119)' is the verse that they cite as the basis for their viewpoint. According to this verse,

Allah will provide an explanation for any rule that they have. Individuals have no authority to interfere with the situation. On the other hand, this proof and argument from the Quran is refuted by other people according to the fact that the verse is connected to what is already mentioned in the Quran. Since the Quran does not specifically address the issue, it is irrelevant.

On top of that, the opinion of the first group is also founded on a statement made by the Prophet, in which the Prophet stated that:

> Both legal and illegal things are obvious, and in between them are (suspicious) doubtful matters. . . . So, whoever forsakes those doubtful things lest he may commit a sin, will avoid what is clearly illegal, and whoever indulges in these (suspicious) doubtful things bravely, is likely to commit what is clearly illegal.
>
> (Al-Bukhari 1978)

According to their interpretation, the Prophet asked in the hadith to leave what is unclear between halal and haram open to interpretation. In addition, he did not consider that ambiguity to be something that was initially enabled. The reason that their understanding of this hadith is incorrect is because the hadith does not specifically and literally make the initial position of a thing as forbidden.

The second group of scholars are of the opinion that the initial rule of something is undetermined until it is decided by *shara'*. Some Shafiites and Hanbalites hold this viewpoint. In the same way as the previous group, their viewpoint is founded on the hadith that was discussed earlier. The hadith that they use is comparable, but their interpretations and conclusions regarding it are different. According to this group, the fact that the hadith prohibits using, consuming, or exploiting the uncertain matters indicates that the status of anything must be determined before it can be used. If this were not the case, the situation would be indecisive, and nothing would be able to be exploited in any situation.

According to their point of view, the status of something is not determined unless it is specifically mentioned as halal or haram in the Quran or Hadith. In this case, a ruling from Islamic law is required to determine its status (Butt 2020). According to the third school of thought, everything is regarded as permissible (*mubah*) unless it can be demonstrated on a jurisprudential level that it is not. This is the viewpoint held by most legal experts. The source of their viewpoint is found in a verse in the Quran, which states, '*He who has created for you what is on the earth wholly. . .*' (The Holy Quran 2:29). It has been made clear in this verse that everything that exists on this planet was designed with the human being in mind.

This indicates that people have the right to make use of or exploit them. Because of this, the idea of total freedom of use and consumption reflects the interpretation that everything is permitted to be exploited in the beginning, and it is in accordance with the principle that everything is permissible. This is how the third school of thought's reasoning manifests itself. As a result, regardless of whether a particular ruling from Islamic authority declares something to be forbidden (haram), it is permissible for consumption or use in Islam (Kashim et al. 2015). The third group holds a viewpoint that is more pragmatic and in agreement with maqasid al-shariah and its principles.

The above viewpoint is the most feasible because of its logic. It is not possible to determine or examine all the things that are under the sky before we can consume them. Given the findings and approach of this group, it is simpler for an individual to live their life because they can consume any substance so long as it is in accordance with the shariah, which will be discussed further on. The reason why it is commensurate with the *maqasid al-shariah* is that it regards the principle of *al-taysīr*, which is the preservation of the facility and easement. This principle is one of the most important principles in *maqasid al-shariah* doctrine. In conclusion, the varying perspectives among scholars regarding the permissibility of doubtful matters in Islamic law can be categorised into three main groups.

First, some scholars adopt a cautious approach, considering any doubtful matter as inherently haram and advocating for its avoidance based on the principle of precaution. Second, another group of scholars emphasises the importance of explicit guidance from the Quran and hadith to determine the halal or haram status of matters not clearly addressed in religious texts, requiring scholarly interpretation and rulings from Islamic law. Lastly, the third group of scholars takes a more permissive stance, asserting that everything is initially considered permissible in the absence of specific prohibitions outlined in Islamic law.

Scholars following the Maliki and Hanafi schools of thought often align with this view, suggesting that unless a clear ruling declares something as haram, it is deemed permissible for consumption or use in Islam. As such, future foods such as lab-grown meats, insects, and other unconventional sources of food would in general be considered permissible unless explicitly prohibited by Islamic law. This analytical framework illustrates the complexity and diversity of perspectives within Islamic jurisprudence regarding dietary matters.

12.4 Specific Reasons of Permissibility and Non-Permissibility

In addition to the explicit prohibitions outlined in Islamic law, there exist various specific reasons rendering a food or beverage impermissible for consumption. One such reason pertains to the presence of harmful substances within the food or beverage, whether poisonous or venomous in nature. This prohibition is grounded in a Quranic verse where Allah explicitly forbids self-harm, stating, 'Do not kill yourselves' (The Holy Quran, 3:29). This verse is understood to encompass all forms of self-inflicted harm, without specifying the method. Consequently, consuming substances that harm or endanger one's wellbeing is deemed impermissible, as it falls under the category of self-inflicted harm that may lead to death.

Moreover, a hadith further underscores the severity of self-harm, stating, 'And whoever throws himself from a mountain to kill himself, then he will be continually throwing himself into the Fire of Jahannam, dwelling in that state eternally' (Al-Bukhari 1978). This hadith serves as a stark warning against self-inflicted harm, highlighting the dire consequences that await those who engage in such actions. Implicitly, this prohibition extends to those who endanger their lives through the consumption of harmful substances, as it constitutes a form of self-inflicted harm condemned within Islamic teachings.

Second, Islam unequivocally prohibits the consumption of intoxicating substances due to their detrimental effects on cognitive function and rationality. Any substance that induces a state of cognitive impairment is deemed impermissible in Islamic teachings. This prohibition is explicitly outlined in the Quranic verse that condemns intoxicants, where it states, 'O believers! Intoxicants, gambling, idols, and divining arrows are abominations devised by Satan; avoid them, so that you may prosper' (The Holy Qur'an, 5:90). The term 'intoxicants' (*al-khimar*) mentioned in this verse is understood by scholars to encompass any substance that impairs cognitive faculties. Hence, the consumption of such intoxicating substances is deemed contrary to the teachings of Islam and falls within the scope of the prohibition outlined in the verse.

Third, the concept of impurity serves as a fundamental shariah basis for the prohibition of certain foods and beverages within Islamic dietary law. It is essential to clarify that impurity in this context is not to be interpreted in its literal sense but rather in a technical manner, where the determination of impurity is guided by established shariah principles. Impurity can manifest in various forms, commonly stemming from human or animal waste such as faeces and urine. In addition, animals themselves may be deemed forbidden if they become carcasses through natural, accidental, or non-shariah compliant slaughter. According to the Hanbali school of thought, a vegetable or fruit may be considered impure if it has been irrigated with impure water unless subsequent irrigation sufficiently removes the impurity.

Fourth, the concept of filthiness also serves as a determining factor for the non-permissibility of certain substances according to shariah. While a substance may be considered physically pure, it may still be prohibited on the grounds of filthiness. For instance, according to the Shafi'i school of thought, substances like semen and sweat are not inherently impure but are prohibited for consumption due to their perceived filthiness. In addition, within the Shafi'i tradition, filthiness is also influenced by Arab customs and practices, whereby if something is deemed filthy by Arabs, it is considered forbidden for consumption. This criterion is rooted in the perception that Arabs historically maintained meticulous hygiene standards in food selection.

However, the ambiguity arises from the challenge of accurately determining the customary perceptions of ancient Arabs regarding certain food items. The fifth reason for the prohibition of certain foods pertains specifically to animals categorised as predatory (*al-iftirās*), possessing catching or killing teeth and claws. This prohibition is based on prophetic sayings, wherein the Prophet explicitly forbade the consumption of animals possessing hunting or killing teeth from the category of predatory animals, as well as those with claws from the category of birds. This prohibition underscores the importance of adhering to the teachings and guidance of the Prophet Muhammad in determining the permissibility of food items within Islamic dietary law.

Lastly, the rationale behind shariah's regulations concerning food and beverage may extend beyond inherent physical characteristics to encompass external factors. Among these external factors, illegality, such as theft, misappropriation, or embezzlement, plays a significant role. Foods and beverages obtained through such unlawful means are deemed impermissible. However, should these factors cease to exist, the prohibition may be lifted, in accordance with the Islamic legal maxim, 'a rule shall depend on its cause for its existence and shall cease to be if the cause ceases to exist' (Shettima et al. 2016). This principle asserts that the legality or illegality of a matter is contingent upon its underlying reason. For instance, stolen food is prohibited due to theft, but if the rightful owner forgives the thief and gifts the food, the act of theft is nullified, rendering the food permissible. This serves as a quintessential example illustrating the application of this maxim.

In conclusion, the Quran emphasises the obligation for Muslims to consume only halal and tayyib (good) food. To ensure compliance with these standards, the Quran and hadith have provided explicit and implicit rules, establishing a comprehensive framework. Islamic jurists meticulously address the permissibility and non-permissibility of food and beverage through general and specific shariah parameters, drawing upon Quranic verses and prophetic traditions. Thus, adherence to these guidelines ensures that Muslims maintain a diet that is not only permissible but also wholesome and in accordance with the teachings of Islam.

12.5 Halal Certification in Malaysia: Process and Regulations

The Department of Islamic Development Malaysia (JAKIM) oversees the crucial aspect of halal certification within Malaysia's regulatory framework (Halal 2024). The role of JAKIM is crucial in overseeing the comprehensive halal certification procedure, guaranteeing that products and services adhere to the rigorous criteria of Islamic law and are deemed acceptable for consumption by individuals who identify as Muslims. The halal certification regulatory framework is carefully designed to uphold Islamic principles and protect the integrity of halal products.

The acquisition of halal certification in Malaysia entails a thorough evaluation of the complete production process, encompassing the procurement of raw materials to the dissemination of the end product. A comprehensive assessment is conducted, which involves careful examination of ingredients, production facilities, and cleaning procedures to mitigate the risk of contamination with non-halal substances. JAKIM's objective is to certify products that are truly halal and adhere to Islamic dietary regulations by thoroughly analysing every stage of production.

Moreover, the halal certification procedure in Malaysia encompasses comprehensive surveillance of the complete supply chain to minimise the potential for non-halal components to infiltrate the manufacturing process. The implementation of this monitoring system guarantees the preservation of halal integrity throughout all stages, encompassing sourcing and distribution. The halal certification system in Malaysia aims to cultivate consumer confidence and maintain the country's standing as a prominent halal centre through the implementation of rigorous standards and comprehensive inspections.

To gain a more comprehensive understanding of the importance of halal certification in Malaysia, it is imperative to emphasise its wider ramifications for the economy, trade, and consumer trust. The halal certification not only enables Malaysian products to trade and access markets, but also bolsters the country's global reputation as a reliable provider of halal goods. Furthermore, an in-depth analysis of the precise regulations and criteria governing the acquisition of halal certification, in conjunction with the accompanying obstacles and advantages, will yield a thorough comprehension of the intricacies entailed in guaranteeing adherence to halal standards within Malaysia's multifaceted market.

12.6 Understanding the Concept of Halal Certification in Malaysia

Halal encompasses food and beverages that adhere to the principles of Islamic law and are deemed permissible for consumption within the framework of Islamic dietary laws. It extends beyond the concept of food edibility itself to encompass the entirety of the production process, encompassing sourcing, manufacturing, and distribution. This concept holds profound religious and cultural significance for Muslims, as it reflects their commitment to upholding Islamic principles in their daily lives. Halal certification plays a pivotal role in ensuring compliance with these principles, providing assurance to Muslim consumers that the products they consume align with their religious beliefs.

The importance of halal certification in Malaysia transcends its religious significance and extends to economic and trade considerations. Numerous studies have highlighted the influence of halal certification on business performance within the food manufacturing sector in Malaysia (Kurniati et al. 2022). Obtaining halal certification is not only a means of verifying the halal status of products but also a prerequisite for legal compliance; essential for companies operating in the halal market (Prabowo et al. 2015). Malaysia has emerged as a key global hub for halal products and services, with its halal certification system enjoying international recognition.

This recognition has bolstered Malaysia's position as a leading player in the halal industry, fostering increased trade and investment in halal products and services. The stringent regulations and criteria governing halal certification in Malaysia play a pivotal role in fostering consumer confidence, both domestically and internationally. Malaysia's adherence to rigorous standards has facilitated the export of halal products to various countries, enhancing its standing in the global halal market. The certification process covers a broad spectrum of aspects including the sourcing of raw materials, production processes, hygiene standards, and the use of additives.

Each stage of production is subject to meticulous assessment to ensure compliance with Islamic principles and the exclusion of any non-halal elements. The Department of Islamic Development Malaysia spearheads the halal certification process, setting clear guidelines and implementing comprehensive documentation and inspection procedures. This commitment to transparency and rigour instils trust among both consumers and businesses; further solidifying Malaysia's reputation as a trusted provider of halal products and services on the global stage.

12.6.1 Halal Certification Challenges

Obtaining halal certification in Malaysia presents a series of challenges, particularly for small- and medium-sized enterprises (SMEs) that may encounter difficulties in meeting the stringent requirements set forth by regulatory authorities. Despite these challenges, the advantages of halal certification, such as access to global halal markets, enhanced consumer confidence, and potential business expansion, outweigh the obstacles and offer long-term benefits for certified entities.

The Manual Procedure for Malaysia Halal Certification (Third Revision) 2014 (MPPHM 2014) serves as a comprehensive guide to the halal certification process in Malaysia, acting in tandem with the Malaysia Halal Standards. This manual encompasses various facets of halal certification, elucidating the intricacies of the certification process, where it provides the following structure:

a) Scope and Definition: The MPPHM 2014 delineates the scope of the manual and provides definitions for key terms pertinent to the halal certification process.
b) Certification Scheme: It elucidates the certification scheme, delineating the different types of halal certification available to businesses.
c) Conditions for Certification: The manual outlines the conditions that must be fulfilled for a product or service to be certified as halal.
d) Requirements for Certification: Both general and specific requirements for halal certification are detailed, ensuring adherence to halal standards.
e) Application Procedure: The manual delineates the step-by-step procedure for applying for halal certification, facilitating a systematic approach to the certification process.
f) Certification Fee: Information regarding the fees associated with halal certification is provided, ensuring transparency in cost considerations for businesses.
g) Audit Procedure: The manual elaborates on the audit procedure, elucidating how audits are conducted to verify compliance with halal standards.

h) Monitoring and Enforcement: Mechanisms for monitoring and enforcing compliance with halal standards are discussed, ensuring ongoing adherence to certification requirements.
i) Malaysia Halal Certificate and Malaysia Halal Logo: Details pertaining to the Malaysia Halal Certificate and Malaysia Halal Logo, symbols of compliance with halal standards, are provided.
j) Responsibilities of Malaysia Halal Certificate Holder: The manual outlines the responsibilities incumbent upon holders of Malaysia Halal Certificates, emphasising accountability in maintaining halal integrity.
k) Malaysia Halal Certification Panel: Information regarding the Malaysia Halal Certification Panel, tasked with overseeing the halal certification process, is elucidated.

The MPPHM 2014 serves as an indispensable resource for businesses aspiring to attain halal certification in Malaysia. By offering a comprehensive and transparent road map of the certification process, it facilitates adherence to halal standards and ensures consistency in certification application and enforcement.

12.7 The Impact of Halal Certification on the Economy and Trade

Halal certification stands as a cornerstone of the Malaysian economy and trade (Ruzulan et al. 2021). Beyond its religious underpinnings, the impact of halal certification reverberates throughout Malaysia's economic landscape, driving growth and expansion in trade spheres. Malaysia's distinguished position as a global halal hub underscores substantial economic gains and trade advancements. The burgeoning demand for halal-certified products and services has catalysed investments, employment opportunities, and the establishment of a robust halal industry infrastructure.

Malaysia's leadership in halal certification has forged lucrative trade partnerships with numerous nations, fostering a conducive economic milieu for local and international stakeholders alike. The cornerstone of any industry lies in consumer confidence, and halal certification plays a pivotal role in assuring Muslim consumers of product integrity. Malaysia's stringent regulatory framework and meticulous certification process have engendered confidence domestically and abroad, fuelling heightened consumption of halal products domestically and cementing Malaysia's status as a trusted exporter to global markets.

The regulatory framework for halal certification in Malaysia is multifaceted and comprehensive, encompassing aspects such as raw material sourcing, production processes, hygiene standards, and additive usage. The Department of Islamic Development Malaysia has set exacting standards for halal certification, ensuring that each certified product epitomises the pinnacle of halal integrity. While navigating the halal certification process in Malaysia presents its fair share of challenges, such as stringent requirements and resource constraints for smaller enterprises, the benefits far outweigh these impediments.

Businesses that secure halal certification gain access to global markets, positioning themselves for international trade and expansion. Moreover, the certification process instils a culture of quality and adherence to best practices, augmenting the overall competitiveness and sustainability of certified entities. In short, Malaysia's robust and stringent halal certification process not only upholds Islamic principles but also serves as a catalyst for economic growth, trade fortification, and consumer confidence. It stands as a testament to Malaysia's unwavering commitment to maintaining the highest standards of halal integrity, exerting a meaningful influence on the global halal industry landscape.

12.8 Regulatory Framework for Halal Certification in Malaysia

The regulatory framework for halal certification in Malaysia is firmly established to ensure the highest standards of halal integrity. JAKIM oversees the entire procedure and lays out precise rules and regulations for obtaining halal certification. These regulations cover various aspects, including the sourcing of raw materials, production processes, hygiene standards, use of additives, and prevention of cross-contamination with non-halal substances. Overall, the halal certification process in Malaysia is a comprehensive and stringent system that covers various aspects of production and ensures adherence to Islamic requirements (Ruzulan et al. 2021).

The certification process involves comprehensive documentation and rigorous inspections to verify compliance with halal requirements. This transparency and thoroughness instil trust in consumers and businesses, bolstering the credibility of halal products both within the domestic market and on the international stage.

Businesses must first apply to JAKIM along with the necessary paperwork, such as manufacturing manuals, ingredient lists, and evidence of halal standard compliance to obtain halal certification in Malaysia. After the initial application, JAKIM conducts an inspection of the premises and production processes to assess compliance with halal requirements. Once the inspection is completed, JAKIM may issue a preliminary certificate if all requirements are met. However, the process does not end there. Rather, JAKIM continues to monitor certified entities through regular audits and inspections to ensure ongoing compliance with halal standards.

These measures to uphold halal integrity not only serve the religious needs of Muslim consumers but also contribute to economic growth. By ensuring that halal products meet the highest standards of integrity, Malaysia's halal certification framework enhances consumer confidence. This, in turn, attracts both domestic and international consumers, leading to increased business opportunities for Malaysian halal manufacturers. Moreover, the halal certification process in Malaysia is not limited to food products. It also extends to other sectors such as cosmetics, pharmaceuticals, and tourism services (Siaw and Rani 2012).

In addition to the thorough inspection process, Malaysia also has strict regulations in place regarding the sourcing of raw materials for halal products. These regulations ensure that the entire supply chain, from sourcing to production to distribution, is aligned with halal standards. As a result, businesses in Malaysia must carefully vet their suppliers and ensure that all ingredients used in halal products are certified halal. In addition, Malaysia has established regulations that require companies to clearly label their products as halal and provide proper documentation to support their claims.

By implementing these regulations and requirements, Malaysia aims to prevent any potential fraud or misrepresentation in the halal industry. In Malaysia, several legislative measures have been implemented to govern halal food products. These include the Trade Descriptions Act 1972 (TDA 1972), Animal Act 1953 (revised 2006), Food Act 1983, Food Regulations 1985, Consumer Protection Act 1999, and the Local Government Act 1976. The TDA 1972 holds great significance as it functions as the principal legislation that governs the production of halal food. According to the provisions of this legislation, the current Ministry of Domestic Trade and Cost of Living possesses the jurisdiction to issue orders concerning halal food products (Rahman et al. 2018).

In conclusion, the stringent and comprehensive regulatory framework for halal certification in Malaysia not only upholds Islamic principles, but also fosters economic growth, strengthens trade relations, and enhances consumer confidence. JAKIM has set the bar high for halal certification, ensuring that every certified product meets the highest standards of halal integrity. This dedication to maintaining the integrity of halal products has led to a solid position for Malaysia as a global halal hub, resulting in substantial economic growth, trade expansion, and increased investment.

12.9 Thoughts on Future Food: Halal Considerations

The emergence of lab-grown meat presents novel challenges within the context of Islamic dietary laws, known as halal and *ṭayyib*. Lab-grown meat produced from cell cultures challenges the traditional notions of food production and consumption. Islamic legal scholars are now tasked with evaluating whether lab-grown meats align with the principles outlined in the Quran and Hadith. The key consideration lies in determining the permissibility of lab-grown meats based on their source and origin. Unlike traditional livestock farming, which involves the slaughter of animals, lab-grown meats are cultivated from animal cells.

Scholars must deliberate on the ethical implications of this process, including its impact on animal welfare and the environment. In addition, the aspect of impurity and filthiness, central to traditional dietary laws, requires re-examination in the context of lab-grown meats, as their production methods differ from conventional slaughtering practices. As technology advances,

Islamic scholars must engage with these emerging issues to provide guidance to Muslim communities navigating their religious dietary obligations amidst modern developments.

The dynamic nature of contemporary food production necessitates a thorough analysis within the Islamic legal framework to ensure that rulings uphold the principles of halal and *ṭayyib* while addressing the ethical and environmental concerns associated with lab-grown meats (Salamon et al. 2021). Likewise, the consumption of insects has garnered attention as a sustainable and nutritious food source. This trend prompts discussions within Islamic communities regarding its permissibility under halal and *ṭayyib* dietary laws. Islamic jurists face the challenge of evaluating the characteristics and properties of insects to determine their suitability as food (Rahim 2018).

The Quran and hadith provide principles for assessing the permissibility of food and beverage, yet the consumption of insects introduces complexities that require careful consideration. Scholars must weigh factors such as the biological nature of insects, their ecological role, as well as the potential benefits or harms associated with their consumption. Furthermore, ethical and environmental considerations, including insect welfare and the ecological impact of insect farming, must be factored into the analysis. To address these evolving challenges, Islamic jurists are tasked with providing guidance that reflects the principles of halal and *ṭayyib* while considering the needs and interests of Muslim communities in the modern world especially while dealing with the impending issue of food scarcity.

12.10 Addressing Food Scarcity: A Muslim Challenge

As discussions on the compatibility of future foods with halal considerations progress, addressing food scarcity emerges as a critical issue. Innovative food sources like lab-grown meats and insects must be viewed within the broader context of global challenges, including food insecurity. With the world's population growing, environmental degradation worsening, and geopolitical instability persisting, ensuring food security becomes increasingly complex.

Future food discussions must not only assess the alignment of new food technologies with Islamic dietary laws but also consider the ethical imperative of promoting sustainable agriculture and equitable food distribution to mitigate food scarcity. Connecting the discourse on future foods with the need to address food scarcity highlights the multifaceted nature of the challenges and opportunities in pursuing halal and *ṭayyib* consumption. As Islamic teachings emphasise compassion, charity, and stewardship of the Earth. Confronting food scarcity requires a multifaceted approach that includes ethical agricultural practices, equitable food distribution, and sustainable food production. The Quran provides guidance on the proper and just use of resources, offering a framework for Muslims to address food scarcity in their communities and beyond. Promoting ethical and sustainable agricultural practices is one way to tackle this issue within an Islamic framework. The concept of responsible land stewardship, as mentioned in the Quran, underscores the importance of sustainable farming techniques that prioritise environmental wellbeing and community welfare. Muslims can advocate for and implement farming methods that are halal and *ṭayyib*, as well as environmentally conscious and socially responsible.

By embracing practices such as organic farming, permaculture, and regenerative agriculture, Muslims can contribute to biodiversity preservation, soil health, water conservation, and sustainable food production. Additionally, the Islamic principle of zakat, or obligatory almsgiving, offers an opportunity to alleviate food scarcity. Muslims are encouraged to allocate a portion of their wealth to those in need, and addressing food insecurity is a key aspect of zakat. By supporting initiatives that provide access to nutritious and permissible food for underprivileged communities, Muslims can actively combat food scarcity while fulfilling their religious obligations.

All the previous, if applied, has the potential of promoting community resilience and self-sufficiency which is also essential in addressing food scarcity. This is in line with Islamic teachings that emphasise cooperation and mutual support within communities. Muslims can work towards establishing local and regional food initiatives that prioritise halal and *ṭayyib* food production and distribution, thereby enhancing community food security.

Thus, addressing food scarcity requires a holistic and ethical approach rooted in Islamic teachings. By advocating for sustainable agriculture, fulfilling charitable obligations, fostering community resilience, and embracing ethical innovation, Muslims can play a transformative role in mitigating food scarcity while upholding the principles of halal and *ṭayyib* principles.

12.11 Conclusion – Malaysia's Stance on Future Foods and Islam

In conclusion, the discourse on halal considerations in the context of future food presents a multifaceted exploration that encompasses various dimensions, from emerging food technologies to addressing global challenges such as food scarcity. Throughout this chapter, we delved into the intricacies of halal certification processes, ethical considerations surrounding food production, and the implications of innovative food sources within Islamic dietary laws. Halal certification in Malaysia, governed by stringent regulations and guidelines, serves as a cornerstone in ensuring the integrity of halal products and bolstering consumer confidence. The regulatory framework provides a comprehensive roadmap for businesses seeking certification, emphasising transparency, rigour, and adherence to Islamic principles.

The discussion extends to emerging food technologies such as lab-grown meats and insect consumption, raising pertinent questions about their compatibility with halal requirements and the ethical implications they entail. Islamic scholars are tasked with navigating these complexities while upholding the principles of halal and *ṭayyib* consumption, considering factors such as source authenticity, environmental sustainability, and societal welfare. Furthermore, the imperative of addressing food scarcity emerges as a central theme, highlighting the need for holistic approaches rooted in Islamic teachings.

Ethical agricultural practices, equitable food distribution, and community resilience play pivotal roles in mitigating food insecurity while aligning with Islamic principles of compassion, stewardship, and social responsibility. As we navigate the evolving landscape of future food, it is imperative to engage in informed discourse that transcends traditional boundaries and embraces the dynamic interplay of religious, ethical, scientific, and socioeconomic factors. By fostering dialogue, promoting collaboration, and embracing ethical innovation, we can chart a path forward that reconciles the pursuit of halal and *ṭayyib* consumption in addressing global food challenges, ultimately contributing to a more sustainable, equitable, and resilient future for all.

References

Ab Rahim, H, Ahmad, H & Ab Rahim, MH 2023, 'Istihalah Contention in Halal Food Ingredients', *International Journal of Humanities Technology and Civilization*, *8*(1), pp.17–21.

Abdullah, YA 2000, *The Holy Qur'an,* Wordsworth Editions Limited, UK.

Al-Bukhari, M 1978, *Sahih al-bukhari*, Dar-ul Hadith, Cairo.

Alzeer, J, Rieder, U & Abou Hadeed, K 2018, 'Rational and practical aspects of Halal and Tayyib in the context of food safety', *Trends in Food Science & Technology*, *71*, pp.264–267.

Butt, MMZ 2020, 'Halal and Shariah Law', in Ramadan, Y, Spear, S & Ibrahim, HA (eds.), *The halal food handbook*, John Wiley & Sons, New Jersey.

Halal, JAKIM 2024, accessed 10 January 2024, www.halal.gov.my/v4/.

Hamdan, MN, Ramli, MA, Huri, NMFZ, Abd Rahman, NNH & Abdullah, A 2021, 'Will Muslim consumers replace livestock slaughter with cultured meat in the market?', *Trends in Food Science & Technology*, *109*, pp.729–732.

Hossain, MS 2019, 'Consumption of stem cell meat: An Islamic perspective', *IIUM Law Journal*, *27*(1), pp.233–257.

Kashim, MIAM, Haris, AAA, Mutalib, SA, Anuar, N & Shahimi, S 2023, 'Scientific and Islamic perspectives in relation to the Halal status of cultured meat', *Saudi Journal of Biological Sciences*, *30*(1), p.103501.

Kashim, MIAM, Majid, LA, Adnan, AHM, Husni, AB, Nasohah, Z, Samsudin, MA & Yahaya, MZ 2015, 'Principles regarding the use of haram (forbidden) sources in food processing: A critical Islamic analysis', *Asian Social Science*, *11*(22), p.17.

Kurniati, E, Rahayu, S & Nurmiyati, N 2022, 'Halal quality management and adaptive strategy under uncertainty post covid-19', *JOSBEF*, pp.1–16.

Mujar, NAH & Hassan, N 2014, *The economics of halal industry*, Universiti Teknologi Malaysia, Skudai.

Nurrachmi, R 2018, 'The global development of halal food industry: A survey', *Tazkia Islamic Finance and Business Review*, [Online] *11*(1).

Prabowo, S, Abd Rahman, A, Ab Rahman, S & Samah, AA 2015, 'Revealing factors hindering halal certification in East Kalimantan Indonesia', *Journal of Islamic Marketing*, *6*(2), pp.268–291.

Quoquab, F, Mohamed Sadom, NZ & Mohammad, J 2020. 'Driving customer loyalty in the Malaysian fast food industry: The role of halal logo, trust and perceived reputation', *Journal of Islamic Marketing*, *11*(6), pp.1367–1387.

Rahim, SF 2018, 'Islamic jurisprudence and the status of arthropods: As alternative source of protein and with regard to E120', *MOJ Food Process Technology*, *6*(4), pp.330–340.

Rahman, AA, Ismail, CT & Abdullah, NA 2018, 'Regulating halal food consumption: Malaysian scenario', *International Journal of Law, Government and Communication*, *3*(13), pp.313–321.

'Ruling on eating synthetic meat produced by using stem cells', 14 September, 2018, https://islamqa.info/en/answers/252773/ruling-on-eating-synthetic-meat-produced-by-using-stem-cells.

Ruzulan, Z, Jamaludin, MA & Ishak, AH 2021, 'Meat and meat-based products: Challenges and opportunities in halal food security', *IOP Conference Series: Earth and Environmental Science*, *756*(1), p.012017, IOP Publishing.

Salamon, HB, Salbi, NM, Rosman, ASB, Rosli, MRB, Noor, SSBM, Muhamad, NHBN, Hamdan, MNB, Bashiron, BB & Hussin, ERB 2021, 'Halalan Tayyiba: An Islamic perspective on healthy food', *Revista Geintec-Gestao Inovacao E Tecnologias*, *11*(2), pp.1001–1014.

Shettima, M, Biu, HA & Deribe, MAA 2016, 'The relevance of Islamic legal maxims in determining some contemporary legal issues', *IIUMLJ*, *24*, p.415.

Siaw, CL & Rani, NSA 2012, 'A critical review on the regulatory and legislation challenges faced by halal start-up SMEs food manufacturers in Malaysia', *Procedia-Social and Behavioral Sciences*, *57*, pp.541–548.

Wahyudi, R & Ali, MB 2021, 'Halal food based on maqâshid al-syarî'ah perspective', *Journal of Halal Science and Research*, *2*(2), pp.43–50.

Zafar, S, Amir-ud-Din, R & Bukhari, AA 2023, 'The role of the halal food certification on the growth of the Islamic economic system: A global review', *COMSATS Journal of Islamic Finance (CJIF)*, *8*(1).

Index

Note: **Boldfaced** page references indicate tables.

AANA Code of Ethics 104
'absolute capability failure' 166–167
access and equitable sharing (ABS) 19–20
Advisory Committee on Novel Foods 91
Africa 13
agencies, enforcement 105–106, 110, 154, 164, 167, 169–170; *see also specific name*
Agreement on Agriculture (AoA) 19
Agreement on Trade-Related Aspects of Intellectual Property Rights (TRIPS) 18–19
agricultural sector 14, 138–140; *see also* agriculture; food systems
agriculture: in Africa 13; agrobiodiversity and 40; agroecology and 32, 38–41, 77, 79; biodiversity in 24, 189; cellular 3; cereal 62–63; climate change and 31, 137–138; colonialism and 15; community-supported 78; Diamond's view of 64; digital farming 139; domestication of animals/plants and 5, 51; as double-edged sword 64; ecosystem and 31, 37, 54; fertilisers and 20, 24, 39, 57, 63, 128, 135, 138–139; food production and 11; food security and 137, 144; globalisation and 73; greenhouse gas emissions and 24–25, 31, 52, 138; importance of 31; industrial 14, 16, 20, 39–40, 52, 73, 121; intellectual property rights and 141; migrant population and 74; organic 37–38; precision 139; research in 138–140; resilience-promoting policies for 77–79; sustainability and 4–5, 23–24, 32, 39, 52, 137–138, 153, 188–189; trade and 17–19, 130; transition from nomadic lifestyle 13; water consumption and 24–25, 121; *see also* regenerative agricultural practices
agrobiodiversity 40
agroecology 32, 38–41, 77, 79
agroforesty 42–48
Albania 125
algae 3, 84–86, 89, 91, 93, 175
Alíagr-Ortega, L 22
Alkire, Sabina 166–169
alternative protein products 3, 6, 84, 86, 88, 90–94; *see also* novel food; *specific type*
Alternative Proteins Council of Australia 92
Altieri, MA 39
animal-based food systems 3
Aristotle 163
Atrato River 125
Australia: Corporate Social Responsibility in 159; diet in 59; functional food regulation 100, 104–106, 108–110, **109**, 113; health claims regulation 100, 104–106, 113; indigenous population of 57–59; land usage in 12; legislation 90–92, 100, 104–106, 108–110, **109**, 113; novel food legislation 90–92; sheep and, introduction of 57–60
Australian Competition and Consumer Act 104
Australian Consumer Law (ACL) 104
Australia New Zealand Food Standards Code 105

Better Meat 88
biodiversity 1–4, 7–8, 14, 16, 20, 24, 39–40, 45, 122–123, 128–130, 138–139, 154, 189
birth of rights to nature 122–126
Bonsu, S 149
Brazil 143–144
Brillat-Savarain, JA 64
Brundland Report 151
Bugelli, Ugo 44
Burcon NutraScience Corporation 88
Business and Sustainable Development Commission Report 24

capability approach 161–169
capability failure 166–167
capitalism 4, 13–14, 16–19, 58, 155–156, 163
carbon dioxide (CO2) 25; *see also* greenhouse gas emissions
Cargill, Inc. 88
cattle 60–62, 65
Cavicchia, M 152
cellular agriculture 3
Centre for Food Policy Research Brief 26
cereal agriculture 62–63
Chacoan phenomenon 54
chestnut groves 43–48
Child Development Index (CDI) 165
Childe, V. Gordon 51
Chile 127, 131
China 25, 52, 143–144, 150
Choudhary, N 165
Clara Foods 88
climate action 2, **36**, 154
climate change: agriculture and 31, 137–138; Chacoan phenomenon and 54; chestnut groves and 48; civilisations' demise and 54; education and 47; European court of Human Rights' rulings and 123–124; food production and past 53–54; food security and 138; food systems and 12, 72; genetically modified organisms and 135; legislation and 125; net neutrality and 124; plantetary boundaries and 2; sustainability and 5, 23, 77; threat of 3–4, 6–7; wildfires and 53
Cnservation Act 123
Coca-Cola company 155
Cochamó Valley 131
Codex Alimentarius 102–104, 130
Codex Alimentarius Commission (CAC) 102
Colombian Amazon 125
colonialism 4, 13–16
commodification of food 4, 13, 16–19, 130
Common Agricultural Policy (CAP) 16, 21, 87
common good 129–131, 152, 163
Common Market 87
communism 163
community-supported agriculture 78
Condeza, Rodrigo 131
Conscious Capitalism 155–156
conservation 5, 42–47, 72, 123, 137
consumption, responsible 2, **36**, 153
Convention on Biological Diversity (CBD) 19–20
conversion factors 170
Corporate Social Responsibility (CSR): in Australia 159; as business model choice 155; business perspective 149–150; Conscious Capitalism and 155–156; consumer good and 149–150; description of 148; environment and 148; in European Union 157–159; examples 155; global perspective 150–154; importance of 154–156, 159; mandatory reporting and 157–159; movement toward 148, 156–157; overview 7–8, 159–160; Stakeholder Theory and 149; statistics 156–157; Sustainable Development Goals and 152–154; 'triple bottom line position' and 150, 152
Corporate Sustainability Due Diligence Directive 8
Corporate Sustainability Reporting Directive (CSRD) 8, 157–159
Coursin, DB 165
COVID-19 pandemic: food choice during 76; food insecurity and 71; food systems and 5–6, 71–72; government challenges and 110; home-cooked meals during 5; lessons from 79; lockdowns during 75; recovery from 71–72; restrictions during 75; supply chain disruptions 74–77; *see also* post-COVID-19 future
Creamar (food company) 88
crisis management for farmers 78

CRISPR-Cas9 86
culinary modernism 73
cultured meat 86, 91, 93

Dairy Product Act 90
Dawson, Peter 7
decent work, access to 2, **34–35**, 153
deforestation 8, 24, 31, 61, 94, 121, 139
Deforestation Regulation EU 2023/1115 8
degradation 5, 11, 20, 31–32, 46, 52, 57–60, 62, 188
de-marketing food 3
Department of Islamic Development Malaysia (JAKIM) 174, 176, 182, 184–186
desertification 7, 139
Diamond, Jared 64
diet 5, 59–60, 62, 71, 76, 92, 98, 102–104, 106–107, 161–162, 182; *see also* food choice
diet-related diseases 21–22; *see also* malnutrition
digital farming 140
disease biomarkers 106
domestication of animals/plants 5, 51; *see also specific animal*
double materiality principle 158
Doughnut model 2–3

economic growth 2, 23, **34–35**, 142, 148, 153, 186–187
economic sustainability 5, 23, 43
economic viability 31, 42–47
ecosystem: agriculture and 31, 37, 54; agroecology and 32, 38–41, 77, 79; biodiversity 4; chestnut groves and 43, 45, 48; disruption in 14, 131; environmental law protecting 121–129; exploitation of 11; food choice and 51; food policies and 27; food systems and 119; human-food-environmental nexus and 51, 54–55, 58, 63, 131; importance of 7–8, 24; nature rights and 6, 120–123, 125–129; post-COVID-19 future and 72, 79; rights of 123
education 2–3, 8, **33**, 46–47, 51, 138, 140, 153–154, 161, 167–171
emergency preparedness 77–78
energy, clean/affordable 2, **34**, 125, 144, 153, 155
Engels, F 61
environmental law: ecosystem protection 121–129; food insecurity and, eliminating 119; human rights and 119, 121–129; landmark case 131; nature rights and 119–122; overview 6–7, 131–132; *see also* legislation; nature rights
environmental sustainability 23–26, 31
EU Directive 2022/2464 157–159
European Commission 87, 106–107
European Court of Human Rights (ECHR) 123–124
European Court of Justice 87
European Environment Agency (EEA) 24
European Environmental Bureau (EEB) 2–3
European Food Safety Authority (EFSA) 106–107, 110
European Green Deal 87
European Novel Food Regulation 84–85
European Union (EU): Corporate Social Responsibility in 157–159; Corporate Sustainability Reporting Directive 8, 157–159; food security and 20–21; functional food regulation 106–108, **109**, 110–111; health claims regulation 106–108, **109**, 110–111; legislation 8, 84–87, 106–108, **109**, 110–111; Non-Financial Reporting Directive 157; novel food legislation 84–87; Sustainable Development Goals and, commitment to 25; Unfair Commercial Practices Directive 158
European Union Health Claims Act 110–111
European Union Novel Food Catalogue 85
EverGrain 88

farming *see* agriculture
Federal Food, Drug, and Cosmetics Act (FDCA) 88–89
Federal Trade Commission 101
Fernando, J 155
fertilisers 20, 24, 39, 57, 63, 128, 135, 138–139
Ficek, R 65
Fillios, Melanie 5
Food and Agriculture Organization (FAO) 11, 25, 71, 85, 102, 136–137
food choice 52–54; *see also* diet; food consumption

food commodification 4, 13, 16–19, 130
food consumption 5, 38, 93, 108, 119, 153, 176; *see also* diet; food choice
food culture 5, 65–66, 71–73, 77, 86, 119
Food and Drug Administration (FDA) 85, 89–90
food insecurity 22, 71, 119
food labelling 87, 89–90, 92, 103–104; *see also* health claims
food law *see* legislation; *specific law*
food policies 3, 20, 22, 24, 26–27, 130, 161
food processing sector 75
food production 11, 38, 43–47, 53–54, 74, 84, 94; *see also* agriculture; food systems
food scarcity 188–189
food security: agriculture and 137, 144; challenge of 130; climate change and 138; European Union and 20–21; human rights and 131; intellectual property rights and 136–140; management of natural resources and, fair 37–42; natural resource management and 37–42; natural resources and 37–42, 136; nature rights and 130–131; research and 135; sustainability and 8, 137, 144; Sustainable Development Goals and 31, **33–37**; *see also* Malaysian perspective of food security
Food Standard Australia New Zealand (FSANZ) 91, 104–106
Food Standards Code 109
food supply chain disruptions 74–77
food systems: actions for sustainability and 26–27; agroecology and 38–39; animal-based 3; capitalism and 13–14, 16–19; challenges 11, 26; changes in 8–9, 113; climate change and 12, 72; colonialism and 13–16; COVID-19 pandemic and 5–6, 71–72; criticalities of current 20–26; ecosystem and 119; environmental sustainability and 23–26; evolution of 11; geopolitics and 16; governance, call for 20–26; health sustainability and 21–22; human-food-environmental nexus and, insights into 66; industrialisation and 5–6; integrated approach to 5, 26–27; interconnectedness of 26, 52; international trade and 12; intervention areas 26–27; land usage and 11–13; natural resource management and 19–20; natural resources and 23–25; resilient, future policies for 77–79; revenue from 12–13; social sustainability and 22–23; supply chain disruptions 74–77; sustainability and 20–26; sustainable Development Goals and 32; trade 12; value chains and, global 12; *see also specific type*
food trade 12
food waste 25, 38, 52, 73–74, 76–79, 137–138, 153
foodways 55–56, 61
Forbes 12–13
forest fires 53, 125
Freeman, E 149
Fresh Hemp Foods 88
functional food: Australia regulation of 100, 104–106, 108–110, **109**, 113; benefits of 98; Codex Alimentarius and 102–104; consumer confidence in 112; dilemma in classifying as medicinal 100–102; European Union regulation of 106–108, **109**, 110–111; functions of 98; growth in 112; institutional framework for health claims on 108, **109**; marketing of 98; overview 99, 102, 113–114; perception of 98; regulation of health claims in 104–110; *see also* health claims
Function Health Claims 107
Future Generations v. Ministry of the Environment and Others (2018) 125
Fytexia Corp 88

Ganges River 125
gender equality 2, 23, **34**, 153
gene editing 86, 92
General Agreement on Tariffs and Trade (GATT) 4, 16–20
General Agreement on Trade in Services (GATS) 18
Generally Recognized as Safe (GRAS) 88–89, 91
General Motors 155
genetically modified organisms (GMOs) 84, 86, 135
geopolitics 16
Ghaffarian, Elham 7
Gliessman, SR 39

Global Hunger Index 165
globalisation 5, 15, 40, 73, 130
Global Report on Food Crises 22, 71
global warming 7, 63
GOOD Meat 89, 93
grazing animals 55, 57–62
green algae 85
greenhouse gas emissions 24–25, 31, 52, 60–61, 124–125, 138
green intellectual property rights/ patents 143–144
green patents 136, 143–144
Green R&D 139–140
Green Revolution 13, 139
Gulati, Vandana 6
Guterres, Antonio 22

hadith 174–176, 178–179, 188
Hagermann, Robert 131
halal certification 174, 182–187
halal consumption 176–177, 182–183, 187–188
Hanbali school of thought 181
Harari,YN 126
harmony between man and nature 129–130
health as basic capability 168–169
health claims of food: Australia regulation of 100, 104–106, 108–110, **109**, 113; background information 98–99; children's development 107; Codex Alimentarius and 102–104; dilemma in classifying functional foods as medicinal 100–102; European Union regulation of 106–108, 110–111; on functional food 6, 99, 101; loopholes in 112; marketing law and 112; medicalisation of 100; overview 6, 99–100, 113–115; power of 6; probiotic bacteria 107–108; regulation of 104–108; risk reduction 107
health sustainability 21–22
health and wellbeing, good 1, **33**, 71, 98, 153, 162, 167
herbicides 63
Home Depot 155
human-food-environmental nexus: background information 51; case studies 54–64; case studies, archaeological and historical 54–64; cattle grazing in Americas 60–62; cereal agriculture in Near East and Mediterranean 54, 62–64; civilisation and 51; cultural change and 65–66; cultural identity and 51–54, 64–65; ecosystem and 51, 54–55, 58, 63, 131; food choice and 51–54, 64–65; food systems and, insight into 66; foodways and 55–56, 61; future and 64–66; nutritious food and 8; overview 5; sheep in Australia 57–60
Human Food Made with Cultured Animal Cells inventory 89
human nature 119
human rights: agreements 3; Doughnut model and 398; environmental law and 119, 121–122; food security and 131; nature rights and 121–122; overview 6–7
husbandry 60–61, 65
hygiene practices 77

Implementation Committee for Food (ISFR) 105
Impossible Foods 88
India 74, 125–126, 165
industrial agriculture 14, 16, 20, 39–40, 52, 73, 121
industrialisation 5–6, 51, 73
inequality, reduced 2, **35**, 136, 153, 161
infrastructure 2, 4, 12, **35**, 78, 125, 185
innovation 2–3, **35**, 52, 84, 87, 94, 99, 109, 114, 135–136, 138–144, 189–190
insects as food source 3, 84–86, 89, 93, 178
institutions, strong 2, **37**, 154
intellectual property rights: access to 140; agriculture and 141; background information 135–136; food security and 136–140; green 143–144; importance of 141; knowledge flow and 141–143; overview 7, 144; perspectives on 141–142
interconnectedness 2, 8, 15, 26, 31–32, 52, 119–120, 129, 131, 149, 152, 159, 171, 176
intergenerational equity 152
Intergovernmental Panel on Climate Change (IPCC) 138
International Assessment of Agriculture Knowledge, Science and Technology for Development (IAASTD) 39

International Fund for Agricultural Development (IFAD) 41
International Symposium on Food Self-Sufficiency (1988) 17
international trade and food systems 12
IPES-Food 1
Iran 150
Islam and future food *see* Malaysian perspective of food security
Italian Constitutional Court 128
Italy 43–47, 127–128

Kaljonen, M 3
Kanwar, Abhay Vir Singh 8
Karskens, G 66
Keeble, B 151
Kent, K 74
Kenton, W 155–156
KlimaSeniorinnen v. Switzerland 123–124
!Kung San of Kalahari 64

labelling food 87, 89–90, 92, 103–104; *see also* health claims
lab-grown meats 178, 187
Lähteenmäki-Uutela, Anu 6–7
Lancet 1
land usage 11–13, 24, 84
least developed countries (LDC) 7; *see also specific name*
Lege of Peugeot (Harari) 126
legislation: in Australia 90–92, 100, 104–106, 108–110, **109**, 113; climate change and 125; in European Union 84–87, 106–108, **109**, 110–111; nature rights and 126–129; patent 19, 136, 141; regulatory frameworks 8, 87, 92, 99, 103–104, 124, 174, 182, 185–187, 189; in Singapore 92–93; United States 88–90
life below water 2, **36**, 154
life cycle assessment (LCA) 23, 25, 27
life on land 2, **36**, 154
livestock 55, 57–62
Lonkila, A 3, 6
Lundgren, BO 42
Lyle(food company) 88

macroalgae 85–86, 89, 91, 93
Malaysian perspective of food security: food scarcity and, addressing 188–189; future food and 187–190; halal certification and 174, 182–187; halal consumption and 176–177, 182–183, 187–188; Hanbali school of thought and 181; intersection between future food and Islam and 175–176; JAKIM and 174, 176, 182, 184–186; *Manual Procedure for Malaysia Hala Certification* (Third Revision) and 184–185; Ministry of Domestic Trade and Cost of Living and 187; overview 8, 174–175, 189–190; permissibility and non-permissibility under shariah and 174, 177–182; *tayyib* consumption and 175–176, 182, 187–190
malnutrition: capability approach and 161–169; capability failure and 166–167; definition of 162; education and 167–169; health and 168–169; incidence of 21, 135, 162; in India 165; nutritious food and, access to 164–170; overview 8, 170–171; poverty and 166–167
Mancuso, Stefano 127
Manual Procedure for Malaysia Hala Certification (Third Revision) (MPPHM 2014) 184–185
maqasid al-shariah 177–180
Marimuthu, Siva Barathi (Sharl) 4–7
marketing food 6, 8, 12, 41, 75, 84, 94, 98, 104, 108, 112–113, 149
Marx, Karl 163
materiality 158–159
'meaty' imitation products 87
medicalisation of health claims 100
medicinal food classification 100–102
Mediterranean countries 54, 62–64
microalgae 89, 93
Middle East 105
Millennium Ecosystem Assessment 122
modern culinary practices 73
modern industrial farming 63
Monsanto 92
Murphy, C 154–155
Murray-Darling River System Bill (2021) 125–126
Musa, Murshamshul Kamariah 8
mushrooms 45–46

natural resources: conservation of 5, 72, 137; depletion of 14, 137–138; distribution of 11, 13–14, 129, 164; exploitation of 11, 15–16, 20,

55; food production and 84, 94; food security and 37–42, 136; food systems and 23–25; fungible 130; industrial agriculture and 16; limited 12, 78; management of 19–20, 31–32, 37–42, 47, 137; non-fungible 130–131; reliance on 12–13; security 55; *see also specific type*
nature rights: challenges to 126–129; in Chile 127; ecosystem and 6, 120–123, 125–129; environmental law and 119–122; first instances of recognizing 122–126; food security and 130–131; harmony between man and nature and 129–130; human rights-based approach and 121–122; importance of 129; interconnectedness and 119–120; in Italy 127–128; legislation 126–129; meaning of 119–121; overview 6, 131–132; prerequisites, legal and cultural 126–129; transitioning from food as commodity to food as common good 129–131
Near East 54, 62–64
Nemecek, T 25
net neutrality 124
New Zealand 104–106, 125–126
Non-Financial Reporting Directive (NFRD) 157
Nordenskiöld, Adolf Erik 123
novel food: algae 3, 84–85, 91, 175; alternative protein products 3, 6, 84, 86, 88, 90–94; Australia legislation 90–92; barriers to 94; compliance with legislation 93–94; European legislation 84–87; overview 6, 94; Singapore legislation 92–93; United States legislation 88–90; *see also specific type*
Novel Food Virtual Clinics 92
Nussbaum, Martha 161, 163
Nutrition and Health Claim Regulation EC 111
nutritious food: access to 164–170; capability approach and 164–169; definition of 161–162; human rights and 8; overview 170–171

ocean acidification 2, 8
ocean levels, rising 7
organic agriculture 37–38
overnutrition 162

Palasuberniam, ? 161
Pantazi, T 157–158
Paris Agreement (2015) 3–4, 123
Parthasarathy, D 165
partnerships 2, 37, 140, 154, 185
patent rights/protection 19, 135–136, 140–144
Paul, A 75
Perry, Mark 7
pesticides 20, 24, 39, 57, 63, 79, 135, 138–139
Piccoli, Lodovico 48
planetary boundaries 1–2, 8, 37, 84, 94, 120
Plant-Based Foods Association 90
plant-based products 25, 84, 86–90, 90, 92–93, 111, 175; *see also specific type*
pollution 24
Ponce de Leon, Juan 15
Poore, J 25
population growth 1, 12, 20, 55, 137, 188
post-COVID-19 future: community-supported agriculture and 78; crisis management for farmers and 78; ecosystem and 72, 79; emergency preparedness and 77–78; food cultures and, traditional 72–73; food as necessity and 71–72; food waste management strategies and 78; globalisation and 73; hygiene practices and 77; industrialisation and 73; modern culinary practices and 73; overview 5–6, 79; policies for more resilient food systems and 77–79; resilient food systems and, future policies for 77–79; supply chain disruptions and 74–77; trade agreements 78–79
poverty 1–2, 13, 20, 32, 152–154, 161, 164, 166–167
precision agriculture 139
precision fermentation 92
process-oriented approach 40
Puelo Patagonia 131

Quintero, Marcela 41
Quran 174–176, 178–180, 188

R&D in agriculture sector 138–140
Rahim, Mia 8
Raintree, JB 42
Rawlsian principle 163

regenerative agricultural practices: agrobiodiversity 40; agroecology 38–41, 42; agroforestry 42–48; chestnut groves 43–48; overview 31; process-oriented approach 40; sustainability and 40; Sustainable Development Goals and 31, 48
regulatory fitness and performance programme (REFIT) 111
regulatory frameworks 8, 87, 92, 99, 103–104, 124, 174, 182, 185–187, 189
renewable energy 125, 144, 155
resources *see* natural resources
Rio Declaration 123
Ritchie, Mark 17
Ruger, JP 168–169
Russia 150

sanitation 2, **34**, 76–77, 153
Santo Domingo 61–62
Schedule 25 of Food Standards Code 91
sea levels, rising 7
Sen, Amartya 161, 163, 167
shariah 177–180
Sheedy, C 159
sheep 57–60
Singapore Food Agency 92
Singapore novel food legislation 92–93
sky farming 79
Slow Food Chestnut Growers Network 45
social sustainability 22–23
Solar Foods 93
Solein (alternative protein) 93
South Korea 52
Stakeholder Theory 149
Starbucks 155
Stifting, Heinrich Böll 13
Stobierski, T 156–157
Stone, Christopher 126
supply chain disruptions of COVID-19 pandemic 74–77
sustainability: actions for food system 26–27; agriculture and 4–5, 23–24, 32, 39, 52, 137–138, 153, 188–189; agroecology and 38–39; animal-based food systems and 3; Brundland Report and 151–152; challenges 137–138; chestnut groves and 43–48; cities/communities 2, **35**, 153; climate change and 5, 23, 77; duty to move toward 1–4; economic 5, 23, 43; environmental 23–26, 31, 43; food security and 8, 137, 144; food systems 20–26; governance for food systems, call for 20–26; health 21–22; overview 5; regenerative agricultural practice and 40; reporting 157–159; social 5, 22–23; Sustainable Development Goals and 1
Sustainable Accounting Standards Board (SASB) 152
Sustainable Development Goals (SDGs): Corporate Social Responsibility and 152–154; establishment of 31, 152; European Union's commitment to 25; food security and 32, **33–37**; food systems and 32; food waste 25; interconnectedness of 31–32; list of **33–37**, 153–154; objectives of 31–32, **33–37**; regenerative agricultural practices and 31, 48; sustainability and 1; zero hunger 2, 22
Sweden 123
Switzerland 123–124

Tate (food company) 88
ṭayyib consumption 175–176, 182, 187–190
tea plants 74
Telch, Alessandra 4–7
Terzi, L 167
'Third Mission' 140
Trade-Related Aspects of Intellectual Property Rights (TRIPS) 18, 136, 141–143
trade/trade agreements 17–19, 78–79, 130
'triple bottom line position' 150, 152
Triton Algae Innovations, Ltd. 85, 89

Unfair Commercial Practices Directive (UCPD) 158
United Nations (UN) 25
United Nations Environment Programme (UNEP) 1
United Nations Food and Agriculture Organization 11, 25, 71, 85, 102, 136
United Nations Human Rights Committee 3
United Nations International Trade Organization 17

United Nations Special Rapporteur on the Right to Food Hilal Elver 39
United States 25, 60–62, 88–90
United States Department of Agriculture (USDA) 17, 89
Universal Declaration of Human Rights (UDHR) 121, 141–142
university R&D 140
UPSIDE Foods 89
Uruguay Round (1986-1994) 19

Venkatapuram, S 168
vertical farming 79
Visa company 155
vitamin D 106–107

water, clean 2, 27, **34**, 76, 153
water consumption 24–25, 121
Whanganui River 125–126
wildfires 53, 125
Wild River National Park 125
World Agroforestry Centre (ICRAF) 42
World Commission on Environment and Development 151
World Health Organization (WHO) 102
World Intellectual Property Organization 135–136, 141
World Trade Organisation (WTO) 18–19

Yamuna River 125
Yanomamo of Brazil 64
Yellowstone National Park 123
Yuso, Mohd Lotpi Mohd 8

Zakariah, Asril Amirul 8
zero hunger 1–2, **33**, 136, 153
Zierock, R 129–130